שיח שולחן

Around the Family Table

Songs and Prayers for the Jewish Home

with

Insights and Commentary by

 Rabbi Shlomo Riskin

הוקרה אישית

לזכר נשמת סבתי מורתי

חיה בילא בת הרב שלמה הכהן ומינדל ז״ל

שנתנה לי לינוק קדושת שבת וחג מסביב לשולחנה

ובזכות אשתי אהובתי

אביבה פרידא לאה בת דוד בער ושרה שינא תלחט״א

שהקימה משפחה למופת ועשתה נפשות לאבינו שבשמים הודות לשולחן שבת וחג שערכה

Special thanks and appreciation to

Jonathan and Marcia Javitt

who encouraged me to write a commentary on Birkat Hamazon,
the first edition of which was distributed at their son Zachary's Bar Mitzva.

Around the Family Table: Songs and Prayers for the Jewish Home
With Insights and Commentary by Rabbi Shlomo Riskin

Editorial Consultant: Kaeren Fish

Design & Typesetting: Leshon Limudim, Ltd., Jerusalem
leshon@netvision.net.il

Printed at Hemed Press, Israel. First Pocket Edition
ISBN 965-7108-73-x

Urim Publications
P.O. Box 52287, Jerusalem 91521 Israel

Ohr Torah Stone Colleges
P.O. Box 1037 Efrat, Israel
www.ohrtorahstone.org.il

Lambda Publishers, Inc.
3709 13th Avenue Brooklyn, New York 11218 USA
Tel.: 718-972-5449; Fax: 718-972-6307

benchers@UrimPublications.com for bulk orders
www.UrimPublications.com

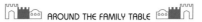
Table of Contents

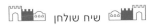
FAMILY LIFE-CYCLE EVENTS

MARRIAGE

A NEW CHILD

INTRODUCTION

E very Jewish family begins with our great-grandparents, Abraham and Sarah, whose faith in the God of compassion and justice inspired them to constantly welcome into their tent strangers in need of companionship and / or nourishment; every Jewish family anxiously anticipates the birth of a great-grandchild of King David who will redeem Israel and the world.

Every Jewish home was initially formed in Eden amidst the tumultuous, tempestuous rustlings of the Tree of Knowledge and the Tree of Life; every Jewish home will eventually be perfected in Jerusalem under the fragrant protective shade of the grape vine and the fig tree.

Every Jewish table, as in Jacob's dream, has its legs rooted on earth and its light-giving candelabrum extending to the spiritual, celestial, supernal realms on high.

Every Jewish family celebration experiences what was, what is, and what will be; every Jewish family celebration embraces the present and touches hands with eternity, reaching out to those who are close by and reaching upward to our Parent in Heaven.

TABLE CULTURE

A recent statistical survey determined that the average American family sits down at the table together for a meal only once a month. My own observation is that most secular American families are like train stations: everyone is on his/her own schedule so that the trains rarely meet; when they do, it usually causes a collision! Judaism believes that the family meal is not only crucial to ensure family togetherness, but is also the highest expression of religious service. It is no accident that all of our sacred religious institutions have the

Hebrew word for "home" (*bayit*, or *bet* — when joined with another noun) as part of their name: *Bet Ha-Mikdash* (the Holy Temple in Jerusalem), *Bet Knesset* (synagogue), *Bet Ha-Midrash* (house of study). Apparently our tradition, both biblical as well as rabbinic, saw the home as an important — perhaps the most important — element in handing over our tradition from generation to generation.

THE HOME IS A SANCTUARY

Indeed, the major accoutrements of the Desert Sanctuary — which served as the model for the Holy Temple in Jerusalem — were the kinds of furnishings that one would find in a home: the Menorah or candelabrum which gives light, the Table for the showbread upon which food is placed, and the Ark, which literally means "closet," which was the repository for the Tablets of Testimony. A central aspect of the Sanctuary was the Altar of Sacrifice, and every parent knows how much sacrifice is necessary in order to raise healthy and productive family members: sacrifice in time, sacrifice in money and especially sacrifice in emotional energy.

It is because Judaism sees the home as the "mother of all religious institutions" that home-centered family ritual celebrations bear a striking parallel to the religious ritual of the Jerusalem Temple even to this day. The most obvious example of this is that mystical and magical evening known as the Passover Seder, modeled upon the Paschal Meal in Jerusalem during Temple times, when every parent becomes a teacher whose primary task is to convey — through songs, stories, explication of biblical passages and special foods — the most seminal experience in Jewish history: the exodus from our Egyptian servitude.

THE FESTIVE FAMILY MEAL IS A JERUSALEM TEMPLE SERVICE

And every Shabbat and Festival meal is a mini Passover Seder. Even before the Friday sun begins to set, the mother of the family kindles the Shabbat lights, reminiscent of the priests' first task each day: to light the Menorah. The blessing over the kiddush wine reminds us of the wine libations accompanying most sacrifices, and the carefully braided hallot, loaves of bread, symbolize the twelve loaves of showbread which were changed in the Temple every Friday just before dusk. Parents bless their children with the same priestly benediction with which the High Priest blessed the congregation in the Temple, and the ritual washing of the hands before partaking of the hallah parallels the hand ablutions of the priests before engaging in Temple service. The salt in which we dip the hallah before reciting the blessing over bread is based upon the biblical decree, "You shall place salt on all of your sacrifices" (Leviticus 2:13), since salt, which is an eternal preservative, is symbolic of the indestructibility of God's covenant with Israel. The songs that are sung and the Torah that is taught during a Friday night meal will hopefully further serve to transport the family participants to the singing of the Levites and the teachings of the priests in the Holy Temple. Such a Shabbat meal links the generations, making everyone feel part of the eternal people participating in an eternal conversation with the Divine.

In large measure my own family — as of this writing, four married children and twelve grandchildren, all living in Efrat, Israel — was formed and shaped, and continues to be directed and inspired, by our family Shabbat and Festival meals. It would not be an exaggeration to say that over the last forty years, thousands of individuals have shared these Shabbat and Festival meals with our family and have likewise discovered meaning and inspiration through their participation. Indeed

I am convinced that the family ritual is a far more authentic and significant expression of Judaism than is any synagogue service. I hope to be able to transmit at least a glimpse into the mystery and majesty of our Jewish table culture by means of this Shabbat bencher and commentary, a kind of Haggadah for Shabbat, Festivals and other family occasions.

A STORY POSTSCRIPT

Many years ago, when I was still a very young rabbi with a very young family in Manhattan, I was riding in a taxicab on the way to a lecture. As is my custom, I engaged the driver in conversation. He was an African-American who had never graduated elementary school. He had raised four children with a wife to whom he was married for over thirty years: one of his children was an engineer, another a lawyer, a third a high-school teacher, and his only daughter a nurse. When I asked him to what he attributed such obvious familial success, he explained to me that as long as his children lived at home, the cardinal family rule was that each had to show up at the dinner table every evening or provide a very good excuse as to why not. These family meals were devoid of television, radio or newspaper; instead, each family member, including himself and his wife, had to recount the most important incident of the day and the most frustrating incident of the day. It was largely as a result of those meals, he believed, that their family loyalty and togetherness was forged, and the strong character of each family member became solidified.

As the taxi driver concluded his description, I burst into tears. What he understood, I had not understood: that every evening meal must be a mini Shabbat meal, with ritual washing, blessing, Torah talk and general discussion. I hope that you will appreciate this while your children are still young.

ברכת המזון

In many communities, Psalm 137 is recited before *Birkat Ha-Mazon* on regular weekdays:

עַל נַהֲרוֹת בָּבֶל שָׁם יָשַׁבְנוּ גַּם בָּכִינוּ בְּזָכְרֵנוּ אֶת צִיּוֹן. עַל עֲרָבִים בְּתוֹכָהּ
תָּלִינוּ כִּנֹּרוֹתֵינוּ. כִּי שָׁם שְׁאֵלוּנוּ שׁוֹבֵינוּ דִּבְרֵי שִׁיר וְתוֹלָלֵינוּ שִׂמְחָה שִׁירוּ לָנוּ
מִשִּׁיר צִיּוֹן. אֵיךְ נָשִׁיר אֶת שִׁיר יְיָ עַל אַדְמַת נֵכָר. אִם אֶשְׁכָּחֵךְ יְרוּשָׁלָיִם,
תִּשְׁכַּח יְמִינִי. תִּדְבַּק לְשׁוֹנִי לְחִכִּי אִם לֹא אֶזְכְּרֵכִי אִם לֹא אַעֲלֶה אֶת יְרוּשָׁלַיִם
עַל רֹאשׁ שִׂמְחָתִי. זְכֹר יְיָ לִבְנֵי אֱדוֹם אֵת יוֹם יְרוּשָׁלָיִם, הָאֹמְרִים עָרוּ עָרוּ עַד
הַיְסוֹד בָּהּ. בַּת בָּבֶל הַשְּׁדוּדָה אַשְׁרֵי שֶׁיְשַׁלֶּם לָךְ אֶת גְּמוּלֵךְ שֶׁגָּמַלְתְּ לָנוּ.
אַשְׁרֵי שֶׁיֹּאחֵז וְנִפֵּץ אֶת עֹלָלַיִךְ אֶל הַסָּלַע:

On Shabbat, Festivals, and other occasions of celebration, *Birkat Ha-Mazon* is preceded by Psalm 126:

שִׁיר הַמַּעֲלוֹת בְּשׁוּב יְיָ אֶת שִׁיבַת צִיּוֹן הָיִינוּ כְּחֹלְמִים. אָז יִמָּלֵא שְׂחוֹק פִּינוּ
וּלְשׁוֹנֵנוּ רִנָּה. אָז יֹאמְרוּ בַגּוֹיִם הִגְדִּיל יְיָ לַעֲשׂוֹת עִם אֵלֶּה, הִגְדִּיל יְיָ לַעֲשׂוֹת
עִמָּנוּ הָיִינוּ שְׂמֵחִים. שׁוּבָה יְיָ אֶת שְׁבִיתֵנוּ כַּאֲפִיקִים בַּנֶּגֶב. הַזֹּרְעִים בְּדִמְעָה
בְּרִנָּה יִקְצֹרוּ. הָלוֹךְ יֵלֵךְ וּבָכֹה נֹשֵׂא מֶשֶׁךְ הַזָּרַע. בֹּא יָבֹא בְרִנָּה נֹשֵׂא אֲלֻמֹּתָיו:

תְּהִלַּת יְיָ יְדַבֶּר פִּי וִיבָרֵךְ כָּל־בָּשָׂר שֵׁם קָדְשׁוֹ לְעוֹלָם וָעֶד. וַאֲנַחְנוּ נְבָרֵךְ יָהּ
מֵעַתָּה וְעַד־עוֹלָם הַלְלוּיָהּ. הוֹדוּ לַיְיָ כִּי טוֹב כִּי לְעוֹלָם חַסְדּוֹ: מִי יְמַלֵּל
גְּבוּרוֹת יְיָ יַשְׁמִיעַ כָּל תְּהִלָּתוֹ:

On Shabbat and Festivals, as well as at family life-cycle celebrations, it is customary to recite Psalm 126, A Song of Ascents, as the introduction to *Birkat Ha-Mazon*. Both this song and *Birkat Ha-Mazon* itself deal with the subject of redemption and there are many who customarily sing this song to the tune of *Ha-Tikvah*. When we return to Zion, the psalmist tells us, we will be like dreamers. The great Talmudic Sage, Rabbi Yohanan, teaches us that there are four types of dreams which are eventually realized: a dream of dawn, a dream which is also dreamed by one's friend, a dream with its interpretation as part of the dream, and a dream which repeats itself (B.T. Berakhot 55b). I once heard from the great scholar Rabbi Professor Shmuel Kalman Mirsky that this refers to the dream of modern Zionism, which began to be fulfilled with the establishment of the State of Israel. The Zionist enterprise was a "dream of dawn": a dream that was dreamed not only at night when the dreamer was asleep, but also in the morning when the dreamer awoke; it was also a dream of redemption because

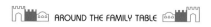
BIRKAT HA-MAZON

GRACE AFTER THE MEAL

In many communities, Psalm 137 is recited before Birkat Ha-Mazon on regular weekdays:

By the rivers of Babylon — there we sat and also wept when we remembered Zion. On the willows within it we hung our lyres. There our captors requested words of song from us, and our joyous lyres: "Sing for us from Zion's song!" How can we sing the song of God upon the alien soil? If I forget you, O Jerusalem, let my right hand forget its skill. Let my tongue adhere to my palate if I fail to recall you, if I fail to elevate Jerusalem above my foremost joy. Remember, O God, for these offspring of Edom, the day of Jerusalem — for those who say, "Destroy! Destroy to its very foundation." O violated daughter of Babylon — fortunate is he who repays you commensurate with your recompense to us. Fortunate is he who will clutch and dash your infants against the rock.

On Shabbat, Festivals, and other occasions of celebration, Birkat Ha-Mazon is preceded by Psalm 126:

A Song of Ascents: When God brought Zion out of captivity, we were like people in a dream. At that time our mouth was filled with laughter and our tongue with cries of joy; at that time it was said among the nations, "The Lord has done great things for them." The Lord has done great things for us; we were happy. O God, return our captivity like the suddenly flowing streams in the Negev. Those who sow in tears shall reap in joy. He who weeps as he trails the seed along will return with joy, carrying his sheaves.

My mouth shall declare the Lord's praise, and let all flesh bless His holy name for all time. As for us, we will bless the Lord from now on and forever more: Praise the Lord! Give thanks to God for He is good, for His kindness is everlasting! Who can describe the mighty deeds of the Lord, or utter all His praise?

dawn is a rabbinic metaphor for redemption. Continuing the parallel, the dream of Zionism was shared by many co-workers, it was a dream which included a detailed program which interpreted the stages necessary for its realization (witness Theodor Herzl's "The Jewish State") and it was a dream that repeated itself, giving the dreamers no rest. We must continue to dream our dreams in such a fashion if we wish them to be realized. ⦿

זימון לברכת המזון

When three or more adults have eaten together, one invites the others to join in the Blessing After the Meal:

The leader begins:

רַבּוֹתַי, נְבָרֵךְ:

The others answer:

יְהִי שֵׁם יְיָ מְבֹרָךְ מֵעַתָּה וְעַד עוֹלָם:

The leader repeats:

יְהִי שֵׁם יְיָ מְבֹרָךְ מֵעַתָּה וְעַד עוֹלָם:

And continues:

בִּרְשׁוּת (אורח: בַּעַל (בַּעֲלַת/בַּעֲלֵי) הַבַּיִת הַזֶּה) מָרָנָן וְרַבָּנָן וְרַבּוֹתַי נְבָרֵךְ (בעשרה או יותר: אֱלֹהֵינוּ) שֶׁאָכַלְנוּ מִשֶּׁלּוֹ:

The others say:

בָּרוּךְ (בעשרה או יותר: אֱלֹהֵינוּ) שֶׁאָכַלְנוּ מִשֶּׁלּוֹ וּבְטוּבוֹ חָיִינוּ:

The leader repeats:

בָּרוּךְ (בעשרה או יותר: אֱלֹהֵינוּ) שֶׁאָכַלְנוּ מִשֶּׁלּוֹ וּבְטוּבוֹ חָיִינוּ:

All say:

בָּרוּךְ הוּא וּבָרוּךְ שְׁמוֹ:

ZIMUN

When three or more males or three or more females are reciting *Birkat Ha-Mazon* together, one invites the others to join in praise of God in a special introductory blessing. (When three or more females eat together the Vilna Gaon rules that they are obliged to recite this *zimun*, while other authorities rule that it is voluntary.)

It is also customary, when three or more adult males are present, to recite Grace over wine. The leader holds the cup in his hand until לעולם על יחסרנו and at the conclusion of the entire

ZIMUN

When three or more adults have eaten together, one invites the others to join in the Blessing After the Meal. The leader begins:

My masters (or friends), let us say the blessing.

The others answer:

May the name of the Lord be blessed from now on and forever more.

The leader repeats:

May the name of the Lord be blessed from now on and forever more.

And continues:

With the consent of (*if one is a guest, say:* "my honored host[s] and") all present, let us bless Him (*if there are ten or more men present, say* "our God") Whose food we have eaten.

The others say:

Blessed is He (our God) whose food we have eaten and through whose goodness we live.

The leader repeats:

Blessed is He (our God) whose food we have eaten and through whose goodness we live.

All say:

May He be blessed and may His name be blessed.

Birkat Ha-Mazon he recites the blessing over the wine. Since the vision of *Birkat Ha-Mazon* is one of redemption, the wine symbolizes the verse, "The cup of salvation do I lift up as I call upon the name of the Lord." If ten males are present for the *zimun*, the addition of אלהינו is included where indicated in parentheses.

Our sages believed that one of the important ways of forging and solidifying a relationship is by a shared meal (note that the English word "companion" literally means "with bread" — *cum pane*). Hence a meal shared by three or more adults takes on the added dimension of companionship, obligating the extra blessing of *zimun* or invitation. ⚹

בָּרוּךְ אַתָּה יְיָ אֱלֹהֵינוּ מֶלֶךְ הָעוֹלָם, הַזָּן אֶת הָעוֹלָם כֻּלּוֹ בְּטוּבוֹ בְּחֵן בְּחֶסֶד וּבְרַחֲמִים, הוּא נוֹתֵן לֶחֶם לְכָל בָּשָׂר כִּי לְעוֹלָם חַסְדּוֹ. וּבְטוּבוֹ הַגָּדוֹל תָּמִיד לֹא חָסַר לָנוּ וְאַל יֶחְסַר לָנוּ מָזוֹן לְעוֹלָם וָעֶד בַּעֲבוּר שְׁמוֹ הַגָּדוֹל, כִּי הוּא אֵל זָן וּמְפַרְנֵס לַכֹּל וּמֵטִיב לַכֹּל וּמֵכִין מָזוֹן לְכָל בְּרִיּוֹתָיו אֲשֶׁר בָּרָא. כָּאָמוּר, פּוֹתֵחַ אֶת יָדֶךָ וּמַשְׂבִּיעַ לְכָל חַי רָצוֹן. בָּרוּךְ אַתָּה יְיָ, הַזָּן אֶת הַכֹּל:

נוֹדֶה לְךָ יְיָ אֱלֹהֵינוּ עַל שֶׁהִנְחַלְתָּ לַאֲבוֹתֵינוּ אֶרֶץ חֶמְדָּה טוֹבָה וּרְחָבָה וְעַל שֶׁהוֹצֵאתָנוּ יְיָ אֱלֹהֵינוּ מֵאֶרֶץ מִצְרַיִם וּפְדִיתָנוּ מִבֵּית עֲבָדִים, וְעַל בְּרִיתְךָ שֶׁחָתַמְתָּ בִּבְשָׂרֵנוּ וְעַל תּוֹרָתְךָ שֶׁלִּמַּדְתָּנוּ וְעַל חֻקֶּיךָ שֶׁהוֹדַעְתָּנוּ וְעַל חַיִּים חֵן וָחֶסֶד שֶׁחוֹנַנְתָּנוּ וְעַל אֲכִילַת מָזוֹן שָׁאַתָּה זָן וּמְפַרְנֵס אוֹתָנוּ תָּמִיד בְּכָל יוֹם וּבְכָל עֵת וּבְכָל שָׁעָה:

WHY BLESS GOD?

What does it mean to bless God? We can all understand the concept of God blessing us, but the idea of humans blessing God is rather strange! The recitation of *Birkat Ha-Mazon* has its biblical source in the verse, "And you shall eat and be satisfied and bless the Lord your God for the good land that He has given you" (Deuteronomy 8:10).

Had the verse instructed us to "thank God," using the term "*hoda'ah,*" this would be perfectly understandable — everybody accepts the importance of expressing gratitude to the Creator of the universe for His munificence in sustaining us. But for a human being to bless God sounds almost paradoxical; God may want our thanks, but why should He want our blessings? What can we possibly give the Creator of the universe that He doesn't already have?

Since the phrase "*u-verakhta et Hashem*" (you shall bless the Lord) does not appear anywhere else in the Torah, we can safely assume that the concept of blessing God must be associated with *Birkat Ha-Mazon* which, from the point of view of Jewish law, is only required when we eat bread, as implied by the verse, "you shall eat and be satisfied...." ✦

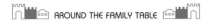
THE FIRST BLESSING

You are blessed, Lord our God, Sovereign of the world, Who provides food for the entire world in His goodness, with grace, kindness and mercy; He supplies bread for all living beings, for his kindness is everlasting. Because of His great goodness, we have never lacked food, nor will we ever lack it — on account of His great name — since He is God who feeds and provides sustenance, and performs good and supplies food for all His creatures which He brought into being. You are blessed, Lord, Who provides food for all.

THE SECOND BLESSING

We thank You, Lord our God, for having given the heritage of a lovely, fine and spacious land to our fathers, and for having brought us out, Lord our God, from Egypt, and for rescuing us from slavery, and also for Your covenant which You sealed in our flesh, as well as for Your Torah which You taught us, and Your laws which You have made known to us, and for the life, grace and kindness that you have granted us, and for the consumption of the food that You provide, giving us sustenance constantly, every day, at all times, at every hour.

THE UNIQUE QUALITY OF BREAD: BREAD VS. THE SEVEN SPECIES, SANCTITY AS A FUNCTION OF HUMAN INVOLVEMENT

But what is so special about bread, more than any other food? And even more to the point, only several biblical verses later, we find that the Torah praises a different category of sustenance: "For God your Lord brings you into a good land, a land of brooks of water, of fountains and depths... a land of wheat and barley, and vines and fig trees and pomegranates, a land of olive trees and honey dates." (Deuteronomy 8:7-8) These are the Seven Species with which the land of Israel is specially blessed, the seven special fruits for which the seven hills of Efrat are named. These luscious and colorful fruits are far more attractive and inspiring than a prosaic and commonplace loaf of bread. Indeed the biblical scouts chose to bring back juicy grapes, pomegranates and figs (Numbers 13:23) in order to demonstrate the uniqueness of Israel — not dry, crusty bread!

On Hannukah:

עַל הַנִּסִּים וְעַל הַפֻּרְקָן וְעַל הַגְּבוּרוֹת וְעַל הַתְּשׁוּעוֹת וְעַל הַמִּלְחָמוֹת, שֶׁעָשִׂיתָ
לַאֲבוֹתֵינוּ בַּיָּמִים הָהֵם בַּזְּמַן הַזֶּה:

בִּימֵי מַתִּתְיָהוּ בֶּן יוֹחָנָן כֹּהֵן גָּדוֹל חַשְׁמוֹנַאי וּבָנָיו, כְּשֶׁעָמְדָה מַלְכוּת יָוָן הָרְשָׁעָה
עַל עַמְּךָ יִשְׂרָאֵל לְהַשְׁכִּיחָם תּוֹרָתֶךָ וּלְהַעֲבִירָם מֵחֻקֵּי רְצוֹנֶךָ, וְאַתָּה בְּרַחֲמֶיךָ
הָרַבִּים עָמַדְתָּ לָהֶם בְּעֵת צָרָתָם, רַבְתָּ אֶת רִיבָם, דַּנְתָּ אֶת דִּינָם, נָקַמְתָּ אֶת
נִקְמָתָם, מָסַרְתָּ גִבּוֹרִים בְּיַד חַלָּשִׁים וְרַבִּים בְּיַד מְעַטִּים וּטְמֵאִים בְּיַד טְהוֹרִים
וּרְשָׁעִים בְּיַד צַדִּיקִים וְזֵדִים בְּיַד עוֹסְקֵי תוֹרָתֶךָ וּלְךָ עָשִׂיתָ שֵׁם גָּדוֹל וְקָדוֹשׁ
בְּעוֹלָמֶךָ וּלְעַמְּךָ יִשְׂרָאֵל עָשִׂיתָ תְּשׁוּעָה גְדוֹלָה וּפֻרְקָן כְּהַיּוֹם הַזֶּה. וְאַחַר כֵּן בָּאוּ
בָנֶיךָ לִדְבִיר בֵּיתֶךָ וּפִנּוּ אֶת הֵיכָלֶךָ וְטִהֲרוּ אֶת מִקְדָּשֶׁךָ וְהִדְלִיקוּ נֵרוֹת בְּחַצְרוֹת
קָדְשֶׁךָ, וְקָבְעוּ שְׁמוֹנַת יְמֵי חֲנֻכָּה אֵלּוּ לְהוֹדוֹת וּלְהַלֵּל לְשִׁמְךָ הַגָּדוֹל:

On Purim:

עַל הַנִּסִּים וְעַל הַפֻּרְקָן וְעַל הַגְּבוּרוֹת וְעַל הַתְּשׁוּעוֹת וְעַל הַמִּלְחָמוֹת, שֶׁעָשִׂיתָ
לַאֲבוֹתֵינוּ בַּיָּמִים הָהֵם בַּזְּמַן הַזֶּה:

בִּימֵי מָרְדְּכַי וְאֶסְתֵּר בְּשׁוּשַׁן הַבִּירָה, כְּשֶׁעָמַד עֲלֵיהֶם הָמָן הָרָשָׁע, בִּקֵּשׁ לְהַשְׁמִיד
לַהֲרֹג וּלְאַבֵּד אֶת כָּל הַיְּהוּדִים מִנַּעַר וְעַד זָקֵן טַף וְנָשִׁים בְּיוֹם אֶחָד, בִּשְׁלוֹשָׁה
עָשָׂר לְחֹדֶשׁ שְׁנֵים עָשָׂר הוּא חֹדֶשׁ אֲדָר וּשְׁלָלָם לָבוֹז. וְאַתָּה בְּרַחֲמֶיךָ הָרַבִּים
הֵפַרְתָּ אֶת עֲצָתוֹ וְקִלְקַלְתָּ אֶת מַחֲשַׁבְתּוֹ וַהֲשֵׁבוֹתָ לּוֹ גְּמוּלוֹ בְּרֹאשׁוֹ, וְתָלוּ אוֹתוֹ
וְאֶת בָּנָיו עַל הָעֵץ:

⋆∘∘∘⋅⟨∾⟩⋅∘∘∘⋆

Rav Soloveitchik, my rebbe and mentor, once addressed the issue of why bread should be singled out with three biblically ordained blessings (four in all — the first composed by Moses, the second by Joshua, the third by David and Solomon, and the fourth by the Sages after the destruction of Betar) — while the Seven Species, even though they grace the land of Israel like a crown of glory, are honored with only a single blessing following their consumption (*al ha-mihya, al ha-etz*)?

Not only that, but when three or more eat bread together, a formal *"zimun"* (literally "invitation") precedes the actual *Birkat Ha-Mazon*, in which one of the participants "invites" the others present to respond to the praises of God. On the Shabbat and Festivals, there is even a custom followed by many Jews to perform this *zimun* while lifting a cup of wine. This "formal invitation," however, is also exclusive to bread, and not the Seven Species.

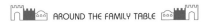
On Hannukah:

We thank You for the miracles, for the liberation, for the mighty acts, for the victories and for the wars which You waged for our ancestors in those days on this occasion. It was in the days of Mattityahu, son of Yohanan, the High Priest, a Hasmonean, and his sons, that the wicked Hellenistic regime confronted Your people Israel to make them forget Your Torah and to drive them away from the laws of Your will. Then You, in Your great mercy, stood up for them in their time of trouble. You pleaded their cause, argued their case, and avenged their wrong; You delivered the strong into the power of the weak, the many into the power of the few, the impure into the power of the pure, the wicked into the power of the righteous, and the sacrilegious into the power of those immersed in Torah. Thus You made for Yourself a great and holy Name in Your world, and for Your people Israel You brought about a great victory and liberation on this day. And afterwards, Your children came to the sanctuary of Your house, cleared your Holy place, purified Your Temple, and kindled lights in Your holy courts, and they established these eight days of Hannukah for giving thanks and praise to Your great Name.

On Purim:

We thank You for the miracles, for the liberation, for the mighty acts, for the victories, and for the wars which You waged for our ancestors in those days on this occasion. It was in the days of Mordekhai and Esther, in the capital of Shushan, that the wicked Haman rose up against them, seeking to wipe out, to murder and to destroy all the Jews, young and old, women and children. On one day, on the thirteenth day of the twelfth month which is the month of Adar, plundering them for spoil. But You, in Your great mercy, frustrated his plan, and thwarted his intention, and turned the tables on him, so that they hanged him and his sons on the gallows.

Rav Soloveitchik explained as follows: Concerning the Seven Species, the partnership between God and humans is limited, with humans performing a largely custodial task. Once we plant the seed, God does all the rest, with the possible exception of our watering and protecting the fruits; indeed, even the water is generally rainwater from God. The truth is that when an individual comes across a pomegranate tree in an open field, and takes a bite into the fruit, he/ she is almost experiencing the "manna from heaven"! God does almost everything! ⸙

BREAD SYMBOLIZES THE HUMAN PARTNERSHIP WITH GOD

In contrast, bread's extraordinary transitional journey from the field to the mouth requires a series of specific procedures. According to the Mishna's categorization of the thirty-nine forbidden activities on Shabbat, eleven are devoted to the preparation of bread: "Sowing, plowing, reaping, binding sheaves, threshing, winnowing, selecting, grinding, sifting, kneading, baking...." (Shabbat 74b)

וְעַל הַכֹּל יְיָ אֱלֹהֵינוּ אֲנַחְנוּ מוֹדִים לָךְ וּמְבָרְכִים אוֹתָךְ, יִתְבָּרַךְ שִׁמְךָ בְּפִי כָּל חַי תָּמִיד לְעוֹלָם וָעֶד, כַּכָּתוּב וְאָכַלְתָּ וְשָׂבָעְתָּ וּבֵרַכְתָּ אֶת יְיָ אֱלֹהֶיךָ עַל הָאָרֶץ הַטֹּבָה אֲשֶׁר נָתַן לָךְ. בָּרוּךְ אַתָּה יְיָ, עַל הָאָרֶץ וְעַל הַמָּזוֹן:

רַחֶם נָא יְיָ אֱלֹהֵינוּ עַל יִשְׂרָאֵל עַמֶּךָ וְעַל יְרוּשָׁלַיִם עִירֶךָ וְעַל צִיּוֹן מִשְׁכַּן כְּבוֹדֶךָ וְעַל מַלְכוּת בֵּית דָּוִד מְשִׁיחֶךָ, וְעַל הַבַּיִת הַגָּדוֹל וְהַקָּדוֹשׁ שֶׁנִּקְרָא שִׁמְךָ עָלָיו. אֱלֹהֵינוּ אָבִינוּ רְעֵנוּ זוּנֵנוּ פַרְנְסֵנוּ וְכַלְכְּלֵנוּ וְהַרְוִיחֵנוּ וְהַרְוַח לָנוּ יְיָ אֱלֹהֵינוּ מְהֵרָה מִכָּל צָרוֹתֵינוּ. וְנָא אַל תַּצְרִיכֵנוּ, יְיָ אֱלֹהֵינוּ, לֹא לִידֵי מַתְּנַת בָּשָׂר וָדָם וְלֹא לִידֵי הַלְוָאָתָם, כִּי אִם לְיָדְךָ הַמְּלֵאָה הַפְּתוּחָה הַקְּדוֹשָׁה וְהָרְחָבָה, שֶׁלֹּא נֵבוֹשׁ וְלֹא נִכָּלֵם לְעוֹלָם וָעֶד:

Clearly, the production of bread is a major project, and even though the seed and the earth and sun and the rain are provided by God, what comes up from the ground will turn into hay unless man first turns it into bread. In the production of bread, the concept of our partnership with God is clearly evident, with human ingenuity and exertion very much in the foreground; the eating of a pomegranate, in contrast, is basically receiving a Divine gift; it is simply a function of God bestowing His loving kindness upon us.

For the same reason, Jewish custom ordains that we place both our hands (ten fingers) over the Shabbat *hallot* before reciting the *"Ha-Motzi"* blessing. We are demonstrating that the bread came about as a result of Divine creation combined with human ingenuity and exertion. Rav Soloveitchik therefore suggests as an answer to our query that the greater the degree of human input, the greater the degree of sanctity. I might suggest a further elucidation of this profound insight. God might have created a world in which we were spectators and recipients — but then human beings would be no more than puppets or pawns in a Divine chess game, with the Almighty the sole player. God chose instead to create an imperfect, incomplete world in which we are to be His partners, in which He waits for us to perfect it — and to perfect ourselves. Insofar as we express our Divine-given function as His Partners, we do indeed "bless" God, and it is for the privilege of being God's co-workers — for the pride which comes from the knowledge that He thinks us worthy of being His partners — that we praise and bless Him especially when we are intimately involved in developing His creation. Since bread expresses — to a greater extent than the Seven Species — human effort and ingenuity, human partnership with God, the "mother of all blessings" is recited over bread! ♦

So for everything, Lord our God, we thank You and bless You; may the mouths of all living things bless Your name constantly, for all time. As it is written, "And you shall eat, and be satisfied, and bless the Lord your God for the good land that He has given you." You are blessed, Lord, for the land and for the food.

THE THIRD BLESSING

Have mercy, Lord our God, upon Israel Your people, upon Jerusalem, Your city, upon Zion — the home of Your glory, on the kingdom of the house of David, Your anointed one, and on the great and holy house which is called by Your name. Our God, our Father: look after us and feed us, give us a livelihood and support us, and provide a respite for us, Lord our God — soon, from all our troubles. And please, let us not be dependent, Lord our God, neither on a gift nor on a loan from a human being, but rather on Your full, open, holy and generous hand, so that we should never feel embarrassed or ashamed.

THE SECOND BLESSING: WHY THANK GOD FOR THE LAND?

"And you shall eat and be satisfied, and bless the Lord your God for the good land which He has given you." (Deuteronomy 8:11)

So does the Torah command the recitation of *Birkat Ha-Mazon*, the paradigm for our thanksgiving to God, whenever we partake in objects that give physical enjoyment. But the formulation of this verse seems strange, at the very least. I would have expected the text to read: "And you shall eat and be satisfied and bless the Lord your God for the good food which He has given you" — not necessarily for the "good land". Why do we thank God for the land when we have just become satisfied because of the food? ◈

THE HOMELAND SINGS

The first response I would offer to this question is that the land is, after all, the most basic source of food — since grains, fruits and vegetables grow on, and develop out of, the land. And the Torah portion Ekev (Deut. 8:7-9) is a paean of praise to the natural resources of the land of Israel. Even more to the point, if the land is not yours, the Gentile owner of the land can refuse to permit you to eat of its produce — and unfortunately, this has happened all too often in our exile-ridden history.

On Shabbat:

רְצֵה וְהַחֲלִיצֵנוּ יְיָ אֱלֹהֵינוּ בְּמִצְוֹתֶיךָ וּבְמִצְוַת יוֹם הַשְּׁבִיעִי הַשַּׁבָּת הַגָּדוֹל וְהַקָּדוֹשׁ הַזֶּה, כִּי יוֹם זֶה גָּדוֹל וְקָדוֹשׁ הוּא לְפָנֶיךָ לִשְׁבָּת בּוֹ וְלָנוּחַ בּוֹ בְּאַהֲבָה כְּמִצְוַת רְצוֹנֶךָ. וּבִרְצוֹנְךָ הָנִיחַ לָנוּ יְיָ אֱלֹהֵינוּ שֶׁלֹּא תְהֵא צָרָה וְיָגוֹן וַאֲנָחָה בְּיוֹם מְנוּחָתֵנוּ, וְהַרְאֵנוּ יְיָ אֱלֹהֵינוּ בְּנֶחָמַת צִיּוֹן עִירֶךָ וּבְבִנְיַן יְרוּשָׁלַיִם עִיר קָדְשֶׁךָ, כִּי אַתָּה הוּא בַּעַל הַיְשׁוּעוֹת וּבַעַל הַנֶּחָמוֹת:

On Rosh Hodesh (the beginning of a new month) and on a Festival:

אֱלֹהֵינוּ וֵאלֹהֵי אֲבוֹתֵינוּ, יַעֲלֶה וְיָבֹא וְיַגִּיעַ וְיֵרָאֶה וְיֵרָצֶה וְיִשָּׁמַע וְיִפָּקֵד וְיִזָּכֵר זִכְרוֹנֵנוּ וּפִקְדּוֹנֵנוּ וְזִכְרוֹן אֲבוֹתֵינוּ, וְזִכְרוֹן מָשִׁיחַ בֶּן דָּוִד עַבְדֶּךָ וְזִכְרוֹן יְרוּשָׁלַיִם עִיר קָדְשֶׁךָ, וְזִכְרוֹן כָּל עַמְּךָ בֵּית יִשְׂרָאֵל לְפָנֶיךָ לִפְלֵיטָה לְטוֹבָה לְחֵן וּלְחֶסֶד וּלְרַחֲמִים לְחַיִּים וּלְשָׁלוֹם בְּיוֹם

On Rosh Hodesh: רֹאשׁ הַחֹדֶשׁ הַזֶּה.

On Rosh Ha-Shanah: הַזִּכָּרוֹן הַזֶּה.

On Sukkot: חַג הַסֻּכּוֹת הַזֶּה.

On Shemini Atzeret/Simhat Torah: הַשְּׁמִינִי חַג הָעֲצֶרֶת הַזֶּה.

On Pesach: חַג הַמַּצּוֹת הַזֶּה.

On Shavuot: חַג הַשָּׁבוּעוֹת הַזֶּה.

זָכְרֵנוּ יְיָ אֱלֹהֵינוּ בּוֹ לְטוֹבָה, וּפָקְדֵנוּ בּוֹ לִבְרָכָה, וְהוֹשִׁיעֵנוּ בּוֹ לְחַיִּים טוֹבִים. וּבִדְבַר יְשׁוּעָה וְרַחֲמִים חוּס וְחָנֵּנוּ וְרַחֵם עָלֵינוּ וְהוֹשִׁיעֵנוּ, כִּי אֵלֶיךָ עֵינֵינוּ, כִּי אֵל מֶלֶךְ חַנּוּן וְרַחוּם אָתָּה:

Perhaps this is what the late Yaakov Hazan, one of the founders of the secular Kibbutz Ha-Shomer Ha-Tza'ir movement, meant when he recounted, in a radio interview shortly before his death, the earliest source of his Zionism. He told how, as a ten-year-old child in the Lithuanian city of Brisk, a doctor suggested that the best cure for his anemia would be exercise in the open summer air. His father apprenticed him to a Gentile farmer, with whom he tilled the ground diligently from dawn to dusk. Despite the arduous work, he noticed that the farmer had a perennial smile on his lips, which young Yaakov asked him to explain. "Don't you hear the land singing?" asked the farmer incredulously. Yaakov cupped his ear to the ground, but disappointedly reported that he heard nothing. "I know why," responded the farmer. "It is not your land!". (I would add that the Torah itself calls the special fruits and nuts of Israel "the song

On Shabbat:

Be pleased, Lord our God, to strengthen us through Your commandments, especially the commandment of the seventh day — this great and holy Shabbat. For this is day is great and holy before You, to rest and to be at ease, with love — as the command of Your will. So may it be Your will to grant us rest, Lord our God, that there should be no trouble, or unhappiness, or weeping on our day of rest. And let us witness, Lord our God, the consolation of Zion, Your city, and the rebuilding of Jerusalem, Your holy city, for You are the Lord of redemption and the Lord of consolation.

On Rosh Hodesh (the beginning of a new month) and on a Festival:

Our God and God of our fathers: may a reminder and remembrance of us, and of our fathers, and of the Messiah — son of David Your servant, and of Jerusalem — Your holy city, and of all Your people — the House of Israel, ascend and arrive, reach, and be noticed, and be accepted, heard, noted and remembered before You, for deliverance and well-being, for grace, kindness, and mercy, for life and peace on this day of

On Rosh Hodesh: **Rosh Hodesh**
On Rosh Ha-Shanah: **Remembrance**
On Sukkot: **the Festival of Sukkot**
On Shemini Atzeret/Simhat Torah: **the Eighth Day of Assembly Festival**
On Pesach: **the Festival of Unleavened Bread**
On Shavuot: **the Festival of Shavuot**

Be mindful of us, Lord our God, on this day, for good; take note of us for blessing and preserve us in life. And with a word of redemption and mercy, have pity on us and be gracious to us, and be merciful to us and save us, for our eyes are directed toward You, for You are a gracious and merciful Divine Ruler.

⸱⸱⟞⟞⟢⟣⟢⟣⟞⟞⸱⸱

of the land" — *zimrat ha-aretz* [Genesis 43:18]). At that moment young Yaakov Hazan vowed to come to his homeland, and to hear its song....

The land of Israel is then — literally — the land of the people of Israel: it is uniquely destined to provide us with material sustenance. And this unique relationship between the nation of Israel and the land of Israel works both ways. The Land of Israel — much as an eternally faithful wife — displays its beauty to and provides its sustenance only for the children of Israel. After all, during the nearly 2000 years that other nations occupied our land — Romans, Byzantines, Mamaluks, Turks, Arabs — its valleys and mountains remained barren and arid. It was only when the nation Israel returned to its homeland that luscious fruits and blazing flowers returned to the landscape, and a "green line" of separation could easily be demarcated.

On regular weekdays, continue here:

וּבְנֵה יְרוּשָׁלַיִם עִיר הַקֹּדֶשׁ בִּמְהֵרָה בְיָמֵינוּ. בָּרוּךְ אַתָּה יְיָ, בּוֹנֵה בְּרַחֲמָיו יְרוּשָׁלָיִם. אָמֵן:

בָּרוּךְ אַתָּה יְיָ אֱלֹהֵינוּ מֶלֶךְ הָעוֹלָם, הָאֵל אָבִינוּ מַלְכֵּנוּ אַדִּירֵנוּ בּוֹרְאֵנוּ גֹּאֲלֵנוּ יוֹצְרֵנוּ קְדוֹשֵׁנוּ קְדוֹשׁ יַעֲקֹב, רוֹעֵנוּ רוֹעֵה יִשְׂרָאֵל, הַמֶּלֶךְ הַטּוֹב וְהַמֵּטִיב לַכֹּל שֶׁבְּכָל יוֹם וָיוֹם, הוּא הֵטִיב הוּא מֵטִיב הוּא יֵיטִיב לָנוּ, הוּא גְמָלָנוּ הוּא גוֹמְלֵנוּ הוּא יִגְמְלֵנוּ לָעַד לְחֵן וּלְחֶסֶד וּלְרַחֲמִים וּלְרֶוַח הַצָּלָה וְהַצְלָחָה בְּרָכָה וִישׁוּעָה נֶחָמָה פַּרְנָסָה וְכַלְכָּלָה וְרַחֲמִים וְחַיִּים וְשָׁלוֹם וְכָל טוֹב וּמִכָּל טוּב לְעוֹלָם אַל יְחַסְּרֵנוּ:

הָרַחֲמָן הוּא יִמְלֹךְ עָלֵינוּ לְעוֹלָם וָעֶד: הָרַחֲמָן הוּא יִתְבָּרַךְ בַּשָּׁמַיִם וּבָאָרֶץ: הָרַחֲמָן הוּא יִשְׁתַּבַּח לְדוֹר דּוֹרִים וְיִתְפָּאַר בָּנוּ לָעַד וּלְנֵצַח נְצָחִים וְיִתְהַדַּר בָּנוּ לָעַד וּלְעוֹלְמֵי עוֹלָמִים: הָרַחֲמָן הוּא יְפַרְנְסֵנוּ בְּכָבוֹד: הָרַחֲמָן הוּא יִשְׁבֹּר עֻלֵנוּ מֵעַל צַוָּארֵנוּ וְהוּא יוֹלִיכֵנוּ קוֹמְמִיּוּת לְאַרְצֵנוּ: הָרַחֲמָן הוּא יִשְׁלַח לָנוּ בְּרָכָה מְרֻבָּה בַּבַּיִת הַזֶּה וְעַל שֻׁלְחָן זֶה שֶׁאָכַלְנוּ עָלָיו: הָרַחֲמָן הוּא יִשְׁלַח לָנוּ אֶת אֵלִיָּהוּ הַנָּבִיא זָכוּר לַטּוֹב וִיבַשֶּׂר לָנוּ בְּשׂוֹרוֹת טוֹבוֹת יְשׁוּעוֹת וְנֶחָמוֹת.

~~~

Hence there are two blessings relating to the land of Israel in our daily Amidah: the blessing for prosperity ("And provide blessing on the face of the land and satisfy us with its goodness") and the blessing of the ingathering of exiles. After all, material sustenance must include a homeland which can provide safe borders and which will always take you in, despite world condemnation and persecution. The sanctity of the Land of Israel is bound up inextricably with the people of Israel; it emanates from its ability to provide food and shelter — a home — for the nation Israel. And on this basis we can well understand Maimonides' position that in the main, when the Jews are no longer living on the land, the land is no longer sacred (Laws of the Chosen House, Chapter 6, Law 15). ✿

THE THIRD BLESSING: THE UNIQUE SANCTITY OF JERUSALEM

From thanksgiving for food and the Land of Israel, the prayer moves to the subject of Jerusalem — obviously bound up with the Land of Israel, but conceptually separated from it.

On regular weekdays, continue here:

And may You rebuild Jerusalem, the holy city, soon — in our lifetimes.
You are blessed, Lord, Who in His mercy builds up Jerusalem. Amen.

THE FOURTH BLESSING

You are blessed, Lord our God, Sovereign of the world — God Who is our Father, our King, our Mighty One, our Creator, our Redeemer, our Maker, our Holy One — the Holy One of Jacob; our Shepherd — the Shepherd of Israel, the King Who is good and Who does good to all, Who each and every day has been good, is good and will be good to us. He gave, gives and will always give us grace, kindness and mercy, and respite, deliverance and triumph, blessing and salvation, comfort, a livelihood and sustenance, and mercy and life and peace and all that is good. And may He never let us lack anything that is good.

The Merciful One — He will rule over us forever. May the Merciful One be blessed in heaven and on earth. May the Merciful One be praised for generation upon generation, and may He be glorified through us forever and ever, and may He be honored through us eternally. May the Merciful One grant us an honorable livelihood. May the Merciful One break the yoke from our neck and lead us upright to our land. May the Merciful One send a plentiful blessing upon this house, and upon this table at which we have eaten. May the Merciful One send us Elijah the prophet — who is remembered for good — who will bring us good tidings of salvation and consolation.

Jerusalem has a deeper sanctity — one which Maimonides insists is eternal: "The sanctity of Jerusalem is the sanctity of the Divine Presence, and the Divine Presence can never be nullified" (ibid). In order to attempt to understand what this really means, we must turn to the daily *Amidah* prayer. Here there are two blessings relating to Jerusalem, paralleling the two blessings relating to the land. In the first, we ask the Almighty God to "return with great compassion to Your city... to restore the Davidic dynasty and to build it as an everlasting building." In the second, we entreat the Almighty to speedily cause the sprouting of the Messiah since we anxiously await salvation.

Although one might superficially suggest that while Israel the land provides the materialistic and geographical infrastructure for the Jewish nation-state, Jerusalem the city constitutes the political and regal seat of the Davidic dynasty. But that is not really what the blessing is saying. After all, the real subject of the first blessing of Jerusalem is not the king or the political leader, but is rather the Almighty Himself — "And to Jerusalem Your city may You return in compassion." ◆

הָרַחֲמָן הוּא יְבָרֵךְ אֶת מְדִינַת יִשְׂרָאֵל רֵאשִׁית צְמִיחַת גְּאֻלָּתֵנוּ.
הָרַחֲמָן הוּא יְבָרֵךְ אֶת חַיָּלֵי צְבָא הַהֲגַנָּה לְיִשְׂרָאֵל, הָעוֹמְדִים עַל מִשְׁמַר אַרְצֵנוּ.

The following blessings are added according to the individual circumstances:

הָרַחֲמָן הוּא יְבָרֵךְ...

Children at their parents' table say

...אֶת אָבִי מוֹרִי בַּעַל הַבַּיִת הַזֶּה, וְאֶת אִמִּי מוֹרָתִי בַּעֲלַת הַבַּיִת הַזֶּה,

Those eating at their own table recite the following (married people add the appropriate words in parentheses)

...אוֹתִי (וְאֶת אִשְׁתִּי/אִישִׁי וְאֶת זַרְעִי) וְאֶת כָּל אֲשֶׁר לִי, וְאֶת כָּל הַמְסֻבִּין כָּאן,

THE TRUE FUNCTION OF THE KING IN ISRAEL

I believe we will be able to understand the true meaning of the blessing of the *Amidah* as well as of the sanctity of Jerusalem if we investigate the biblical concept of the function of the King of Israel. The Torah records that "when you come to the land and you say, 'Place upon me a king, like all the nations round about,' you shall place upon yourself a king whom the Lord your God shall choose" (Deut. 17:14-18). The text goes on to command that "the king dare not acquire a multitude of horses... nor a multitude of wives, nor may he amass a great deal of gold and silver... But he shall write a copy of this Torah scroll which shall remain with him... to observe all the words of this Torah."

The king of Israel was never slated to be the usual autocratic potentate who reveled in materialistic trappings of monarchy; rather, he was supposed to be the representative of the Almighty God, of the King of all Kings, Whose laws he had to inspire all of Israel — and eventually all of the world — to respect and maintain. After all, the biblical general and judge, Gideon, told those who asked him to rule over them, "I shall not rule over you, and my sons shall not rule over you; God shall rule over you" (Judges 8:23). From a Torah perspective, the king is merely God's representative, who would read the Torah to the assemblage every seven

May the Merciful One bless the State of Israel — the beginning of the flowering of our redemption.
May the Merciful One bless and shield the defenders of the State of Israel.

The following blessings are added according to the individual circumstances:

May the Merciful One bless...

Children at their parents' table say:

My father and teacher — the man of this house,
and my mother and teacher — the woman of this house;

Those eating at their own table recite the following (married people add the appropriate words in parentheses)

Me (and my wife/husband, and our children), together with everything that is mine, and all those who dine here,

years during the celebration of *Hakhel* in order to reenact the Revelation at Sinai (Maimonides, Laws of Hagigah, Chapter 3). And Jerusalem, the city of God, is the place from where the word of God is to emanate in order to communicate ethical monotheism to the world, the vision that "nation dare not lift up sword against nation; humanity dare not learn war any more" (Isaiah 2). ✦

THE SANCTITY OF JERUSALEM IS THE SANCTITY OF GOD'S VISION OF WORLD PEACE

The sanctity of the land of Israel derives from the sanctity of the nation of Israel; the sanctity of Jerusalem derives from God's teaching of ethical monotheism and universal peace. The name "Jerusalem" means City of Peace, and one of God's names is Peace. Our Temple of God is to be a "house of prayer for all nations." The nation of Israel is invested with the Divine mission of communicating God's will to the world through Jerusalem — whose sanctity is as inviolate and as eternal as is the sanctity of the Divine Presence itself. Just ponder the genius of a nation that commands the message of such profound and relevant theological-national-universal concepts as Israel and Jerusalem every time one of its members eats a piece of bread — even in the Diaspora. Is it any wonder, then, that the dreams of Israel and Jerusalem remained in the forefront of the Jewish mind and consciousness despite two thousand years of exile?! ✦

Guests recite a special blessing that is formulated differently according to custom. The following is adapted from the traditional Yemenite version:

...אֶת בַּעַל/בַּעֲלַת/בַּעֲלֵי הַבַּיִת הַזֶּה. הָרַחֲמָן יְיַשֵּׁר אוֹרְחוֹתֵיהֶם. הָרַחֲמָן יַצְלִיחַ אֶת דַּרְכֵיהֶם. הָרַחֲמָן מִכָּל צָרָה וְנֶזֶק יַצִּילֵם. הָרַחֲמָן יִפְתַּח לֵב בְּנֵיהֶם וּבְנוֹתֵיהֶם לְתַלְמוּד תּוֹרָתוֹ. הָרַחֲמָן יְגַדְּלֵם לַעֲבוֹדָתוֹ וּלְיִרְאָתוֹ. הָרַחֲמָן יְבָרֵךְ אֶת הַשֻּׁלְחָן הַזֶּה וִיסַדֵּר בּוֹ כָּל מַעֲדַנֵּי עוֹלָם וְיִהְיֶה כְּשֻׁלְחָנוֹ שֶׁל אַבְרָהָם אָבִינוּ, כָּל רָעֵב מִמֶּנּוּ יֹאכַל וְכָל צָמֵא מִמֶּנּוּ יִשְׁתֶּה.

All continue here:

אוֹתָם וְאֶת בֵּיתָם וְאֶת זַרְעָם וְאֶת כָּל אֲשֶׁר לָהֶם, אוֹתָנוּ וְאֶת כָּל אֲשֶׁר לָנוּ, כְּמוֹ שֶׁנִּתְבָּרְכוּ אֲבוֹתֵינוּ אַבְרָהָם יִצְחָק וְיַעֲקֹב בַּכֹּל מִכֹּל כֹּל. כֵּן יְבָרֵךְ אוֹתָנוּ כֻּלָּנוּ יַחַד בִּבְרָכָה שְׁלֵמָה, וְנֹאמַר אָמֵן:

בַּמָּרוֹם יְלַמְּדוּ עֲלֵיהֶם וְעָלֵינוּ זְכוּת שֶׁתְּהֵא לְמִשְׁמֶרֶת שָׁלוֹם, וְנִשָּׂא בְרָכָה מֵאֵת יְיָ וּצְדָקָה מֵאֱלֹהֵי יִשְׁעֵנוּ, וְנִמְצָא חֵן וְשֵׂכֶל טוֹב בְּעֵינֵי אֱלֹהִים וְאָדָם:

On Shabbat:

הָרַחֲמָן הוּא יַנְחִילֵנוּ יוֹם שֶׁכֻּלּוֹ שַׁבָּת וּמְנוּחָה לְחַיֵּי הָעוֹלָמִים:

On Rosh Hodesh (the beginning of a new month):

הָרַחֲמָן הוּא יְחַדֵּשׁ עָלֵינוּ אֶת הַחֹדֶשׁ הַזֶּה לְטוֹבָה וְלִבְרָכָה:

On a Festival:

הָרַחֲמָן הוּא יַנְחִילֵנוּ יוֹם שֶׁכֻּלּוֹ טוֹב:

On Rosh Ha-Shanah:

הָרַחֲמָן הוּא יְחַדֵּשׁ עָלֵינוּ אֶת הַשָּׁנָה הַזֹּאת לְטוֹבָה וְלִבְרָכָה:

On Sukkot

הָרַחֲמָן הוּא יָקִים לָנוּ אֶת סֻכַּת דָּוִד הַנּוֹפָלֶת:

Guests recite a special blessing that is formulated differently according to custom. The following is adapted from the traditional Yemenite version:

The owner(s) of this house; may He direct his (her, their) paths to be straight-forward. May He prosper all of his (her, their) ways, may He save him (her, them) from all trouble and distress. May He open the hearts of his (her, their) children to the Torah and Divine Service. May He bless this table and place upon it all the fine delicacies of the world; may He make it like the table of Avraham our father and Sarah our mother, so that anyone who is hungry may eat of it and anyone who is thirsty may drink of it.

All continue here:

— them, their household, their children and all that is theirs; we, and all that is ours, just as our fathers, Abraham, Isaac and Jacob were blessed — with everything — so may He bless all of us together with a complete blessing, and let us say Amen.

May we and they be judged favorably on high, resulting in the security of peace. And may we receive a blessing from the Lord, and righteousness from the God of our salvation. And may we find favor and understanding in the sight of God and man.

On Shabbat:

May the Merciful One bequeath to us a day that will be totally Shabbat and rest, for eternal life.

On Rosh Hodesh (the beginning of a new month):

May the Merciful One start this month for us with goodness and with blessing.

On a Festival:

May the Merciful One bequeath to us a day that is totally good.

On Rosh Ha-Shanah:

May the Merciful One start this year for us with goodness and with blessing.

On Sukkot

May the Merciful One raise up for us the fallen *sukkah* of David.

If, on Hannukah or Purim, the עַל הַנִּסִים addition was not included in its proper place, the following introductory sentence is recited, followed by either "In the days of Mordekhai..." or "In the days of Matityahu...."

הָרַחֲמָן הוּא יַעֲשֶׂה לָנוּ נִסִּים וְנִפְלָאוֹת כְּמוֹ שֶׁעָשָׂה לַאֲבוֹתֵינוּ בַּיָּמִים הָהֵם בַּזְּמַן הַזֶּה.

הָרַחֲמָן הוּא יְזַכֵּנוּ לִימוֹת הַמָּשִׁיחַ וּלְחַיֵּי הָעוֹלָם הַבָּא.

מַגְדִּיל (On days when the Mussaf service is added, say: מִגְדּוֹל) יְשׁוּעוֹת מַלְכּוֹ וְעֹשֶׂה חֶסֶד לִמְשִׁיחוֹ לְדָוִד וּלְזַרְעוֹ עַד עוֹלָם. עֹשֶׂה שָׁלוֹם בִּמְרוֹמָיו הוּא יַעֲשֶׂה שָׁלוֹם עָלֵינוּ וְעַל כָּל יִשְׂרָאֵל, וְאִמְרוּ אָמֵן:

יְראוּ אֶת יְיָ קְדֹשָׁיו כִּי אֵין מַחְסוֹר לִירֵאָיו. כְּפִירִים רָשׁוּ וְרָעֵבוּ וְדֹרְשֵׁי יְיָ לֹא יַחְסְרוּ כָל טוֹב. הוֹדוּ לַיְיָ כִּי טוֹב כִּי לְעוֹלָם חַסְדּוֹ. פּוֹתֵחַ אֶת יָדֶךָ וּמַשְׂבִּיעַ לְכָל חַי רָצוֹן. בָּרוּךְ הַגֶּבֶר אֲשֶׁר יִבְטַח בַּיְיָ וְהָיָה יְיָ מִבְטַחוֹ. נַעַר הָיִיתִי גַּם זָקַנְתִּי, וְלֹא רָאִיתִי צַדִּיק נֶעֱזָב וְזַרְעוֹ מְבַקֶּשׁ לָחֶם. יְיָ עֹז לְעַמּוֹ יִתֵּן, יְיָ יְבָרֵךְ אֶת עַמּוֹ בַשָּׁלוֹם:

THE FOURTH BLESSING: HA-TOV VE-HA-METIV

The Sages of the Talmud explain that although the basic content of the first three blessings of *Birkat Ha-Mazon* are biblically mandated (Deuteronomy 8), the actual wording of each was instituted during different periods: Moses instituted the words of the first blessing when the Almighty sent the manna in the desert; Joshua instituted the language of the second blessing when the Israelites entered the land of Israel, and Kings David and Solomon instituted the language of the third blessing with the sanctity of Jerusalem and the building of the Holy Temple.

The fourth blessing is considered to be rabbinical in origin, harking back to the fall of Betar at the conclusion of the abortive Bar Kokhba rebellion (135 C.E.). The Hadrianic persecutions, devastatingly executed by the Romans, brought untold misery to the defeated Judeans. When the Jews were finally allowed to bury their dead, the sages of Yavneh composed this fourth blessing, which gives thanks to the beneficent God (ha-Tov) Who miraculously did not allow the bodies to decompose, and to the benevolent God (ha-Metiv) Who permitted the bodies to

If, on Hannukah or Purim, the **על הנסים** addition was not included in its proper place, the following introductory sentence is recited, followed by either "In the days of Mordekhai..." or "In the days of Mattityahu..."

May the Merciful One perform miracles and wonders for us as He did for our ancestors in those days at this time.

May the Merciful One make us worthy of experiencing the days of the Messiah, and the life of the World to Come.

He brings about great victories for His king and shows kindness to His anointed one — to David and to his descendants forever. He Who makes peace in His high places, may He bring about peace for us and for all of Israel, and say — Amen.

Fear the Lord, you who are His holy ones, for there is nothing lacking for those who stand in awe of Him. Even young lions may suffer want and hunger, but those who seek the Lord will have no lack of all that is good. Praise the Lord for He is good, for His kindness is everlasting. You open Your hand and satisfy all living things. Blessed is the man who trusts in the Lord, and who makes the Lord the object of his trust. I was young and have become old, but never have I overlooked a deserving man who was destitute, with his children begging for bread. May the Lord give strength to His people; may the Lord bless His people with peace.

be buried. There can be no greater example of the ability of the Jew to give thanks to his God even in the most difficult of times, and to retain his faith in ultimate redemption even when experiencing cruel persecution, than this blessing of thanksgiving and hope. ✦

Note the English translation: not "I have never seen a deserving person who was destitute, with his/her children begging for bread," but rather, "I have never overlooked...." I have never seen such a tragedy without attempting to remedy or at least ameliorate the situation. We find such a usage for the verb *ra'oh* in Megillat Esther, when Esther asks Ahasverosh to rescind the permission granted to Haman to destroy the Jews of Persia: "for how can I look [— and not act, i.e., overlook] the evil which has befallen my nation; how can I look [— and not act, i.e., overlook] the destruction of my birth-people" (*ve-ra'iti* — look and not act; overlook — Esther 8:6). ✦

ברכת המזון בבית האבל

Three changes are made to the regular Birkat Ha-Mazon when it is recited in a house of mourning:

1. The *zimun* to *Birkat Ha-Mazon* is adapted as follows:

The leader begins:

רַבּוֹתַי, נְבָרֵךְ:

The others answer:

יְהִי שֵׁם יְיָ מְבֹרָךְ מֵעַתָּה וְעַד עוֹלָם:

The leader repeats:

יְהִי שֵׁם יְיָ מְבֹרָךְ מֵעַתָּה וְעַד עוֹלָם:

And continues:

בִּרְשׁוּת (בַּעַל (בַּעֲלַת/בַּעֲלֵי) הַבַּיִת הַזֶּה) מָרָנָן וְרַבָּנָן וְרַבּוֹתַי נְבָרֵךְ (בעשרה או יותר: אֱלֹהֵינוּ) מְנַחֵם אֲבֵלִים שֶׁאָכַלְנוּ מִשֶּׁלּוֹ:

The others say:

בָּרוּךְ (בעשרה או יותר: אֱלֹהֵינוּ) מְנַחֵם אֲבֵלִים שֶׁאָכַלְנוּ מִשֶּׁלּוֹ וּבְטוּבוֹ חָיִינוּ:

The leader repeats:

בָּרוּךְ (בעשרה או יותר: אֱלֹהֵינוּ) מְנַחֵם אֲבֵלִים שֶׁאָכַלְנוּ מִשֶּׁלּוֹ וּבְטוּבוֹ חָיִינוּ:

All say:

בָּרוּךְ הוּא וּבָרוּךְ שְׁמוֹ:

BIRKAT HA-MAZON IN THE HOUSE OF A MOURNER

Three changes are made to the regular Birkat Ha-Mazon when it is recited in a house of mourning:

1. The *zimun* (invitation) to *Birkat Ha-Mazon* is adapted as follows:

The leader begins:

My masters (or friends), let us say the blessing.

The others answer:

May the name of the Lord be blessed from now on and forever more.

The leader repeats:

May the name of the Lord be blessed form now on and forever more.

And continues:

With the consent of (my honored host[s] and)
all present, let us bless Him (if there are ten or more men present, say: "our God,") Comforter of mourners, Whose food we have eaten.

The others say:

Blessed is He (our God), Comforter of mourners, Whose food we have eaten and through whose goodness we live.

The leader repeats:

Blessed is He (our God), Comforter of mourners, Whose food we have eaten and through whose goodness we live.

All say:

May He be blessed and may His name be blessed.

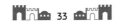

2. At the end of the third blessing, **רחם**, in the house of a mourner, the following replaces the blessing's conclusion (from **ובני ירושלים עיר הקדש** until the final blessing, (ברוך אתה ה' בונה...:

נַחֵם יְיָ אֱלֹהֵינוּ אֶת אֲבֵלֵי צִיּוֹן וְאֶת אֲבֵלֵי יְרוּשָׁלַיִם וְאֶת הָאֲבֵלִים הַמִּתְאַבְּלִים בָּאֵבֶל הַזֶּה. נַחֲמֵם מֵאָבְלָם וְשַׂמְּחֵם מִיגוֹנָם, כָּאָמוּר כְּאִישׁ אֲשֶׁר אִמּוֹ תְּנַחֲמֶנּוּ כֵּן אָנֹכִי אֲנַחֶמְכֶם וּבִירוּשָׁלַיִם תְּנֻחָמוּ. בָּרוּךְ אַתָּה יְיָ מְנַחֵם צִיּוֹן וּבוֹנֵה יְרוּשָׁלָיִם:

3. After this, recite this substitute fourth blessing, which concludes Birkat Ha-Mazon in the House of a Mourner:

בָּרוּךְ אַתָּה יְיָ אֱלֹהֵינוּ מֶלֶךְ הָעוֹלָם, הָאֵל אָבִינוּ מַלְכֵּנוּ אַדִּירֵנוּ גּוֹאֲלֵנוּ קְדוֹשֵׁנוּ קְדוֹשׁ יַעֲקֹב, הַמֶּלֶךְ הַחַי הַטּוֹב וְהַמֵּטִיב, אֵל אֱמֶת שׁוֹפֵט בְּצֶדֶק, לוֹקֵחַ נְפָשׁוֹת שַׁלִּיט בְּעוֹלָמוֹ לַעֲשׂוֹת כִּרְצוֹנוֹ וַאֲנַחְנוּ עַמּוֹ וַעֲבָדָיו. וְעַל הַכֹּל אֲנַחְנוּ חַיָּבִים לְהוֹדוֹת לוֹ וּלְבָרְכוֹ, גּוֹדֵר פְּרָצוֹת הוּא יִגְדֹּר אֶת הַפִּרְצָה הַזֹּאת מֵעָלֵינוּ וּמֵעַל עַמּוֹ יִשְׂרָאֵל בְּרַחֲמִים. עֹשֶׂה שָׁלוֹם בִּמְרוֹמָיו הוּא יַעֲשֶׂה שָׁלוֹם עָלֵינוּ וְעַל כָּל יִשְׂרָאֵל, וְאִמְרוּ אָמֵן:

2. At the end of the third blessing, **רחם**, in the house of a mourner, the following replaces the blessing's conclusion (from **הקדש עיר ירושלים ובני** until the final blessing, בָּרוּךְ אַתָּה ה' בּוֹנֵה...):

Comfort, O Lord our God, the mourners of Zion and the mourners of Jerusalem and the mourners who mourn at this advent of mourning. Grant them comfort from their mourning, and grant them joy from their sorrow, as it is said, "As an individual whose mother gives him comfort, so do I (God) comfort you," and "in Jerusalem shall you be comforted." You are blessed, Lord, Who comforts those who mourn and builds Jerusalem.

3. After this, recite this substitute fourth blessing, which concludes *Birkat Ha-Mazon* in the House of a Mourner:

Blessed are You, Lord our God, Sovereign of the world, God Who is our Father, our King, our Mighty One, our Redeemer, our Holy One, the Holy One of Jacob. The King Who lives, Who is good and performs good, the God of truth Who judges in righteousness, Who takes souls and rules in His world in accordance with His [often inscrutable] will.

We are His nation and His servants; for everything we are obligated to praise Him and to bless Him. The One who heals breaches, may He heal this breach from upon us and from upon His nation Israel with compassion.

May He Who makes peace in His high, heavenly places — may He bring about peace for us and for all Israel, and say Amen.

ברכה אחרונה

The following blessing is recited after (a) drinking wine or grape juice, or (b) eating one or more of the fruits (olives, dates, grapes, figs, pomegranates) associated with the land of Israel, or (c) one of the grains (wheat, barley, spelt, rye, oats).

If the snack includes none of these — e.g., a peach, a chocolate bar — then only the final blessing *"borei nefashot"* is recited.

בָּרוּךְ אַתָּה יְיָ אֱלֹהֵינוּ מֶלֶךְ הָעוֹלָם

For grain products:

עַל הַמִּחְיָה וְעַל הַכַּלְכָּלָה

For fruits:

עַל הָעֵץ וְעַל פְּרִי הָעֵץ

For wine:

עַל הַגֶּפֶן וְעַל פְּרִי הַגֶּפֶן

For grain products and wine consumed:

עַל הַמִּחְיָה וְעַל הַכַּלְכָּלָה וְעַל הַגֶּפֶן וְעַל פְּרִי הַגֶּפֶן

וְעַל תְּנוּבַת הַשָּׂדֶה, וְעַל אֶרֶץ חֶמְדָּה טוֹבָה וּרְחָבָה שֶׁרָצִיתָ וְהִנְחַלְתָּ לַאֲבוֹתֵינוּ לֶאֱכוֹל מִפִּרְיָהּ וְלִשְׂבּוֹעַ מִטּוּבָהּ. רַחֶם נָא יְיָ אֱלֹהֵינוּ עַל יִשְׂרָאֵל עַמֶּךָ וְעַל יְרוּשָׁלַיִם עִירֶךָ וְעַל צִיּוֹן מִשְׁכַּן כְּבוֹדֶךָ וְעַל מִזְבְּחֶךָ וְעַל הֵיכָלֶךָ. וּבְנֵה יְרוּשָׁלַיִם עִיר הַקֹּדֶשׁ בִּמְהֵרָה בְיָמֵינוּ. וְהַעֲלֵנוּ לְתוֹכָהּ וְשַׂמְּחֵנוּ בְּבִנְיָנָהּ וְנֹאכַל מִפִּרְיָהּ וְנִשְׂבַּע מִטּוּבָהּ וּנְבָרֶכְךָ עָלֶיהָ בִּקְדֻשָּׁה וּבְטָהֳרָה...

BLESSING AFTER A SNACK
The blessing recited after a snack is a shortened form of the first three blessings of Birkat Ha-Mazon. It is very clear from the content of the blessing that our central thanksgiving to God after partaking of food is our gratitude for the land of Israel.
When different types of food are to be eaten together, one ought choose what to eat first (and therefore to recite the appropriate blessing for first) in the following order:

 36

BLESSING AFTER A SNACK

The following blessing is recited after (a) drinking wine or grape juice, or (b) eating one or more of the fruits (olives, dates, grapes, figs, pomegranates) associated with the land of Israel, or (c) one of the grains (wheat, barley, spelt, rye, oats).

If the snack includes none of these — e.g., a peach, a chocolate bar — then only the final blessing *"borei nefashot"* is recited.

You are blessed, Lord our God, Sovereign of the world,

For grain products:

For the sustenance and nourishment

For fruits:

For the trees and their fruit

For wine:

For the vine and its fruit

For grain products and wine consumed:

For the substance and nourishment, and the vine and its fruit

...and for the produce of the field, and for the lovely, fine and spacious land which You graciously gave to our ancestors as a heritage, to eat its fruit and to be sated with its goodness. Have mercy, Lord our God, upon Israel — Your nation, upon Jerusalem — Your city, upon Zion — the home of Your glory, upon Your altar and upon Your Sanctuary. May You build up Jerusalem, the holy city, soon in our lifetimes, and may You bring us there so that we may rejoice in its rebuilding, eat of its fruit and be sated with its goodness. And there we shall bless You, in holiness and in purity...

1) grain products (cakes, cookies, cereals); 2) wine, grape juice or grapes; 3) olives; 4) dates; 5) figs; 6) pomegranates.

This order is based upon the biblical verse in praise of the land of Israel: "A land of wheat and barley, grapes, figs and pomegranates, a land of olive oil and date honey" (Deut. 8:8). The food closest to the words "land" has priority in importance.

On Shabbat:

וּרְצֵה וְהַחֲלִיצֵנוּ בְּיוֹם הַשַּׁבָּת הַזֶּה.

On Rosh Hodesh (beginning of a new month):

וְזָכְרֵנוּ לְטוֹבָה בְּיוֹם רֹאשׁ הַחֹדֶשׁ הַזֶּה.

On Festivals:

וְשַׂמְּחֵנוּ בְּיוֹם חַג הַמַּצּוֹת/הַשָּׁבֻעוֹת/הַסֻּכּוֹת הַזֶּה.

On Shemini Atzeret/Simhat Torah:

וְשַׂמְּחֵנוּ בְּיוֹם חַג הַשְּׁמִינִי, חַג הָעֲצֶרֶת הַזֶּה.

On Rosh Ha-Shanah:

וְזָכְרֵנוּ לְטוֹבָה בְּיוֹם הַזִּכָּרוֹן הַזֶּה.

כִּי אַתָּה יְיָ טוֹב וּמֵטִיב לַכֹּל, וְנוֹדֶה לְךָ עַל הָאָרֶץ...

For fruit: For grain products:

וְעַל הַפֵּרוֹת   וְעַל הַמִּחְיָה (וְעַל הַכַּלְכָּלָה)

For wine:

וְעַל פְּרִי הַגָּפֶן.

בָּרוּךְ אַתָּה יְיָ, עַל הָאָרֶץ וְעַל

For fruit: For wine: For grain products:

הַפֵּרוֹת: פְּרִי הַגָּפֶן: הַמִּחְיָה וְעַל הַכַּלְכָּלָה:

בורא נפשות

If the snack included — or consisted entirely of — other foods which are not included in any of the above categories, then recite the following:

בָּרוּךְ אַתָּה יְיָ אֱלֹהֵינוּ מֶלֶךְ הָעוֹלָם בּוֹרֵא נְפָשׁוֹת רַבּוֹת וְחֶסְרוֹנָן עַל כָּל מַה שֶּׁבָּרָאתָ לְהַחֲיוֹת בָּהֶם נֶפֶשׁ כָּל חָי. בָּרוּךְ חֵי הָעוֹלָמִים:

On Shabbat:

And be pleased to strengthen us on this Shabbat day;

On Rosh Hodesh (beginning of a new month):

And remember us for good on this day of Rosh Hodesh;

On Festivals:

And let us rejoice on this day of the Festival of Matza/Shavu'ot/Sukkot

On Shemini Atzeret/Simhat Torah:

And let us rejoice on this festive day of Shemini Atzeret

On Rosh Ha-Shanah:

And remember us for good on this Day of Remembrance

For You, Lord, are good and You perform good for all, and we thank You for the land and for the

For grain products:	For wine:	For fruit:
sustenance (and the nourishment).	fruit of its vine.	fruit.

You are blessed, Lord, for the land and for the

For grain products:	For wine:	For fruit:
sustenance (and the nourishment).	fruit of its vine.	fruit.

BOREI NEFASHOT

If the snack included — or consisted entirely of — other foods which are not included in any of the above categories, then recite the following:

You are blessed, Lord our God, Sovereign of the world, Creator of many souls and their needs: for all that You have created to keep every soul alive, You are blessed, ever living God.

סדר ליל שבת

Candle Lighting

Light the candles, then cover the eyes and recite the blessing. Uncover the eyes and gaze briefly at the candles.

בָּרוּךְ אַתָּה יְיָ אֱלֹהֵינוּ מֶלֶךְ הָעוֹלָם, אֲשֶׁר קִדְּשָׁנוּ בְּמִצְוֹתָיו וְצִוָּנוּ לְהַדְלִיק נֵר שֶׁל שַׁבָּת:

(יְהִי רָצוֹן מִלְּפָנֶיךָ יְיָ אֱלֹהַי וֵאלֹהֵי אֲבוֹתַי, שֶׁיִּבָּנֶה בֵּית הַמִּקְדָּשׁ בִּמְהֵרָה בְיָמֵינוּ, וְתֵן חֶלְקֵנוּ בְּתוֹרָתֶךָ. וְשָׁם נַעֲבָדְךָ בְּיִרְאָה כִּימֵי עוֹלָם וּכְשָׁנִים קַדְמוֹנִיּוֹת. וְעָרְבָה לַיְיָ מִנְחַת יְהוּדָה וִירוּשָׁלַיִם כִּימֵי עוֹלָם וּכְשָׁנִים קַדְמוֹנִיּוֹת:)

It is customary to recite the following prayer after kindling. The words in parentheses are added as applicable.

יְהִי רָצוֹן מִלְּפָנֶיךָ יְיָ אֱלֹהַי וֵאלֹהֵי אֲבוֹתַי, שֶׁתְּחוֹנֵן אוֹתִי (וְאֶת אִישִׁי) וְאֶת כָּל קְרוֹבַי, וְתִתֶּן לָנוּ וּלְכָל יִשְׂרָאֵל חַיִּים טוֹבִים וַאֲרֻכִּים. וְתִזְכְּרֵנוּ בְּזִכְרוֹן טוֹבָה וּבְרָכָה, וְתִפְקְדֵנוּ בִּפְקֻדַּת יְשׁוּעָה וְרַחֲמִים, וּתְשַׁכֵּן שְׁכִינָתְךָ בֵּינֵינוּ, וְזַכֵּנוּ לְגַדֵּל בָּנִים וּבְנֵי בָנִים חֲכָמִים וּנְבוֹנִים, אוֹהֲבֵי יְיָ, יִרְאֵי אֱלֹהִים, אַנְשֵׁי אֱמֶת, זֶרַע קֹדֶשׁ, בַּיְיָ דְּבֵקִים וּמְאִירִים אֶת הָעוֹלָם בַּתּוֹרָה וּבְמַעֲשִׂים טוֹבִים וּבְכָל מְלֶאכֶת עֲבוֹדַת הַבּוֹרֵא. אָנָּא, שְׁמַע אֶת תְּחִנָּתִי בִּזְכוּת שָׂרָה, רִבְקָה, רָחֵל וְלֵאָה אִמּוֹתֵינוּ. וְהָאֵר נֵרֵנוּ שֶׁלֹּא יִכְבֶּה לְעוֹלָם וָעֶד, וְהָאֵר פָּנֶיךָ וְנִוָּשֵׁעָה. אָמֵן:

• ◦ ⟨ ⟩ ⟨ ⟩ ◦ •

CANDLE LIGHTING FOR SHABBAT

Late Friday afternoon, 18 minutes before sunset, the woman of the house kindles the Shabbat lights as a symbol of peace in the home and as an expression of Shabbat joy. In so doing, the woman functions as a Priestess of the Holy Temple, in an act resembling the kindling of the Menorah. It is an established custom that when a girl reaches the age of 12 (bat-mitzvah) she should begin lighting one candle every Friday together with her mother. When she is married, she begins to light two candles, and subsequently adds an additional candle for each additional member born to her family. The proper procedure is for the woman to light the candles, after which she immediately closes her eyes and recites the blessing. She then extends her hands over the fire so that she can feel its warmth. The reason for this inverse order (usually the blessing is recited for a ritual act before its performance) is that once she recites the blessing, she has formally accepted the Shabbat and is now forbidden to kindle fire.

SHABBAT EVENING

Candle Lighting

Light the candles, then cover the eyes and recite the blessing. Uncover the eyes and gaze briefly at the candles.

You are blessed, Lord our God, Sovereign of the world, Who sanctified us with His commandments and commanded us to kindle lights for Shabbat.

(May it be Your will, Lord our God and God of our fathers, that the Temple should be rebuilt soon in our lifetime, and grant us involvement in Your Torah. And there we will serve You reverently as in days gone by, in ancient times. And may the offering of Judah and Jerusalem be sweet to the Lord as in days gone by, in ancient times.)

It is customary to recite the following prayer after kindling. The words in parentheses are added as applicable.

May it be Your will, Lord my God and God of my fathers, to be gracious to me (and to my husband / and children) and to all my family, causing Your Divine Presence of peace to dwell among us. Make me worthy to raise learned children and grandchildren who will bring light to the world with Torah and good deeds, and let the glow of our lives never be dimmed. Show us the light of Your face that we may be saved. Amen.

･〜◦〜◦◈◦〜◦〜･

Hence she must first light the candles, then recite the blessing — and since the blessing must precede some action, she ought then extend her hands to benefit from the warmth of the flame. It is then customary to recite the above prayer. If there is no woman in the house who is at least 12 years and one day old, a man should kindle the lights. ◈

Shalom Aleikhem

The Sages of the Talmud teach us that every individual is accompanied home from the synagogue on Shabbat eve by two ministering angels. If the Shabbat candles are lit and the table set for a special Shabbat meal, the members of the family are blessed by the angels with the wish, "So may it be next Shabbat, with God's help." (Shabbat 119b)

Since Shabbat familial harmony is a glimpse of our vision of ultimate world peace in the period of redemption, the family begins the Shabbat evening festivities with the Song of Peace, asking that the angels of peace bless us with peace. In our home we omit the fourth stanza, in accordance with the view of Rav Yaakov Emden, who did not think it proper to usher the angels out. ◈

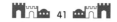

שלום עליכם

שָׁלוֹם עֲלֵיכֶם מַלְאֲכֵי הַשָּׁרֵת מַלְאֲכֵי עֶלְיוֹן,

מִמֶּלֶךְ מַלְכֵי הַמְּלָכִים הַקָּדוֹשׁ בָּרוּךְ הוּא.

בּוֹאֲכֶם לְשָׁלוֹם מַלְאֲכֵי הַשָּׁלוֹם מַלְאֲכֵי עֶלְיוֹן,

מִמֶּלֶךְ מַלְכֵי הַמְּלָכִים הַקָּדוֹשׁ בָּרוּךְ הוּא.

בָּרְכוּנִי לְשָׁלוֹם מַלְאֲכֵי הַשָּׁלוֹם מַלְאֲכֵי עֶלְיוֹן,

מִמֶּלֶךְ מַלְכֵי הַמְּלָכִים הַקָּדוֹשׁ בָּרוּךְ הוּא.

(**צֵאתְכֶם** לְשָׁלוֹם מַלְאֲכֵי הַשָּׁלוֹם מַלְאֲכֵי עֶלְיוֹן,

מִמֶּלֶךְ מַלְכֵי הַמְּלָכִים הַקָּדוֹשׁ בָּרוּךְ הוּא:)

כִּי מַלְאָכָיו יְצַוֶּה לָּךְ לִשְׁמָרְךָ בְּכָל דְּרָכֶיךָ.

יְיָ יִשְׁמָר צֵאתְךָ וּבוֹאֶךָ מֵעַתָּה וְעַד עוֹלָם:

אשת חיל

אֵשֶׁת־חַיִל מִי יִמְצָא וְרָחֹק מִפְּנִינִים מִכְרָהּ.

בָּטַח בָּהּ לֵב בַּעְלָהּ וְשָׁלָל לֹא יֶחְסָר.

גְּמָלַתְהוּ טוֹב וְלֹא־רָע כֹּל יְמֵי חַיֶּיהָ.

דָּרְשָׁה צֶמֶר וּפִשְׁתִּים וַתַּעַשׂ בְּחֵפֶץ כַּפֶּיהָ.

A WOMAN OF VALOR

The song in praise of a woman of valor comprises the last 22 verses of the Book of Proverbs. It is clear from the text that the biblical view of the woman's role was not necessarily to be

SHALOM ALEIKHEM

Welcome, ministering angels, messengers of the Most High,
of the supreme King of Kings, the Holy One, blessed be He.

Come in peace, ministering angels, messengers of the Most High,
of the supreme King of Kings, the Holy One, blessed be He.

Bless me with peace, ministering angels, messengers of the Most High,
of the supreme King of Kings, the Holy One, blessed be He.

May your departure be in peace, ministering angels, messengers of the Most
High, of the supreme King of Kings, the Holy One, blessed be He.

He will command His angels to watch over you in all your ways.
The Lord will watch over your comings and going
from now on and forever more.

ESHET HAYIL — A WOMAN OF VALOR

A woman of valor who can find? She is more precious than pearls.
Her husband places his trust in her, and only profits thereby.
She brings him good, and no evil, all the days of her life.
She seeks out wool and flax and cheerfully performs her handiwork.
She is like the trading ships, bringing food from afar.

fulfilled exclusively in the home; the woman described here takes care of her household but is likewise involved in business and agriculture as well as the pursuit of wisdom and loving kindness. There is a beautiful Sefardi custom for the husband and children to dance around the woman of the house while chanting Eshet Hayil, and even kissing her hand.

הָיְתָה כָּאֳנִיּוֹת סוֹחֵר מִמֶּרְחָק תָּבִיא לַחְמָהּ.

וַתָּקָם בְּעוֹד לַיְלָה וַתִּתֵּן טֶרֶף לְבֵיתָהּ וְחֹק לְנַעֲרֹתֶיהָ.

זָמְמָה שָׂדֶה וַתִּקָּחֵהוּ מִפְּרִי כַפֶּיהָ נָטְעָה כָּרֶם.

חָגְרָה בְעוֹז מָתְנֶיהָ וַתְּאַמֵּץ זְרוֹעֹתֶיהָ.

טָעֲמָה כִּי־טוֹב סַחְרָהּ לֹא־יִכְבֶּה בַלַּיְלָה נֵרָהּ.

יָדֶיהָ שִׁלְּחָה בַכִּישׁוֹר וְכַפֶּיהָ תָּמְכוּ פָלֶךְ.

כַּפָּהּ פָּרְשָׂה לֶעָנִי וְיָדֶיהָ שִׁלְּחָה לָאֶבְיוֹן.

לֹא־תִירָא לְבֵיתָהּ מִשָּׁלֶג כִּי כָל־בֵּיתָהּ לָבֻשׁ שָׁנִים.

מַרְבַדִּים עָשְׂתָה־לָּהּ שֵׁשׁ וְאַרְגָּמָן לְבוּשָׁהּ.

נוֹדָע בַּשְּׁעָרִים בַּעְלָהּ בְּשִׁבְתּוֹ עִם־זִקְנֵי־אָרֶץ.

סָדִין עָשְׂתָה וַתִּמְכֹּר וַחֲגוֹר נָתְנָה לַכְּנַעֲנִי.

עֹז־וְהָדָר לְבוּשָׁהּ וַתִּשְׂחַק לְיוֹם אַחֲרוֹן.

פִּיהָ פָּתְחָה בְחָכְמָה וְתוֹרַת־חֶסֶד עַל־לְשׁוֹנָהּ.

צוֹפִיָּה הֲלִיכוֹת בֵּיתָהּ וְלֶחֶם עַצְלוּת לֹא תֹאכֵל.

קָמוּ בָנֶיהָ וַיְאַשְּׁרוּהָ בַּעְלָהּ וַיְהַלְלָהּ.

רַבּוֹת בָּנוֹת עָשׂוּ חָיִל וְאַתְּ עָלִית עַל־כֻּלָּנָה.

שֶׁקֶר הַחֵן וְהֶבֶל הַיֹּפִי אִשָּׁה יִרְאַת־יְיָ הִיא תִתְהַלָּל.

תְּנוּ־לָהּ מִפְּרִי יָדֶיהָ וִיהַלְלוּהָ בַשְּׁעָרִים מַעֲשֶׂיהָ:

❧ ⚜ ❧

Eshet Hayil does not only apply to the woman of the house, however. The Talmud records that "When Rav Yosef would hear the sound of the footsteps of his mother he would declare, 'I must rise before the Shekhinah (Divine Presence) who is coming'" (Kiddushin 31b). The woman is a symbol of the Divine Presence, the compassionate and loving aspect of God, Who is present at every Shabbat table.

She arises while it is still night to provide food for her household and a fair share for her staff.

She considers a field and purchases it, and plants a vineyard with the fruit of her labors.

She girds herself with strength and her arms with energy.

She senses that her trade is profitable, her light is not extinguished at night.

She stretches out her hand to the distaff, while her palms hold the spindle.

She opens her palm to the poor and stretches her hand to the needy.

She has no fear of the snow for her household, for all her household is dressed in fine clothing.

She makes her own coverlets; she is dressed in fine linen and luxurious cloth.

Her husband is known at the gates, where he sits with the elders of the land.

She makes and sells linens; she supplies the merchants with sashes.

She is robed in strength and dignity, and faces the future with optimism.

She opens her mouth with wisdom, and the teaching of kindness is upon her tongue.

She looks after the conduct of her household, never tasting the bread of sloth.

Her children rise up and make her happy; her husband praises her: Many women have been valiant, but you have outshone them all.

Grace is deceptive and beauty is empty; a woman who fears the Lord — she shall be praised.

Give her credit for the fruit of her labors, and let her achievements praise her at the gates.

The custom in some places is not to recite Shalom Aleikhem or Eshet Hayil on the evening of a festival that coincides with Shabbat, although in our home we recite them with added fervor. After all, there is usually even more work in preparing for the festival than in preparing for Shabbat, and since the extended family is often present at the festival home celebrations, the angels of peace have an especially important role to play! ♦

ברכת הבנים

The parents (either only one, each separately, or both together, depending on custom) place their hands upon the head of each child in turn and bless him/her.

For a daughter:

יְשִׂמֵךְ אֱלֹהִים כְּשָׂרָה רִבְקָה רָחֵל וְלֵאָה.

For a son:

יְשִׂמְךָ אֱלֹהִים כְּאֶפְרַיִם וְכִמְנַשֶּׁה.

For both, continue:

יְבָרֶכְךָ יְיָ וְיִשְׁמְרֶךָ. יָאֵר יְיָ פָּנָיו אֵלֶיךָ וִיחֻנֶּךָ. יִשָּׂא יְיָ פָּנָיו אֵלֶיךָ וְיָשֵׂם לְךָ שָׁלוֹם.

ברכת הבשמים

בָּרוּךְ אַתָּה יְיָ אֱלֹהֵינוּ מֶלֶךְ הָעוֹלָם, בּוֹרֵא מִינֵי בְשָׂמִים.

BLESSING OF THE CHILDREN

It is interesting that the blessing for a son asks God to make him like Efraim and Menashe, the two sons of Joseph, whereas the blessing for a daughter asks the Almighty to make her like the matriarchs. Why not make the son like the patriarchs?

My wife provided the answer for me many years ago. I once asked her what she prays for above everything else when she kindles the Shabbat candles. She responded that she always prays for everyone's health — but adds that the children always be loving and supportive of one another. All of the siblings in the Torah — from Cain and Abel to Joseph and his brothers — were involved in tragic sibling rivalries. Efraim and Menashe were the only two brothers in the Book of Genesis about whom there is no hint of jealousy, even after the younger brother receives the primary blessing from his grandfather Jacob. We want our sons to be like Efraim and Menashe: loving and supportive siblings. Such a familial bulwark will provide the greatest protection against the often tempestuous waves that life brings upon us. ⸙

BLESSING OVER SPICES

There is a custom which harks back to the Holy Ari, practiced among some Hassidic groups and which we follow in our home, to recite a blessing over two sweet-smelling plants or spices. An individual recites the blessing, partakes of the fragrance, and then passes the spices around the table for all the participants to share.

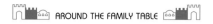
BLESSING FOR THE CHILDREN

The parents (either only one, each separately, or both together, depending on custom) place their hands upon the head of each child in turn and bless him/her.

For a daughter:

May God make you like Sarah, Rebecca, Rachel and Leah.

For a son:

May God make you like Efraim and Menashe.

For both, continue:

May the Lord bless you and watch over you. May the Lord shine His face towards you and show you favor. May the Lord lift His face towards you and grant you peace.

BLESSING OVER SPICES

You are blessed, Lord our God, Sovereign of the world, Creator of the various kinds of spices.

The Talmud records that when Rabbi Shimon Bar Yohai criticized the Roman government he was given a death sentence. He and his son escaped to a cave in Peki'in in the northern part of Israel, where they remained for twelve years, completely absorbed in the study of Torah. When they received a message from Elijah the prophet that the Roman Emperor had died and the death penalty rescinded, they left the cave, and saw a farmer tilling the ground. "How can you forsake the eternal world of Torah and involve yourself in the temporal world of agriculture?" decried Rabbi Shimon — and a fire came forth from his eyes, about to destroy the hapless farmer. Rabbi Shimon and his son began to return to the cave and forsake the materialistic world in which we live when they came upon an old man carrying two myrtle twigs. It was late Friday afternoon, and the old man explained that the myrtle was in preparation for his Shabbat table — one for the verse, "Remember the Shabbat day to keep it holy", and the second for the verse, "Observe the Shabbat day to keep it holy." Rabbi Shimon and his son then understood that every aspect of the material world can be sanctified; after all, the farmer's tilling of the soil could produce those very myrtle twigs which enhance the Shabbat table. They rejoined the world and set out to sanctify it rather than to reject it, thanks to the lessons of the myrtle twigs (Shabbat 33b).

This Talmudic story is the source for the custom of blessing two spices on Shabbat evening. But there is yet another significance to the spices. The Shabbat is set apart from the other days of

קידוש לליל שבת

(וַיַּרְא אֱלֹהִים אֶת כָּל אֲשֶׁר עָשָׂה וְהִנֵּה טוֹב מְאֹד) וַיְהִי עֶרֶב וַיְהִי בֹקֶר,
יוֹם הַשִּׁשִּׁי. וַיְכֻלּוּ הַשָּׁמַיִם וְהָאָרֶץ וְכָל צְבָאָם וַיְכַל אֱלֹהִים בַּיּוֹם
הַשְּׁבִיעִי מְלַאכְתּוֹ אֲשֶׁר עָשָׂה. וַיִּשְׁבֹּת בַּיּוֹם הַשְּׁבִיעִי מִכָּל מְלַאכְתּוֹ
אֲשֶׁר עָשָׂה, וַיְבָרֶךְ אֱלֹהִים אֶת יוֹם הַשְּׁבִיעִי וַיְקַדֵּשׁ אֹתוֹ כִּי בוֹ שָׁבַת
מִכָּל מְלַאכְתּוֹ אֲשֶׁר בָּרָא אֱלֹהִים לַעֲשׂוֹת.

סַבְרִי מָרָנָן וְרַבָּנָן וְרַבּוֹתַי

בָּרוּךְ אַתָּה יְיָ אֱלֹהֵינוּ מֶלֶךְ הָעוֹלָם, בּוֹרֵא פְּרִי הַגָּפֶן.

בָּרוּךְ אַתָּה יְיָ אֱלֹהֵינוּ מֶלֶךְ הָעוֹלָם, אֲשֶׁר קִדְּשָׁנוּ בְּמִצְוֹתָיו וְרָצָה בָנוּ,
וְשַׁבַּת קָדְשׁוֹ בְּאַהֲבָה וּבְרָצוֹן הִנְחִילָנוּ זִכָּרוֹן לְמַעֲשֵׂה בְרֵאשִׁית. (כִּי
הוּא יוֹם) תְּחִלָּה לְמִקְרָאֵי קֹדֶשׁ, זֵכֶר לִיצִיאַת מִצְרָיִם. (כִּי בָנוּ בָחַרְתָּ
וְאוֹתָנוּ קִדַּשְׁתָּ מִכָּל הָעַמִּים) וְשַׁבַּת קָדְשְׁךָ בְּאַהֲבָה וּבְרָצוֹן הִנְחַלְתָּנוּ.
בָּרוּךְ אַתָּה יְיָ, מְקַדֵּשׁ הַשַּׁבָּת:

the week by the Kiddush ceremony with wine at its beginning, and by the Havdalah ceremony with wine at its culmination. (Indeed, Kiddush and Havdalah mean the same thing: separation.) Just as the Havdalah includes a blessing over lights and a blessing over spices, so ought the parallel Kiddush, which is recited to the light of the Shabbat candles, also include fragrant spices. ✦

KIDDUSH

ויַרא אלהים את כל אשר עשה והנה טוב מאד — Why do we include here "And God saw..."? Because that is the beginning of the verse (Gen. 1:31), and a biblical verse should be recited in its entirety.

There are many customs as to precisely how to recite the Kiddush, with some standing, some sitting, and some standing for the first part and sitting for the second. Rav Moshe Isserles rules that the first paragraph, in which we bear testimony to God the Creator of the universe, be recited while standing, since witnesses must give their testimony before the Religious Court while standing. Since our Sages further rule that the Kiddush must be recited in the place where one eats, the blessing over the wine as well as the final blessing sanctifying the Shabbat are to be said while sitting around the table. It is best that one individual recites Kiddush for the entire assembly, since "a multitude of people brings greater glory to the King." The Hebrew word "kiddush" means "sanctification," and we make the sanctification over wine.

KIDDUSH FOR SHABBAT EVENING

(And God saw everything that He had made, and behold , it was very good;) It was evening and it was morning, the sixth day. So the heavens and the earth were finished, with all their complement. Thus on the seventh day, God had completed His work which He had undertaken, and He rested on the seventh day from all His work which He had been doing. Then God blessed the seventh day and made it holy, because on it He rested from all His creative work, which God had brought into being to fulfill its purpose.

You are blessed, Lord our God, Sovereign of the world, Creator of the fruit of the vine.

You are blessed, Lord our God, Sovereign of the world, Who sanctified us with His commandments and favored us, and gave us His holy Shabbat, in love and favor, to be our heritage, as a reminder of the Creation. It is the foremost day of the holy festivals, a memorial to the Exodus from Egypt. For it is us whom You have chosen, and us that You have sanctified, out of all the nations, and You have given us Your holy Shabbat, with love and favor, as our heritage. You are blessed, Lord, Who sanctifies Shabbat.

It is important to note that our sages understood very well the dangers inherent in wine. There is even a Midrash which records that when Noah was about to plant the first vineyard, after emerging safe and sound from the Ark, Satan suggested that he be his partner. The Evil One then killed a lamb, pouring its blood on the ground, followed by the blood of a lion, then the blood of a monkey, and then the blood of a pig.

Therefore, when one drinks a little wine he becomes sleepy like a lamb; after drinking a little more he becomes fearless like a lion; after imbibing still more he begins to engage in all kinds of foolish antics like a monkey; and after truly drinking to excess he becomes disgusting like a pig. Our sages further taught that wine is red because at worst, under its influence one can even come to shed innocent blood; at best, one's face turns red with shame when remembering words spoken or deeds committed when inebriated....

Nevertheless, Judaism believes that there is no aspect of the physical world that cannot be sanctified. And so we take this wine specifically — which has such potential for evil — and lift it up as a symbol of our ability and charge to sanctify every aspect of the physical world.

There are two fundamental motifs within the Kiddush: God the Creator, and God the Liberator. The Shabbat is a reminder of both the Creation of the world and our freedom from Egyptian slavery. The truth is that both of these messages are inextricably interrelated as two sides of

WASHING THE HANDS

Water is poured from a cup over the right hand and then over the left.

Before drying the hands, say:

(שְׂאוּ יְדֵיכֶם קֹדֶשׁ וּבָרְכוּ אֶת יְיָ. וְאֶשָּׂא כַפַּי אֶל מִצְוֹתֶיךָ אֲשֶׁר אָהַבְתִּי וְאָשִׂיחָה בְחֻקֶּיךָ.)

בָּרוּךְ אַתָּה יְיָ אֱלֹהֵינוּ מֶלֶךְ הָעוֹלָם, אֲשֶׁר קִדְּשָׁנוּ בְּמִצְוֹתָיו וְצִוָּנוּ עַל נְטִילַת יָדַיִם.

Placing both hands upon the hallot, say:

בָּרוּךְ אַתָּה יְיָ אֱלֹהֵינוּ מֶלֶךְ הָעוֹלָם, הַמּוֹצִיא לֶחֶם מִן הָאָרֶץ.

the same coin. After all, if God is our Creator, we are all creatures, subjects of the same one and only Lord. Therefore no human being has the right to enslave, lord over, or take advantage of any other human being. The Parenthood of God ensures the siblinghood of every human being and demands that every person be free.

And since God created the entire universe, Shabbat is the day in which we must recognize the right of each creature to live and be seen as a created being with its own individual value — not merely as a means to human ends. Hence we cannot even pluck a flower or ride a horse on Shabbat; we must recognize the right of every creature to be. A Hassidic sage once said that anyone who cannot declare "Shabbat Shalom!" to a tree or a dog doesn't understand the deepest meaning of Shabbat. ◆

WASHING THE HANDS

The ritual washing is not for the sake of cleanliness; it is necessary for the hands to be hygienically clean before the ritual washing. The Priests of the Holy Temple ritually washed their hands before performing the Temple service; Shabbat and Festival meals are considered to be sacred offerings to God. This is clear even from a linguistic perspective: the Hebrew verb for washing is *rahatz*, whereas the word *natal* means uplifting. This is not merely the washing of the hands; it is the uplifting of the hands in preparation for a sacred act.

The sages of the Talmud taught with regard to Kiddush that "there is no sanctification except in the place where you eat," meaning that one must recite the blessing over the wine in the same room where one is about to have the meal. The Hassidic Sages gave this legal requirement an added theological meaning: if one wishes to achieve true sanctity, then one must eat in a sacred manner, with familial love and togetherness amidst songs of praise to God and words of Torah study. Many religions practice sanctity when they fast; Jews attempt to express the highest sanctity when they eat. And hence the introduction to the blessing with the uplifting of the hands:

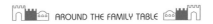

WASHING THE HANDS

Water is poured from a cup over the right hand and then over the left. Before drying the hands, say:

(Raise your hands to the holy place and bless the Lord. I will raise my hands to perform Your commandments, which are dear to me, as I speak of Your laws.)

You are blessed, Lord our God, Sovereign of the world, Who sanctified us with His commandments and commanded us to wash our hands.

Placing both hands upon the hallot, say:

You are blessed, Lord our God, Sovereign of the world, Who brings forth bread from the ground.

"Raise your hands to the Holy Place and bless the Lord." The table becomes an altar and our hands are ministering to the Almighty God as we begin the sacred meal.

There is further significance to the uplifting of the hands before one eats. The psalmist declares, "Who will go up to the mountain of the Lord, and who will stand in His holy place? He who is clean of hands and pure of heart, whose soul has not been given to vanity and who has never sworn deceitfully." (Psalms 24) Our hands must be ethically and morally clean of wrongdoing before we have the right to partake of any food.

The *hallot* — two braided loaves of bread — are covered over with a special cloth cover. This is reminiscent of the manna of the desert, which aimed to teach the Israelites that our food ultimately comes from God, and so we dare not and need not work on the Shabbat day in order to provide material sustenance. To this end, the Almighty provided a double portion of food on Friday that would suffice for Shabbat as well. Hence our Shabbat table features two *hallot* covered over, which was how the generation of the desert received their manna, according to the Midrash. The custom is then to place both hands on the hallah: bread represents — more than anything else — the partnership between man and God in the production of food, and our thanks to God is chiefly for the ability He implanted within us to produce the bread. (There are 11 separate procedures of human ingenuity and exertion from the time that the ground is plowed and prepared to the final product of bread or hallah.)

Our custom is then to slice the bottom hallah first on Shabbat evening, the upper hallah first on Shabbat morning, and both hallot together for the third meal. The upper hallah symbolizes God, the bottom hallah symbolizes the Jewish people; we understand that sometimes Israel may initiate and sometimes God may initiate the steps toward redemption, but our ultimate goal is for us to work together in Divine partnership. The hallah is then dipped in salt and distributed to all participants — the salt (used for preserving) symbolizing both the indestructible covenant with God as well as the ritual sacrifices which were likewise always accompanied by salt. ❧

זמירות ליל שבת

כל מקדש

כָּל **מ**ְקַדֵּשׁ שְׁבִיעִי כָּרָאוּי לוֹ.
כָּל **שׁ**וֹמֵר שַׁבָּת כַּדָּת מֵחַלְּלוֹ.
שְׂכָרוֹ **ה**ַרְבֵּה מְאֹד עַל פִּי פָעֳלוֹ.
אִישׁ עַל מַחֲנֵהוּ וְאִישׁ עַל דִּגְלוֹ.

אוֹהֲבֵי יְיָ הַמְחַכִּים לְבִנְיַן אֲרִיאֵל.
בְּיוֹם הַשַּׁבָּת שִׂישׂוּ וְשִׂמְחוּ כִּמְקַבְּלֵי מַתַּן נַחֲלִיאֵל.
גַּם שְׂאוּ יְדֵיכֶם קֹדֶשׁ וְאִמְרוּ לָאֵל.
בָּרוּךְ יְיָ אֲשֶׁר נָתַן מְנוּחָה לְעַמּוֹ יִשְׂרָאֵל.

דוֹרְשֵׁי יְיָ זֶרַע אַבְרָהָם אוֹהֲבוֹ.
הַמְאַחֲרִים לָצֵאת מִן הַשַּׁבָּת וּמְמַהֲרִים לָבֹא.
וּשְׂמֵחִים לְשָׁמְרוֹ וּלְעָרֵב עֵרוּבוֹ.
זֶה הַיּוֹם עָשָׂה יְיָ נָגִילָה וְנִשְׂמְחָה בוֹ.

ZEMIROT

Just as in the celebration of the Passover Seder, when the meal is merely one aspect of an entire evening dedicated to songs of thanksgiving to God and discussions about our time-hallowed traditions and values, so is to be each of the three Shabbat meals. The Torah portion of the week is generally the main topic of study-discussion; the songs deal with the beauty of the Shabbat as a foretaste of redemption and the importance of parents and children having shared experiences and values. The food, then, is not merely a source of nutrition and gastronomic pleasure; rather, it is the medium through which we establish strong bonds with each other, with our past tradition, and with God. This, we believe, was the main experience of the sacrificial meals in the Holy Temple in Jerusalem.

Zemirot for Sabbath Evening

Kol Mekadesh

Whoever hallows the Shabbat as befits it;

whoever protects the Shabbat properly from desecration,

His reward is exceedingly great — in accordance with his deed —

"Every individual at his own camp; every individual at his own banner."

Lovers of Hashem who long for the building of His holy Temple:

on the Shabbat day rejoice and be glad, as if receiving the gift of God's inheritance.

Raise your hands in holiness and say to God —

"Blessed is Hashem Who bestows tranquility on His people, Israel."

Seekers of Hashem, seed of Abraham — His beloved,

who delay departing from the Shabbat and who rush to welcome it,

glad to safeguard it and set its *eruv* —

"This is the day that Hashem has made; let us rejoice and be glad with it."

KOL MEKADESH

Attributed to R. Moshe ben Kalonymus the Elder, one of the early Ashkenazic sages (11th century).

"Every individual at his own camp; every individual at his own banner" — In its description of the creation of the human being, the Torah teaches: "And the Almighty created the human being in His image, in the image of God created He him, male and female created He them." Just about every English translation so translates the phrase, "in His image". However, I would render the pronoun in the small case, "in his image", since the very next phrase declares, "in the image of God created He him" — a teaching that would be superfluous were the first phrase to be "in His image". Apparently the Torah is telling us that every individual has his/her own image — his/her own particular and specific character, proclivities and set of talents — which is different from everyone else's and which emanates from the fact that each of us, male and female, was created in the image of God. Every parent, teacher and friend must constantly be aware of, and have respect for, the unique and inviolate image of God in each and every single person — and no one ought to try to obliterate that uniqueness. Human beings are not like salamis,

זִכְרוּ תּוֹרַת מֹשֶׁה בְּמִצְוַת שַׁבָּת גְּרוּסָה.

חֲרוּתָה לַיּוֹם הַשְּׁבִיעִי כְּכַלָּה בֵּין רֵעוֹתֶיהָ מְשֻׁבָּצָה.

טְהוֹרִים יִירָשׁוּהָ וִיקַדְּשׁוּהָ בְּמַאֲמַר כָּל אֲשֶׁר עָשָׂה.

וַיְכַל אֱלֹהִים בַּיּוֹם הַשְּׁבִיעִי מְלַאכְתּוֹ אֲשֶׁר עָשָׂה.

יוֹם קָדוֹשׁ הוּא מִבּוֹאוֹ וְעַד צֵאתוֹ.

כָּל זֶרַע יַעֲקֹב יְכַבְּדוּהוּ כִּדְבַר הַמֶּלֶךְ וְדָתוֹ.

לָנוּחַ בּוֹ וְלִשְׂמוֹחַ בְּתַעֲנוּג אָכוֹל וְשָׁתוֹ.

כָּל עֲדַת יִשְׂרָאֵל יַעֲשׂוּ אוֹתוֹ.

מְשֹׁךְ חַסְדְּךָ לְיֹדְעֶיךָ אֵל קַנָּא וְנוֹקֵם.

נוֹטְרֵי לַיּוֹם הַשְּׁבִיעִי זָכוֹר וְשָׁמוֹר לְהָקֵם.

שַׂמְּחֵם בְּבִנְיַן שָׁלֵם בְּאוֹר פָּנֶיךָ תַּבְהִיקֵם.

יִרְוְיֻן מִדֶּשֶׁן בֵּיתֶךָ וְנַחַל עֲדָנֶיךָ תַשְׁקֵם.

עֲזוֹר לַשּׁוֹבְתִים בַּשְּׁבִיעִי בֶּחָרִישׁ וּבַקָּצִיר עוֹלָמִים.

פּוֹסְעִים בּוֹ פְּסִיעָה קְטַנָּה, סוֹעֲדִים בּוֹ לְבָרֵךְ שָׁלֹשׁ פְּעָמִים.

צִדְקָתָם תַּצְהִיר כְּאוֹר שִׁבְעַת הַיָּמִים.

יְיָ אֱלֹהֵי יִשְׂרָאֵל אַהֲבַת תָּמִים.

יְיָ אֱלֹהֵי יִשְׂרָאֵל תְּשׁוּעַת עוֹלָמִים:

which all come out of the meat machine exactly the same size and shape. It is precisely the differences which make us human — and interesting, and creative.

I would suggest that even with regard to the manner in which we observe various commandments, there are legitimate variations on the theme within the parameters of *halakha*, depending upon individual inclinations and preferences. On Shabbat, for example,

Remember Moses' Torah as its Shabbat precept is expounded,

engraved with teachings for the seventh day like a bride bedecked among her companions;

Pure ones bequeath it and hallow it with the statement, "All that He had made" —

"On the seventh day God completed His work which He had done."

It is a holy day from beginning to end;

all of Jacob's seed will honor it according to the King's word and decree.

To rest on it and be glad with the pleasure of food and drink —

"The entire congregation of Israel will observe it."

Extend Your kindness to those who know You, O jealous and vengeful God;

to those who await the seventh day to uphold "Remember" and "Safeguard."

Gladden them with the rebuilt Jerusalem; make them radiant with the light of Your face —

Sate them with the abundance of Your house, and give them drink from the stream of Your Eden.

Always help those who desist from plow and harvest on the seventh,

who walk on it with short strides and feast three times on it in order to bless You.

May their righteousness blaze forth like the light of the Seven Days —

"Hashem, God of Israel, grant completeness!"

Hashem, God of Israel — a perfect love;
Hashem, God of Israel — eternal salvation.

are we to emphasize the aspect of prayer, or family togetherness, or walking along a beautiful nature trail? Do we experience a study-oriented Mitnagdic Shabbat, or a singing-oriented Hassidic Shabbat? The possibilities are certainly variegated enough, the rubric of Shabbat is certainly broad enough, to admit of different variations, all in accordance with *halakha*. It is indeed "every individual at his/her own camp; every individual at his/her own banner."

מנוחה ושמחה

מְנוּחָה וְשִׂמְחָה אוֹר לַיְּהוּדִים, יוֹם שַׁבָּתוֹן יוֹם מַחֲמַדִּים.
שׁוֹמְרָיו וְזוֹכְרָיו הֵמָּה מְעִידִים, כִּי לְשִׁשָּׁה כָּל בְּרוּאִים וְעוֹמְדִים:

שְׁמֵי שָׁמַיִם אֶרֶץ וְיַמִּים, כָּל צְבָא מָרוֹם גְּבוֹהִים וְרָמִים.
תַּנִּין וְאָדָם וְחַיַּת רְאֵמִים, כִּי בְּיָהּ יְיָ צוּר עוֹלָמִים:

הוּא אֲשֶׁר דִּבֶּר לְעַם סְגֻלָּתוֹ, שָׁמוֹר לְקַדְּשׁוֹ מִבֹּאוֹ וְעַד צֵאתוֹ.
שַׁבַּת קֹדֶשׁ יוֹם חֶמְדָּתוֹ, כִּי בוֹ שָׁבַת אֵל מִכָּל מְלַאכְתּוֹ:

בְּמִצְוַת שַׁבָּת אֵל יַחֲלִיצָךְ, קוּם קְרָא אֵלָיו יָחִישׁ לְאַמְּצָךְ.
נִשְׁמַת כָּל חַי וְגַם נַעֲרִיצָךְ, אֱכֹל בְּשִׂמְחָה כִּי כְבָר רָצָךְ:

בְּמִשְׁנֶה לֶחֶם וְקִדּוּשׁ רַבָּה, בְּרֹב מַטְעַמִּים וְרוּחַ נְדִיבָה.
יִזְכּוּ לְרַב טוּב הַמִּתְעַנְּגִים בָּהּ, בְּבִיאַת גּוֹאֵל לְחַיֵּי הָעוֹלָם הַבָּא:

MENUHA VE-SIMHA
Generally attributed to the same R. Moshe ben Kalonymus.
This poetic song refers to the Shabbat as a "day of delightful treasures."
The story is told of a poor Jew who dreamed that if he would journey to a far-distant town,
would go into the forest at the outskirts of the town, and would dig up the earth under the
sixth tree from the entrance to the forest, he would find a map that would lead him to a great

MENUHA VE-SIMHA

Contentment and joy, light for the Jews
on this day of Shabbat — day of delights.
Those who observe it and those who remember it — they bear witness
That in six days all was created and still endures.

The heavenly realms, earth and seas,
all the host above, high and exalted,
Sea giant and man and mighty beasts —
that the Creator, Hashem, is the stronghold of the universe.

It is He Who spoke to His treasured nation:
"Stand guard to hallow it from arrival to departure!"
The holy Shabbat, day of His delight —
For on it the Almighty rested from all His work.

Through the Shabbat command the Almighty will strengthen you;
Arise, beseech Him, that He may rush to fortify you.
Recite "Soul of all living" and also "We proclaim Your strength" —
Eat in gladness, for He has already shown you favor.

With double loaves and the great Kiddush,
with abundant delicacies and generous spirit,
they will merit much good — those who take pleasure in it,
With the coming of the redeemer, for the life of the World to Come.

treasure. He undertook the long and arduous journey, dug up a complex and convoluted map, painstakingly followed the geographic details — only to discover the treasure under a tree in his own backyard!

Many Jews pursue esoteric ideologies, searching out Far Eastern ashrams, never realizing that the most delightful spiritual treasure of all is to be found in their own backyards, in the foundation of their own tradition: the precious Shabbat!

מה ידידות

מַה יְדִידוּת מְנוּחָתֵךְ אַתְּ שַׁבָּת הַמַּלְכָּה.

בְּכֵן נָרוּץ לִקְרָאתֵךְ בּוֹאִי כַלָּה נְסוּכָה.

לְבוּשׁ בִּגְדֵי חֲמוּדוֹת לְהַדְלִיק נֵר בִּבְרָכָה.

וַתֵּכֶל כָּל הָעֲבוֹדוֹת לֹא תַעֲשׂוּ מְלָאכָה:

לְהִתְעַנֵּג בְּתַעֲנוּגִים בַּרְבּוּרִים וּשְׂלָו וְדָגִים:

מֵעֶרֶב מַזְמִינִים כָּל מִינֵי מַטְעַמִּים.

מִבְּעוֹד יוֹם מוּכָנִים תַּרְנְגוֹלִים מְפֻטָּמִים.

וְלַעֲרוֹךְ כַּמָּה מִינִים שְׁתוֹת יֵינוֹת מְבֻשָּׂמִים.

וְתַפְנוּקֵי מַעֲדַנִּים בְּכָל שָׁלֹשׁ פְּעָמִים:

לְהִתְעַנֵּג בְּתַעֲנוּגִים בַּרְבּוּרִים וּשְׂלָו וְדָגִים:

נַחֲלַת יַעֲקֹב יִירָשׁ בְּלִי מְצָרִים נַחֲלָה.

וִיכַבְּדוּהוּ עָשִׁיר וָרָשׁ וְתִזְכּוּ לִגְאֻלָּה.

יוֹם שַׁבָּת אִם תִּשְׁמֹרוּ וִהְיִיתֶם לִי סְגֻלָּה.

שֵׁשֶׁת יָמִים תַּעֲבוֹדוּ וּבַשְּׁבִיעִי נָגִילָה:

לְהִתְעַנֵּג בְּתַעֲנוּגִים בַּרְבּוּרִים וּשְׂלָו וְדָגִים:

⚜️

MAH YEDIDUT
"Jacob's inheritance shall the Shabbat observer inherit; an inheritance without bounds. The wealthy and poor alike shall honor it, and shall thereby merit redemption...."
I knew a very prominent, secular Jewish executive who retired from Manhattan to Jerusalem at the end of her life — when she became a fully Shabbat-observant Jew. She explained to

MAH YEDIDUT

How beloved is your contentment, you Shabbat Queen;

Therefore we run toward you, "Come, O royal bride!"

Dressed in beautiful garments to kindle the flame with blessing,

Then all labors ceased — "You shall not perform work."

       To indulge in delights — fatted fowl, quail, and fish.

From Shabbat Eve they prepare all manner of delicacies,

While yet day, fatted chickens were readied,

To arrange many varieties and to drink scented wines

And luxurious delicacies on all three occasions.

       To indulge in delights — fatted fowl, quail, and fish.

Jacob's inheritance shall the Shabbat observer inherit, without bounds;

Wealthy and poor alike shall honor it, and shall thereby merit redemption.

If you observe the Shabbat day you will be My treasure.

You shall labor for six days, and on the seventh let us rejoice.

       To indulge in delights — fatted fowl, quail, and fish.

me that she had come from a totally observant Jewish family in the deep south, which could barely (actually, rarely) make financial ends meet. Deeply embedded in her memory, however, were the words of her father as he would recline each Saturday afternoon on the outdoor lounge (which her parents called the "lunch"). He always spent the morning in prayer and study in the synagogue, after which he would enjoy a little Kiddush schnapps and herring with his cronies. Upon arriving home, he would eat a leisurely meal with the family, sharing

חֲפָצֶיךָ אֲסוּרִים וְגַם לַחֲשֹׁב חֶשְׁבּוֹנוֹת.

הִרְהוּרִים מֻתָּרִים וּלְשַׁדֵּךְ הַבָּנוֹת.

וְתִינוֹק לְלַמְּדוֹ סֵפֶר לַמְנַצֵּחַ בִּנְגִינוֹת.

וְלַהֲגוֹת בְּאִמְרֵי שֶׁפֶר בְּכָל פִּנּוֹת וּמַחֲנוֹת:

לְהִתְעַנֵּג בְּתַעֲנוּגִים בַּרְבּוּרִים וּשְׂלָו וְדָגִים:

הִלּוּכְךָ תְּהֵא בְנַחַת עֹנֶג קְרָא לַשַּׁבָּת.

וְהַשֵּׁנָה מְשֻׁבַּחַת כְּדָת נֶפֶשׁ מְשִׁיבַת.

בְּכֵן נַפְשִׁי לְךָ עָרְגָה וְלָנוּחַ בְּחִבַּת.

כַּשּׁוֹשַׁנִּים סוּגָה בּוֹ יָנוּחוּ בֵּן וּבַת:

לְהִתְעַנֵּג בְּתַעֲנוּגִים בַּרְבּוּרִים וּשְׂלָו וְדָגִים:

מֵעֵין עוֹלָם הַבָּא יוֹם שַׁבָּת מְנוּחָה.

כָּל הַמִּתְעַנְּגִים בָּהּ יִזְכּוּ לְרֹב שִׂמְחָה.

מֵחֶבְלֵי מָשִׁיחַ יֻצְּלוּ לִרְוָחָה.

פְּדוּתֵנוּ תַצְמִיחַ וְנָס יָגוֹן וַאֲנָחָה:

לְהִתְעַנֵּג בְּתַעֲנוּגִים בַּרְבּוּרִים וּשְׂלָו וְדָגִים:

anecdotes, laughs and Shabbat songs around the table, and then get ready for his afternoon nap. She loved the way he looked on Saturdays — at least ten years younger, his usually tension-creased brow and clouded-over eyes free and clear of worry and anxiety. Before drifting into sleep, he would boast to his eldest daughter: "Maybe Vanderbilt (the furniture magnate in their home city) makes me jealous during the week, but on Shabbat I make him

Your mundane affairs are forbidden on it, and even to calculate accounts;

Reflections are permitted, and to arrange matches for maidens;

To arrange for a child to be taught a text, to sing a song of praise,

And to engage in beautiful words in every corner and community.

　　　　　To indulge in delights — fatted fowl, quail, and fish.

May your walk be calm; declare the Shabbat a delight.

Its sleep is praiseworthy, as sufficient to refresh the soul.

Indeed, my soul yearns for You, to be content in love,

Fenced in like roses — on it son and daughter will rest.

　　　　　To indulge in delights — fatted fowl, quail, and fish.

A foretaste of the World to Come is the Shabbat day of contentment,

All who delight in it will merit much gladness.

From the birthpangs of the Messiah they will be rescued to relief.

Make our redemption flourish, that grief and sighs may flee.

　　　　　To indulge in delights — fatted fowl, quail, and fish.

jealous. After all, at this moment he has far more worries than I, who am privileged to have a twenty-five hour time-out from troubles and a blissful taste of the World to Come every single Shabbat."

"I became Shabbat observant," she concluded with a smile, "because I wanted Vanderbilt to be jealous of me too!" ♦

יוֹם זֶה לְיִשְׂרָאֵל

יוֹם זֶה לְיִשְׂרָאֵל אוֹרָה וְשִׂמְחָה שַׁבָּת מְנוּחָה:

צִוִּיתָ פִּקּוּדִים, בְּמַעֲמַד הַר סִינַי.
שַׁבָּת וּמוֹעֲדִים, לִשְׁמֹר בְּכָל שָׁנַי.
לַעֲרֹךְ לְפָנַי, מַשְׂאֵת וַאֲרוּחָה. שַׁבָּת מְנוּחָה: יוֹם זֶה לְיִשְׂרָאֵל...

חֶמְדַּת הַלְּבָבוֹת, לְאֻמָּה שְׁבוּרָה.
לִנְפָשׁוֹת נִכְאָבוֹת, נְשָׁמָה יְתֵרָה.
לְנֶפֶשׁ מְצֵרָה, תָּסִיר אֲנָחָה. שַׁבָּת מְנוּחָה: יוֹם זֶה לְיִשְׂרָאֵל...

קִדַּשְׁתָּ בֵּרַכְתָּ, אוֹתוֹ מִכָּל יָמִים.
בְּשֵׁשֶׁת כִּלִּיתָ מְלֶאכֶת עוֹלָמִים.
בּוֹ מָצְאוּ עֲגוּמִים, הַשְׁקֵט וּבִטְחָה. שַׁבָּת מְנוּחָה: יוֹם זֶה לְיִשְׂרָאֵל...

לְאִסּוּר מְלָאכָה, צִוִּיתָנוּ נוֹרָא.
אֶזְכֶּה הוֹד מְלוּכָה, אִם שַׁבָּת אֶשְׁמֹרָה.
אַקְרִיב שַׁי לַמּוֹרָא, מִנְחָה מֶרְקָחָה. שַׁבָּת מְנוּחָה: יוֹם זֶה לְיִשְׂרָאֵל...

חַדֵּשׁ מִקְדָּשֵׁנוּ, זָכְרָה נֶחֱרֶבֶת.
טוּבְךָ מוֹשִׁיעֵנוּ, תְּנָה לַנֶּעֱצֶבֶת.
בְּשַׁבָּת יוֹשֶׁבֶת, בְּזֶמֶר וּשְׁבָחָה. שַׁבָּת מְנוּחָה: יוֹם זֶה לְיִשְׂרָאֵל...

YOM ZEH LE-YISRAEL
"This day for Israel is... Shabbat of contented rest."
The Shabbat is our day of rest, in which we are restricted from performing thirty-nine principal categories of physically creative and energy-depleting activities. But what if an individual spends ten hours on Saturday re-arranging the furniture in his house — not technically

YOM ZEH LE-YISRAEL

This day for Israel is light and gladness: Shabbat of contented rest.

You commanded precepts at the assemblage at Sinai,
Shabbat and Festivals — to observe through all my years,
To prepare before me courses and banquets — Shabbat of contented rest.
This day for Israel...

Hearts' beloved of the shattered nation,
For suffering people — an additional soul;
For a troubled soul it removes sighs of grief — Shabbat of contented rest.
This day for Israel...

You hallowed; You blessed it above all other days.
In six days You completed the labor of the universe.
On it grieving people find tranquility and trust — Shabbat of contented rest.
This day for Israel...

Concerning the ban of labor the Awesome One commanded us;
I shall merit kingly glory if I safeguard the Shabbat.
I shall bring an offering to the Fearsome One, a perfumed meal offering —
Shabbat of contented rest.
This day for Israel...

Renew our Sanctuary, remember the ruined city.
Your goodness, our Savior, grant to the saddened one
Who spends Shabbat in song and praise — Shabbat of contented rest.
This day for Israel...

transgressing any of the prohibited categories of work, but not resting, either? Or what if he stays in bed all day — not exerting himself physically, but not engaging in any of the spiritual, intellectual and familial activities that are generally included in the "contented rest" which is supposed to define the Shabbat?

Maimonides insists that in addition to the negative prohibition, "You shall not perform physically creative activities (*melakha*)'" there is a positive command that the Shabbat is given "in order that they contentedly rest (*le-ma'an yanuah*)" (Deut. 5:13). In addition to not working, there must be positive involvement in the contented rest of spiritual, intellectual and family-centered activity! The Shabbat is not only a day of "don'ts"; it is first and foremost a very unique day because of its special "do's"! ✦

צור משלו

הַזָּן אֶת עוֹלָמוֹ רוֹעֵנוּ אָבִינוּ,
אָכַלְנוּ אֶת לַחְמוֹ וְיֵינוֹ שָׁתִינוּ.
עַל כֵּן נוֹדֶה לִשְׁמוֹ וּנְהַלְלוֹ בְּפִינוּ.
אָמַרְנוּ וְעָנִינוּ אֵין קָדוֹשׁ כַּיְיָ:

צוּר מִשֶּׁלוֹ אָכַלְנוּ בָּרְכוּ אֱמוּנַי שָׂבַעְנוּ וְהוֹתַרְנוּ כִּדְבַר יְיָ:

בְּשִׁיר וְקוֹל תּוֹדָה נְבָרֵךְ לֵאלֹהֵינוּ,
עַל אֶרֶץ חֶמְדָּה (טוֹבָה)
שֶׁהִנְחִיל לַאֲבוֹתֵינוּ.
מָזוֹן וְצֵדָה הִשְׂבִּיעַ לְנַפְשֵׁנוּ.
חַסְדּוֹ גָּבַר עָלֵינוּ וֶאֱמֶת יְיָ:
צוּר מִשֶּׁלוֹ אָכַלְנוּ...

רַחֵם בְּחַסְדֶּךָ עַל עַמְּךָ צוּרֵנוּ,
עַל צִיּוֹן מִשְׁכַּן כְּבוֹדֶךָ, זְבוּל בֵּית תִּפְאַרְתֵּנוּ.
בֶּן דָּוִד עַבְדֶּךָ יָבֹא וְיִגְאָלֵנוּ.
רוּחַ אַפֵּינוּ מְשִׁיחַ יְיָ:
צוּר מִשֶּׁלוֹ אָכַלְנוּ...

יִבָּנֶה הַמִּקְדָּשׁ עִיר צִיּוֹן תְּמַלֵּא,
וְשָׁם נָשִׁיר שִׁיר חָדָשׁ וּבִרְנָנָה נַעֲלֶה.
הָרַחֲמָן הַנִּקְדָּשׁ יִתְבָּרֵךְ וְיִתְעַלֶּה,
עַל כּוֹס יַיִן מָלֵא כְּבִרְכַּת יְיָ:
צוּר מִשֶּׁלוֹ אָכַלְנוּ...

TZUR MI-SHELO
Since this beautiful song contains all of the major motifs of *Birkat Ha-Mazon* (God the universal
Sustainer, the gift of the land of Israel, the request to rebuild Jerusalem), it should be sung

TZUR MI-SHELO

He nourishes His universe, our Shepherd, our Father,
We have eaten his bread, and His wine have we drunk.
Therefore let us praise His Name, and praise Him with our mouths —
Let us say, let us declare: There is none as holy as Hashem!

The Rock from Whose sustenance we have eaten — Bless Him, faithful friends. We have eaten our fill and left over, according to Hashem's word.

With song and the sound of thanksgiving let us bless our God
For the lovely and good land that He gave our forefathers as an inheritance.
With nourishment and sustenance He has sated our souls;
His kindness prevailed over us, and Hashem is truth!

The Rock from Whose sustenance we have eaten...

Our Rock — be merciful, in Your kindness, upon Your nation
Upon Zion, resting place of Your glory, the shrine and home of our splendor.
May the son of David, Your servant, come and redeem us —
Breath of our nostrils, anointed of Hashem.

The Rock from Whose sustenance we have eaten...

May the Temple be rebuilt; the city of Zion replenished.
There we shall sing a new song and ascend with great joy.
May the Merciful One, the Holy One, be blessed and exalted
Over a full cup of wine worthy of Hashem's blessing.

The Rock from Whose sustenance we have eaten...

towards the beginning of the meal, or at least when some food will still be served. If it is sung when the meal has been concluded, it renders *Birkat Ha-Mazon* redundant.

יה רבון

יָה רִבּוֹן עָלַם וְעָלְמַיָּא,
אַנְתְּ הוּא מַלְכָּא מֶלֶךְ מַלְכַיָּא.
עוֹבַד גְּבוּרְתֵּךְ וְתִמְהַיָּא, שְׁפַר קָדָמָךְ לְהַחֲוָיָא:

יָה רִבּוֹן עָלַם וְעָלְמַיָּא, אַנְתְּ הוּא מַלְכָּא מֶלֶךְ מַלְכַיָּא.

שְׁבָחִין אֲסַדֵּר צַפְרָא וְרַמְשָׁא,
לָךְ אֱלָהָא קַדִּישָׁא דִּי בְרָא כָּל נַפְשָׁא.
עִירִין קַדִּישִׁין וּבְנֵי אֱנָשָׁא, חֵיוַת בָּרָא וְעוֹפֵי שְׁמַיָּא: יָה רִבּוֹן עָלַם...

רַבְרְבִין עוֹבְדָךְ וְתַקִּיפִין,
מָכִיךְ רְמַיָּא וְזַקִּיף כְּפִיפִין.
לוּ יִחְיֶה גְּבַר שְׁנִין אַלְפִין,
לָא יֵעוֹל גְּבוּרְתֵּךְ בְּחוּשְׁבְּנַיָּא: יָה רִבּוֹן עָלַם...

אֱלָהָא דִּי לֵיהּ יְקַר וּרְבוּתָא,
פְּרוֹק יַת עָנָךְ מִפּוּם אַרְיָוָתָא.
וְאַפֵּיק יַת עַמֵּךְ מִגּוֹ גָלוּתָא,
עַמֵּךְ דִּי בְחַרְתְּ מִכָּל אֻמַּיָּא: יָה רִבּוֹן עָלַם...

לְמִקְדָּשֵׁךְ תּוּב וּלְקֹדֶשׁ קֻדְשִׁין,
אֲתַר דִּי בֵיהּ יֶחֱדוּן רוּחִין וְנַפְשִׁין.
וִיזַמְּרוּן לָךְ שִׁירִין וְרַחֲשִׁין,
בִּירוּשְׁלֵם קַרְתָּא דְשֻׁפְרַיָּא: יָה רִבּוֹן עָלַם...

KAH RIBON

O Creator, Master of this world and all worlds,
You are the King Who reigns over kings;
Your mighty and wondrous deeds — it is beautiful to declare before You.

O Creator, Master of this world and all worlds,
You are the King Who reigns over kings.

Praises shall I prepare day and night
To You, O holy God, Who created all life:
Holy angels and sons of man, beasts of the field and birds of the sky.

O Creator, Master of this world...

Great are Your deeds, and mighty,
Humbling the haughty and straightening the bowed.
Even if man lived for thousands of years
He could not fathom the extent of Your mighty deeds.

O Creator, Master of this world...

God — to Whom honor and greatness belong,
Save Your sheep from the mouth of lions
And bring Your nation out of its exile,
The nation that You chose from all the nations.

O Creator, Master of this world...

Return to Your Sanctuary, and to the Holy of Holies,
The place where spirits and souls will rejoice
And utter songs and praises
In Jerusalem, city of beauty.

O Creator, Master of this world...

KAH RIBON
This song was composed by R. Yisrael, son of R. Moshe the son of R. Levi Najara, who served as the rabbi of Gaza in the 17th century.

A Personal and Historical Testimony

One of the great miracles of the last quarter of the twentieth century was the collapse of the Iron Curtain of the Soviet Union and the close to one million Russian Jews who emigrated to Israel. There are many who maintain that the first and ultimately lethal blow against the Communist "Evil Empire" was dealt by the Soviet Jewish refuseniks — who refused to bow down to Communist atheism. Strangely enough, it was not until the early 60's that news of horrific anti-Semitic oppression against Soviet Jews began to be publicized in the free world, and we (at that time I was chairman of the Center for Russian Jews) began to picket the Russian consulate and the U.N. Always sensitive to public relations, the Communist government dispatched Rav Levin, the Chief Rabbi of Moscow, to New York in June 1969, armed with a newly published Soviet edition of the Jewish prayer book, called The Siddur of Peace. The Rabbi was to demonstrate with this publication the Soviet dedication to the continuity of Jewish religion and culture in the Soviet Union.

Rav Levin stayed in Essex House, where he held a private *minyan* (prayer quorum) each morning, which I attended. The "launch" of the new Soviet prayer book publication was to be that Sunday at the Hunter College auditorium. Since the synagogue closest to Essex House was my own fledgling (at the time) Lincoln Square Synagogue, I was introduced as the Rabbi of the neighborhood, and Rav Levin invited me to breakfast with him that Friday morning.

The Rav had come to New York with two attendants, one of whom (underground rumor had it) was a KGB (Soviet Secret Police) agent sent to "spy" on his activities. Since I was active on behalf of demonstrations for Soviet Jews, I tried to use the breakfast to gain much-needed hard facts about their plight. "Are there synagogues in Russia? Day schools? Zionist

organizations?" I queried. The Rav looked uncomfortable, glanced over at his attendant and answered my questions with counter-questions: "Are there synagogues in America? Day schools, Zionist organizations — in America?"

Seeing that I was getting nowhere, I decided to switch tactics. Knowing that Rav Levin had studied as a youth in the renowned Slobodka Yeshiva, I asked about the curriculum of studies and the various personalities that had made the institution unique. Somewhere in the midst of his lengthy reply, the problematic attendant left the table for the bathroom. Suddenly Rav Levin began to sing — at first in a whisper. He sang *Kah Ribon* — and when he reached the stanza, "God — to Whom honor and greatness belong, Save Your sheep from the mouth of lions...," his voice rose to a great crescendo and tears rolled down his cheeks. He sang these same words again and again as if they were a mantra, and his tears never stopped flowing. The spell was interrupted by the indignant voice of the attendant who had just exited from the bathroom: "Es iz nuch nit shabbes, Rav Levin! Vuss zingt ihr, Rav Levin?!" ("It is not yet Shabbat, Rav Levin! What are you singing, Rav Levin?!")

The sage turned white, and then red. Clearly embarrassed, he mumbled that "the young Rabbi wanted to know how they sang *zemirot* (Shabbat songs) in Slobodka."

I excused myself from the breakfast table. Clearly the Rav couldn't speak — but he had told it all through the immortal words of *Kah Ribon*.

קִידוּשׁ לְיוֹם הַשַּׁבָּת

(אִם תָּשִׁיב מִשַּׁבָּת רַגְלֶךָ עֲשׂוֹת חֲפָצֶךָ בְּיוֹם קָדְשִׁי, וְקָרָאתָ לַשַּׁבָּת
עֹנֶג לִקְדוֹשׁ יְיָ מְכֻבָּד, וְכִבַּדְתּוֹ מֵעֲשׂוֹת דְּרָכֶיךָ מִמְּצוֹא חֶפְצְךָ וְדַבֵּר
דָּבָר: אָז תִּתְעַנַּג עַל יְיָ וְהִרְכַּבְתִּיךָ עַל בָּמֳתֵי אָרֶץ וְהַאֲכַלְתִּיךָ נַחֲלַת
יַעֲקֹב אָבִיךָ כִּי פִּי יְיָ דִּבֵּר:)

וְשָׁמְרוּ בְנֵי יִשְׂרָאֵל אֶת הַשַּׁבָּת לַעֲשׂוֹת אֶת הַשַּׁבָּת לְדֹרֹתָם בְּרִית
עוֹלָם. בֵּינִי וּבֵין בְּנֵי יִשְׂרָאֵל אוֹת הִיא לְעֹלָם, כִּי שֵׁשֶׁת יָמִים עָשָׂה יְיָ
אֶת הַשָּׁמַיִם וְאֶת הָאָרֶץ, וּבַיּוֹם הַשְּׁבִיעִי שָׁבַת וַיִּנָּפַשׁ:

זָכוֹר אֶת יוֹם הַשַּׁבָּת לְקַדְּשׁוֹ. שֵׁשֶׁת יָמִים תַּעֲבֹד וְעָשִׂיתָ כָּל
מְלַאכְתֶּךָ. וְיוֹם הַשְּׁבִיעִי שַׁבָּת לַיְיָ אֱלֹהֶיךָ לֹא תַעֲשֶׂה כָל מְלָאכָה, אַתָּה
וּבִנְךָ וּבִתֶּךָ עַבְדְּךָ וַאֲמָתְךָ וּבְהֶמְתֶּךָ וְגֵרְךָ אֲשֶׁר בִּשְׁעָרֶיךָ. כִּי שֵׁשֶׁת יָמִים
עָשָׂה יְיָ אֶת הַשָּׁמַיִם וְאֶת הָאָרֶץ אֶת הַיָּם וְאֶת כָּל אֲשֶׁר בָּם וַיָּנַח בַּיּוֹם
הַשְּׁבִיעִי.

Some start here and recite only this verse-fragment before the blessing:

עַל כֵּן בֵּרַךְ יְיָ אֶת יוֹם הַשַּׁבָּת וַיְקַדְּשֵׁהוּ:

סַבְרִי מָרָנָן וְרַבָּנָן וְרַבּוֹתַי

בָּרוּךְ אַתָּה יְיָ אֱלֹהֵינוּ מֶלֶךְ הָעוֹלָם, בּוֹרֵא פְּרִי הַגָּפֶן:

ZEMIROT FOR SHABBAT MORNING

If the main theme of the Shabbat evening *zemirot* is the food, family and fellowship around the
Shabbat table, the main theme of the *zemirot* for the Shabbat day is Shabbat as the promise
of redemption. Shabbat is the foretaste of the World to Come. Just as the biblical "Covenant

KIDDUSH FOR SHABBAT MORNING

(If you will restrain your legs from walking beyond the Shabbat limit, your hands from performing your egoistic desires on My sacred day; if you will call the Shabbat a delight and honor the holy day of the Lord; if you will honor it by refraining from going about your personal affairs, from seeking your wants and speaking your mundane words, then you shall find your delight in the Lord, and He will raise you high above the highest towers on the earth; He will nourish you with the heritage of Jacob your father, for the voice of the Lord has spoken.) (Isaiah 58:13-14)

The children of Israel should keep Shabbat, observing Shabbat throughout their generations as an everlasting covenant. It is a sign between Me and the children of Israel for all time, that in six days the Lord made the heavens and the earth, and that on the seventh day He was finished and He rested. (Exodus 31:16-18)

Remember the Shabbat day to make it holy. Six days shall you labor and perform all your work, but the seventh day is Shabbat for the Lord your God: you shall not perform any creative work — neither you nor your son, nor your daughter, nor your male or female worker, nor your cattle, nor the stranger who dwells among you. Because in six days the Lord made the heavens and the earth, the sea, and all that they contain, and He rested on the seventh day. (Exodus 20:7-11)

Some start here and recite only this verse-fragment before the blessing:

That is why the Lord blessed the Shabbat day and made it holy.

You are blessed, Lord our God, Sovereign of the world, Creator of the fruit of the vine.

Between the Pieces" (Gen. 15:17-21) caused a great black fear, a *mysterium tremendum*, to descend upon Abraham when he contemplated Jewish struggle and persecution throughout the generations, its concluding Divine promise that the nation Israel will live eternally fills us with joy. ✦

זמירות ליום השבת
ברוך ה' יום יום

בָּרוּךְ אֲדֹנָי יוֹם יוֹם,
יַעֲמָס לָנוּ יֶשַׁע וּפִדְיוֹם,
וּבִשְׁמוֹ נָגִיל כָּל הַיּוֹם,
וּבִישׁוּעָתוֹ נָרִים רֹאשׁ עֶלְיוֹן,
כִּי הוּא מָעוֹז לַדָּל וּמַחֲסֶה לָאֶבְיוֹן:

שִׁבְטֵי יָהּ לְיִשְׂרָאֵל עֵדוּת,
בְּצָרָתָם לוֹ צָר, בְּסִבְלוֹת וּבְעַבְדוּת,
בְּלִבְנַת הַסַּפִּיר הֶרְאָם עֹז יְדִידוּת,
וְנִגְלָה לְהַעֲלוֹתָם מֵעֹמֶק בּוֹר וָדוּת,
כִּי עִם יְיָ הַחֶסֶד וְהַרְבֵּה עִמּוֹ פְדוּת:

מַה יָּקָר חַסְדּוֹ בְּצִלּוֹ לְגוֹנְנֵימוֹ,
בְּגָלוּת בָּבֶלָה שֻׁלַּח לְמַעֲנֵימוֹ,
לְהוֹרִיד בָּרִיחִים נִמְנָה בֵינֵימוֹ,
וַיִּתְּנֵם לְרַחֲמִים לִפְנֵי שׁוֹבֵימוֹ,
כִּי לֹא יִטֹּשׁ יְיָ אֶת עַמּוֹ, בַּעֲבוּר הַגָּדוֹל שְׁמוֹ:

עֵילָם שָׁת כִּסְאוֹ לְהַצִּיל יְדִידָיו, לְהַעֲבִיר מִשָּׁם מֹאזְנֵי מוֹרְדָיו,
מֵעֲבוּר בַּשֶּׁלַח פָּדָה אֶת עֲבָדָיו,
קֶרֶן לְעַמּוֹ יָרִים תְּהִלָּה לְכָל חֲסִידָיו,
כִּי אִם הוֹגָה וְרִחַם כְּרַחֲמָיו וּכְרֹב חֲסָדָיו:

❧⟨⟨❈⟩⟩❧

BARUKH HASHEM YOM YOM
Composed by R. Shimon, son of R. Isaac the Great of Mainz, 11th century.
This song reviews our Egyptian, Babylonian, Persian, Greco-Roman, Christian and Moslem

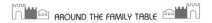
ZEMIROT FOR SHABBAT DAY

BARUKH HASHEM YOM YOM

Blessed is my Lord for every single day;

He will bring us salvation and redemption.

Then in His Name we will sing songs of gladness all day

And in His salvation we will raise our head up high —

For He is a stronghold for the needy and a refuge for the destitute.

That the tribes are God's He bore witness to Israel.

Amid their distress is His distress, in oppression and slavery.

Through a sapphire brick He showed them the strength of His love;

He was then revealed to lift them from the depth of pit and dungeon,

For with God is the loving kindness and His redemption is abundant.

How precious is His loving kindness to shield them with His protection.

Into Babylonian exile was He dispatched for their sake,

When their ships went down He was included among them.

Then He caused them to be treated mercifully by their captors —

For Hashem will not forsake His people because of His great Name.

In Elam He placed His throne to rescue His loved ones, to destroy from there the strongholds of His rebels.

From passage under the sword He redeemed His servants.

Pride for His nation shall He raise, praise for all His devout ones —

For though He afflicts, He then pities in His mercy and His abundant loving kindness.

enemies, each of whom in turn was vanquished (or at least outlived) by Israel. Our ultimate goal remains our desire for world peace, as enunciated in the final stanza. ♦

וּצְפִיר הָעִזִּים הִגְדִּיל עֲצוּמָיו, וְגַם חֲזוּת
אַרְבַּע עָלוּ לִמְרוֹמָיו,
וּבְלִבָּם דִּמּוּ לְהַשְׁחִית אֶת רְחוּמָיו,
עַל יְדֵי כֹהֲנָיו מִגֵּר מִתְקוֹמְמָיו,
חַסְדֵי יְיָ כִּי לֹא תָמְנוּ כִּי לֹא כָלוּ רַחֲמָיו:

נִסְגַּרְתִּי לֶאֱדוֹם בְּיַד רֵעַי מְדָנַי, שֶׁבְּכָל יוֹם וָיוֹם
מְמַלְּאִים כְּרֵסָם מֵעֲדָנַי,
עֶזְרָתוֹ עִמִּי לִסְמוֹךְ אֶת אֲדָנַי,
וְלֹא נְטַשְׁתַּנִי כָּל יְמֵי עִדָּנַי,
כִּי לֹא יִזְנַח לְעוֹלָם אֲדֹנָי:

בְּבֹאוֹ מֵאֱדוֹם חֲמוּץ בְּגָדִים, זֶבַח לוֹ
בְּבָצְרָה וְטֶבַח לוֹ בְּבוֹגְדִים,
וַיִּז נִצְחָם מַלְבּוּשָׁיו לְהַאְדִים,
בְּכֹחוֹ הַגָּדוֹל יְבַצֵּר רוּחַ נְגִידִים,
הָגָה בְּרוּחוֹ הַקָּשָׁה בְּיוֹם קָדִים:

רָאוֹתוֹ כִּי כֵן אֱדוֹמִי הָעוֹצֵר, יַחְשֹׁב לוֹ בְּבָצְרָה תִּקְלֹט כְּבֶצֶר,
וּמַלְאָךְ כְּאָדָם בְּתוֹכָהּ יִנָּצֵר, וּמֵזִיד
כְּשׁוֹגֵג בְּמִקְלָט יֵעָצֵר,
אֶהֱבוּ אֶת יְיָ כָּל חֲסִידָיו אֱמוּנִים נוֹצֵר:

יְצַוֶּה צוּר חַסְדּוֹ קְהִלּוֹתָיו לְקַבֵּץ,
מֵאַרְבַּע רוּחוֹת עָדָיו לְהִקָּבֵץ, וּבְהַר מְרוֹם הָרִים אוֹתָנוּ לְהַרְבֵּץ,
וְאִתָּנוּ יָשׁוּב נִדָּחִים קוֹבֵץ,
יָשִׁיב לֹא נֶאֱמַר כִּי אִם וְשָׁב וְקִבֵּץ:

Then the he-goat exalted itself over mighty ones, and the semblance of the four ascended even to His heights.

In their hearts they intended to destroy the objects of His mercy,

But through His priest He laid low those who rose up against Him —

Hashem's loving kindness surely has not ended, nor are His mercies exhausted.

I was handed over to Edom through my contentious brothers, who daily filled their bellies from my treasures.

His help stayed with me to support my pillars;

You have not forsaken me all the days of my times —

For Hashem does not reject forever.

When He comes from Edom with bloodied clothes He will slaughter in Botzra, executing traitors.

The dripping of their lifeblood will redden His garments.

With His great strength He will cut down the spirit of the nobles,

Sweeping away with His mighty blast like the day of the east wind.

When he sees how it is, the Edomite oppressor, he will think that Botzra can give refuge like Betzer;

That angel, like man, is protected within it, and that the willful, like the unintentional one, is detained in the refuge —

Love Hashem, all His devout ones; His faithful ones He safeguards.

May the Rock command His loving kindness to gather in congregations

From the four winds to be gathered up to Him, upon the loftiest mountain to set us down.

He shall return with us, the Gatherer of outcasts —

"He shall bring back" is not said, but "He shall return," and gather in.

בָּרוּךְ הוּא אֱלֹהֵינוּ אֲשֶׁר טוֹב גְּמָלָנוּ,
כְּרַחֲמָיו וּכְרֹב חֲסָדָיו הִגְדִּיל לָנוּ,
אֵלֶּה וְכָאֵלֶּה יוֹסֵף עִמָּנוּ,
לְהַגְדִּיל שְׁמוֹ הַגָּדוֹל הַגִּבּוֹר וְהַנּוֹרָא
שֶׁנִּקְרָא עָלֵינוּ:

בָּרוּךְ אֱלֹהֵינוּ שֶׁבְּרָאָנוּ לִכְבוֹדוֹ,
לְהַלְלוֹ וּלְשַׁבְּחוֹ וּלְסַפֵּר הוֹדוֹ,
מִכָּל אוֹם גָּבַר עָלֵינוּ חַסְדּוֹ,
לָכֵן בְּכָל לֵב וּבְכָל נֶפֶשׁ וּבְכָל מְאוֹדוֹ,
נַמְלִיכוֹ וּנְיַחֲדוֹ:

שֶׁהַשָּׁלוֹם שֶׁלּוֹ יָשִׂים עָלֵינוּ בְּרָכָה וְחַיִּים וְשָׁלוֹם,
מִשְּׂמֹאל וּמִיָּמִין עַל יִשְׂרָאֵל שָׁלוֹם,
הָרַחֲמָן הוּא יְבָרֵךְ אֶת עַמּוֹ בַשָּׁלוֹם,
וְיִזְכּוּ לִרְאוֹת בָּנִים וּבְנֵי בָנִים עוֹסְקִים בַּתּוֹרָה
וּבְמִצְוֹת עַל יִשְׂרָאֵל שָׁלוֹם,
יוֹעֵץ אֵל גִּבּוֹר אֲבִי עַד שַׂר שָׁלוֹם:

Blessed is our God Who performed good for us,

According to His mercy and His abundant loving kindness He did great things for us.

Both these and their like may He increase with us

To magnify His great, mighty and awesome Name

Which was proclaimed upon us.

Blessed is our God Who created us for His glory;

to praise Him, laud Him and relate His majesty.

More than any nation He strengthened His loving kindness over us.

Therefore with all our heart, with all our soul and with all our resources

Let us proclaim him King and proclaim Him Unique.

May He to Whom peace belongs set upon us blessing and peace

From left and from right, peace upon Israel.

May the Merciful One bless Israel with peace,

And may they merit to see children and grandchildren engaging in Torah and the commandments, bringing peace upon Israel.

Adviser, Mighty God, Eternal Father, Prince of Peace.

ברוך אל עליון

בָּרוּךְ אֵל עֶלְיוֹן אֲשֶׁר נָתַן מְנוּחָה,
לְנַפְשֵׁנוּ פִדְיוֹם מִשֵּׁאת וַאֲנָחָה.
וְהוּא יִדְרוֹשׁ לְצִיּוֹן עִיר הַנִּדָּחָה,
עַד אָנָה תּוּגְיוֹן נֶפֶשׁ נֶאֱנָחָה:
הַשׁוֹמֵר שַׁבָּת הַבֵּן עִם הַבַּת לָאֵל יֵרָצוּ כְּמִנְחָה עַל מַחֲבַת:

רוֹכֵב בָּעֲרָבוֹת מֶלֶךְ עוֹלָמִים,
אֶת עַמּוֹ לִשְׁבּוֹת אִזֵּן בַּנְּעִימִים.
בְּמַאֲכָלֵי עֲרֵבוֹת בְּמִינֵי מַטְעַמִּים,
בְּמַלְבּוּשֵׁי כָבוֹד זֶבַח מִשְׁפָּחָה:
הַשׁוֹמֵר שַׁבָּת הַבֵּן עִם הַבַּת לָאֵל יֵרָצוּ כְּמִנְחָה עַל מַחֲבַת:

וְאַשְׁרֵי כָּל חוֹכֶה לְתַשְׁלוּמֵי כֵפֶל,
מֵאֵת כָּל סוֹכֶה שׁוֹכֵן בָּעֲרָפֶל.
נַחֲלָה לוֹ יִזְכֶּה בָּהָר וּבַשָּׁפֶל,
נַחֲלָה וּמְנוּחָה כַּשֶּׁמֶשׁ לוֹ זָרְחָה:
הַשׁוֹמֵר שַׁבָּת הַבֵּן עִם הַבַּת לָאֵל יֵרָצוּ כְּמִנְחָה עַל מַחֲבַת:

BARUKH KEL ELYON
Composed by R. Barukh, son of R. Samuel of Mainz, 12th century.
"(The Shabbat) is redemption for our souls":
The Shabbat reflects not only spiritual and familial blessings, but political — and even
revolutionary — blessings as well. As we have seen in the Kiddush, Shabbat comes to remind

BARUKH KEL ELYON

Blessed is the most exalted God Who gave contentment;
For our souls it is redemption from ravage and groaning.
May He seek out Zion the outcast city:
how long, the grieving for the groaning soul?!
Whoever keeps the Shabbat — man and woman alike —
May they find God's favor like a meal-offering in a sacred pan.

He Who rides through the heavens, the King of the universe —
He let it be known with pleasantness that His nation should rest on Shabbat,
With tasty foods and every kind of delicacy,
With elegant garments and a family feast.
Whoever keeps the Shabbat — man and woman alike —
May they find God's favor like a meal-offering in a sacred pan.

Praiseworthy is everyone who awaits a double reward
from the One Who sees all but dwells in dense darkness.
He will grant him an inheritance in mountain and valley,
An inheritance and resting place like Jacob upon whom the sun shone.
Whoever keeps the Shabbat — man and woman alike —
May they find God's favor like a meal-offering in a sacred pan.

us that God created the world and that God took us out of Egypt; the parenthood of God
must entail the siblinghood — and individual freedom — of humanity. Hence the *Lekha Dodi*
prayer on Shabbat evening urges the Jewish people to arouse themselves, to rise from the
ashes of despair and to adorn themselves in their garments of majestic splendor. The Shabbat
contains a message of spiritual and political redemption at the same time. ♦

כָּל שׁוֹמֵר שַׁבָּת כַּדָּת מֵחַלְלוֹ,
הֵן הֶכְשַׁר חִבַּת קֹדֶשׁ גּוֹרָלוֹ.
וְאִם יֵצֵא חוֹבַת הַיּוֹם אַשְׁרֵי לוֹ,
אֶל אֵל אָדוֹן מְחוֹלְלוֹ. מִנְחָה הִיא שְׁלוּחָה:
הַשּׁוֹמֵר שַׁבָּת הַבֵּן עִם הַבַּת לָאֵל יֵרָצוּ כְּמִנְחָה עַל מַחֲבַת:

חֶמְדַּת הַיָּמִים, קְרָאוֹ אֵלִי צוּר.
וְאַשְׁרֵי לִתְמִימִים, אִם יִהְיֶה נָצוּר.
כֶּתֶר הִלּוּמִים עַל רֹאשָׁם יָצוּר.
צוּר הָעוֹלָמִים רוּחוֹ בָּם נָחָה:
הַשּׁוֹמֵר שַׁבָּת הַבֵּן עִם הַבַּת לָאֵל יֵרָצוּ כְּמִנְחָה עַל מַחֲבַת:

זָכוֹר אֶת יוֹם הַשַּׁבָּת לְקַדְּשׁוֹ,
קַרְנוֹ כִּי גָּבְהָה נֵזֶר עַל רֹאשׁוֹ.
עַל כֵּן יִתֵּן הָאָדָם לְנַפְשׁוֹ עֹנֶג וְגַם שִׂמְחָה
בָּהֶם לְמָשְׁחָה:
הַשּׁוֹמֵר שַׁבָּת הַבֵּן עִם הַבַּת לָאֵל יֵרָצוּ כְּמִנְחָה עַל מַחֲבַת:

קֹדֶשׁ הִיא לָכֶם שַׁבָּת הַמַּלְכָּה,
אֶל תּוֹךְ בָּתֵּיכֶם לְהָנִיחַ בְּרָכָה.
בְּכָל מוֹשְׁבוֹתֵיכֶם לֹא תַעֲשׂוּ מְלָאכָה,
בְּנֵיכֶם וּבְנוֹתֵיכֶם עֶבֶד וְגַם שִׁפְחָה:
הַשּׁוֹמֵר שַׁבָּת הַבֵּן עִם הַבַּת לָאֵל יֵרָצוּ כְּמִנְחָה עַל מַחֲבַת:

Whoever safeguards the Shabbat properly from desecration
Behold — worthiness for beloved holiness is his lot.
And if he fulfills the day's obligation, praises are due to him.
To God, the Lord Who fashioned him, it is sent as a gift.
Whoever keeps the Shabbat — man and woman alike —
May they find God's favor like a meal-offering in a sacred pan.

"The most beloved of days" is what my God and Rock called it.
Praises are due the wholesome ones if it is protected;
A beaten crown is fashioned upon their heads.
As for the Rock of the universe, His spirit will be content with them.
Whoever keeps the Shabbat — man and woman alike —
May they find God's favor like a meal-offering in a sacred pan.

He who remembers the Shabbat day to hallow it,
His honor will rise like a diadem on his head.
Therefore let each man allow himself pleasure and gladness
Through which he will be exalted.
Whoever keeps the Shabbat — man and woman alike —
May they find God's favor like a meal-offering in a sacred pan.

She is holy to you, the Shabbat Queen,
within your homes to deposit blessing.
In all your dwellings do not work:
Your sons and daughters, slaves and maidservants.
Whoever keeps the Shabbat — man and woman alike —
May they find God's favor like a meal-offering in a sacred pan.

יום זה מכבד

יוֹם זֶה מְכֻבָּד מִכָּל יָמִים, כִּי בוֹ שָׁבַת צוּר עוֹלָמִים:

שֵׁשֶׁת יָמִים תַּעֲשֶׂה מְלַאכְתֶּךָ, וְיוֹם הַשְּׁבִיעִי לֵאלֹהֶיךָ.
שַׁבָּת לֹא תַעֲשֶׂה בוֹ מְלָאכָה, כִּי כֹל עָשָׂה שֵׁשֶׁת יָמִים: יוֹם זֶה ...

רִאשׁוֹן הוּא לְמִקְרָאֵי קֹדֶשׁ, יוֹם שַׁבָּתוֹן יוֹם שַׁבַּת קֹדֶשׁ.
עַל כֵּן כָּל אִישׁ בְּיֵינוֹ יְקַדֵּשׁ, עַל שְׁתֵּי לֶחֶם יִבְצְעוּ תְמִימִים: יוֹם זֶה ...

אֱכֹל מַשְׁמַנִּים שְׁתֵה מַמְתַּקִּים, כִּי אֵל יִתֵּן לְכָל בּוֹ דְבֵקִים.
בֶּגֶד לִלְבּוֹשׁ לֶחֶם חֻקִּים, בָּשָׂר וְדָגִים וְכָל מַטְעַמִּים: יוֹם זֶה ...

לֹא תֶחְסַר כֹּל בּוֹ וְאָכַלְתָּ וְשָׂבָעְתָּ, וּבֵרַכְתָּ אֶת יְיָ אֱלֹהֶיךָ
אֲשֶׁר אָהַבְתָּ, כִּי בֵרַכְךָ מִכָּל הָעַמִּים: יוֹם זֶה ...

הַשָּׁמַיִם מְסַפְּרִים כְּבוֹדוֹ, וְגַם הָאָרֶץ מָלְאָה חַסְדּוֹ.
רְאוּ כִּי כָל אֵלֶּה עָשְׂתָה יָדוֹ, כִּי הוּא הַצּוּר פָּעֳלוֹ תָמִים: יוֹם זֶה ...

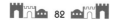

YOM ZEH MEKHUBAD

"This day is more blessed than all other days" — the Shabbat is the crown, and purpose, of all the days of the week. It is for this reason that initially the six days of the week had no names; they were identified as "the first day towards the Shabbat," "the second day towards the Shabbat," etc.

The Roman Tacitus criticized the Israelites for their laziness since they did not work on Shabbat. The Second Commonwealth historian Josephus defended his people by arguing that the opposite was the case: resting one day a week would make them more productive during the

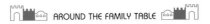

YOM ZEH MEKHUBAD

This day is honored above all days, for on it rested the Rock of the universe.

For six days you may do your work, but the seventh day is for your God.
On the Shabbat — do no work, for He completed all in six days.

This day ...

It is the first of the holy days, a day of rest, the holy Shabbat day. Therefore
let every man recite Kiddush over wine; let him slice two complete loaves.

This day ...

Eat rich foods, drink sweet drinks, for God will give to all who cleave to Him
Clothes to wear and allotted bread, meat and fish and all types of delicacies.

This day ...

You will lack nothing on it; you will eat, be satisfied and bless Hashem,
your God, Whom you love, for He has blessed you beyond all nations.

This day ...

The heavens declare His glory, and the earth as well is full of His kindness.
Perceive that all these have His hand made, for He is the molder — His work
is perfect.

This day ...

other six days, as any industrial psychologist will confirm. But Josephus, although correct in
theory, was wrong with regard to the significance of Shabbat. The laws of *muktzeh* — the
prohibition against moving any vessel on Shabbat which has not been prepared for Shabbat
use during the weekdays — teach us that we do not rest on Shabbat in order to be able to
work more productively during the rest of the week; that would be reducing Shabbat to a
preparatory agent for the other days. Quite the opposite: we work during the week so that
we can be free to enjoy the spiritual and intellectual nourishment that the Shabbat provides.
Shabbat is the purpose and goal of the week and the true significance of our lives. ✦

יום שבתון

יוֹם שַׁבָּתוֹן אֵין לִשְׁכּוֹחַ, זִכְרוֹ כְּרֵיחַ הַנִּיחוֹחַ.
יוֹנָה מָצְאָה בוֹ מָנוֹחַ, וְשָׁם יָנוּחוּ יְגִיעֵי כֹחַ:

הַיּוֹם נִכְבָּד לִבְנֵי אֱמוּנִים,
זְהִירִים לְשָׁמְרוֹ אָבוֹת וּבָנִים.
חָקוּק בִּשְׁנֵי לוּחוֹת אֲבָנִים,
מֵרוֹב אוֹנִים וְאַמִּיץ כֹּחַ:   יוֹנָה מָצְאָה בוֹ מָנוֹחַ, וְשָׁם יָנוּחוּ יְגִיעֵי כֹחַ:

וּבָאוּ כֻלָּם בִּבְרִית יַחַד,
נַעֲשֶׂה וְנִשְׁמַע אָמְרוּ כְּאֶחָד,
וּפָתְחוּ וְעָנוּ יְיָ אֶחָד,
בָּרוּךְ הַנּוֹתֵן לַיָּעֵף כֹּחַ:   יוֹנָה מָצְאָה בוֹ מָנוֹחַ...:

דִּבֶּר בְּקָדְשׁוֹ בְּהַר הַמּוֹר,
יוֹם הַשְּׁבִיעִי זָכוֹר וְשָׁמוֹר.
וְכָל פִּקּוּדָיו יַחַד לִגְמֹר,
חַזֵּק מָתְנַיִם וְאַמֵּץ כֹּחַ:   יוֹנָה מָצְאָה בוֹ מָנוֹחַ...:

הָעָם אֲשֶׁר נָע כַּצֹּאן טָעָה,
יִזְכֹּר לְפָקְדוֹ בִּבְרִית וּשְׁבוּעָה.
לְבַל יַעֲבָר בָּם מִקְרֵה רָעָה,
כַּאֲשֶׁר נִשְׁבַּעְתָּ עַל מֵי נֹחַ: יוֹנָה מָצְאָה בוֹ מָנוֹחַ...:

YOM SHABBATON
Composed by R. Yehudah HaLevi, author of The Kuzari, 11th century.
"On (Shabbat) the dove found rest; there shall rest they who are weary" — The reference is to

YOM SHABBATON

The day of rest should not be forgotten;
its memory is fragrant.
On it the dove found rest;
there shall rest they who are weary.

This day is honored by the faithful ones
Who are scrupulous to safeguard it — parents and children.
Engraved in the two stone tablets given by
The Abundantly Potent and Vigorously Strong.

On it the dove found rest; there shall rest they who are weary.

Then they all joined together in a covenant
"We will do and we will hear," they said as one.
Then they opened their mouths and called out, "Hashem is One!"
Blessed is He Who gives strength to the exhausted.   On it the dove...

He spoke amid His holiness at the mountain of teaching:
"The seventh day — remember and safeguard!"
And all His precepts should equally be studied —
Strengthen loins and be vigorously strong!   On it the dove...

The nation that wandered like bewildered sheep —
May He remember for them His covenant and oath
Lest evil happenings pass among them
As He swore at the Waters of Noah.   On it the dove...

the biblical dove in the time of Noah; the Shabbat is compared to the Ark which served as a protective haven from the raging flood waters, and is therefore by analogy our life-saving raft even in the most tempestuous of times. A most poignant Midrash recounts that when Adam and Eve sinned and were exiled from the Garden of Eden, they complained that their suffering was too great to bear. The Almighty in His compassion armed them with two gifts as they entered the alien and dangerous world: tears, and Shabbat. Said God: "When the situation in exile makes life an almost insufferable burden, weep and you will feel the comfort of release; keep the Shabbat and you will taste the eventual redemption." ✦

שמרו שבתותי

שָׁמְרוּ שַׁבְּתוֹתַי לְמַעַן תִּינְקוּ וּשְׂבַעְתֶּם
מִזִּיו בִּרְכוֹתַי, אֶל הַמְּנוּחָה כִּי בָאתֶם:
וְלְווּ עָלַי בָּנַי וְעֶדְנוּ מַעֲדָנַי, שַׁבָּת הַיּוֹם לַיְיָ:

לְעָמֵל קִרְאוּ דְרוֹר, וְנָתַתִּי אֶת בִּרְכָתִי,
אִשָּׁה אֶל אֲחוֹתָהּ לִצְרוֹר, לִגְלוֹת עַל יוֹם שִׂמְחָתִי,
בִּגְדֵי שֵׁשׁ עִם שָׁנִי, וְהִתְבּוֹנְנוּ מִזְּקֵנִי: שַׁבָּת הַיּוֹם לַיְיָ.

וְלְווּ עָלַי בָּנַי וְעֶדְנוּ מַעֲדָנַי, שַׁבָּת הַיּוֹם לַיְיָ:

מַהֲרוּ אֶת הַמָּנֶה, לַעֲשׂוֹת אֶת דְּבַר אֶסְתֵּר,
וְחִשְׁבוּ עִם הַקּוֹנֶה, לְשַׁלֵּם אָכוֹל וְהוֹתֵר,
בִּטְחוּ בִי אֱמוּנַי, וּשְׁתוּ יַיִן מִשְׁמַנִּי: שַׁבָּת הַיּוֹם לַיְיָ.   וְלְווּ עָלַי בָּנַי...

הִנֵּה יוֹם גְּאֻלָּה, יוֹם שַׁבָּת אִם תִּשְׁמֹרוּ,
וִהְיִיתֶם לִי סְגֻלָּה, לִינוּ וְאַחַר תַּעֲבֹרוּ, וְאָז
תִּחְיוּ לְפָנַי, וּתְמַלְּאוּ צְפוּנַי: שַׁבָּת הַיּוֹם לַיְיָ.   וְלְווּ עָלַי בָּנַי...

חֲזַק קִרְיָתִי, אֵל אֱלֹהִים עֶלְיוֹן, וְהָשֵׁב אֶת נְוָתִי,
בְּשִׂמְחָה וּבְהִגָּיוֹן, יְשׁוֹרְרוּ שָׁם רְנָנַי, לַיְיָ וְכֹהֲנַי,
וְאָז תִּתְעַנַּג עַל יְיָ: שַׁבָּת הַיּוֹם לַיְיָ.   וְלְווּ עָלַי בָּנַי...

❦

SHIMRU SHABTOTAI

Composed by R. Shelomo ibn Gevirol, late 11th century

The usual translation of וְלְווּ עָלַי בָּנַי is God saying to the Jewish people, "Borrow on My account — i.e., perform acts of loving kindness; give charity, expend funds to beautify the Shabbat — and I will repay you." However, the expression וְלְווּ עָלַי also means "join with me." Therefore I have always understood the refrain to mean that the head of the family is calling

SHIMRU SHABTOTAI

Safeguard My Shabbats so that you may be nourished and sated
from the glow of My blessings when you arrive at the day of contentment.
Borrow on My account, My children, and enjoy My delicacies —
Shabbat is the day for Hashem.

From travail, announce freedom. Then I shall confer My blessing
Attaching one to the other, causing joy on My day of gladness.
Wear linen garments and scarlet wool, learn to do so from My Sages —
Shabbat is the day for Hashem.

Borrow on My account, My children, and enjoy My delicacies —
Shabbat is the day for Hashem.

Expedite the portion — fulfill Esther's order; reckon accounts with the Master
Who repays what you ate and what you left.
Trust Me, My faithful ones, and drink wine from My abundance —
Shabbat is the day for Hashem.   Borrow on My account...

Behold — a day of redemption is the Shabbat day if your safeguard it.
And you shall be My treasured one. Endure your exile-night, afterward you shall cross
Then to thrive before Me and be filled with My hidden bounty —
Shabbat is the day for Hashem.   Borrow on My account...

Strengthen my city, O exalted God, and replace my Temple, with gladness song.
There my singers will exult, my Levites and my Priests
And then you shall take pleasure with Hashem —
Shabbat is the day for Hashem.   Borrow on My account...

❦

out to his children and grandchildren, "Join along with me, my children, and enjoy all the unique delicacies. This is the Shabbat day for Hashem."

Obviously, there is no greater satisfaction that any parent can have than seeing children and grandchildren following along in the Jewish tradition, with generations sitting together and singing zemirot together around the Shabbat table. ✦

כי אשמרה שבת

כִּי אֶשְׁמְרָה שַׁבָּת אֵל יִשְׁמְרֵנִי.
אוֹת הִיא לְעוֹלְמֵי עַד בֵּינוֹ וּבֵינִי:

אָסוּר מְצֹא חֵפֶץ, עֲשׂוֹת דְּרָכִים.
גַּם מִלְדַּבֵּר בּוֹ דִּבְרֵי צְרָכִים,
דִּבְרֵי סְחוֹרָה אַף דִּבְרֵי מְלָכִים.
אֶהְגֶּה בְּתוֹרַת אֵל וּתְחַכְּמֵנִי:

כִּי אֶשְׁמְרָה שַׁבָּת אֵל יִשְׁמְרֵנִי.
אוֹת הִיא לְעוֹלְמֵי עַד בֵּינוֹ וּבֵינִי:

בּוֹ אֶמְצָא תָמִיד נֹפֶשׁ לְנַפְשִׁי,
הִנֵּה לְדֹר רִאשׁוֹן נָתַן קְדוֹשִׁי.
מוֹפֵת בְּתֵת לֶחֶם מִשְׁנֶה בַּשִּׁשִּׁי,
כָּכָה בְּכָל שִׁשִּׁי יַכְפִּיל מְזוֹנִי:

כִּי אֶשְׁמְרָה שַׁבָּת אֵל יִשְׁמְרֵנִי.
אוֹת הִיא לְעוֹלְמֵי עַד בֵּינוֹ וּבֵינִי:

KI ESHMERAH SHABBAT
Composed by R. Abraham ibn Ezra, 12th century.
"(The Shabbat) is a sign forever between Him and me (Israel)" — The Midrash teaches that the
Shabbat came before the Almighty with a legitimate complaint: "Every day of the week has a
partner, a spouse: Sunday has Monday, Tuesday has Wednesday, Thursday has Friday. Only

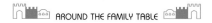

KI ESHMERAH SHABBAT

If I safeguard Shabbat, God will safeguard me;

It is a sign forever and ever between Him and me.

It is forbidden to seek mundane desires

or to engage in such pursuits;

Even to converse concerning matters of need: commercial or political talk.

I shall meditate in the Torah of God — it shall make me wise.

> If I safeguard Shabbat, God will safeguard me;
>
> It is a sign forever and ever between Him and me.

Through it I can always find refreshment for my soul

Behold — to the first generation my Holy One gave a wondrous proof:

By giving doubled food on the sixth day;

so may He double my food every sixth day.

> If I safeguard Shabbat, God will safeguard me;
>
> It is a sign forever and ever between Him and me.

I, Shabbat, am separate and alone." God responded that "Similarly in the world of nations, every nation has an ally, a comrade-in-arms and ideology. Only Israel is separate and alone. Israel shall be wedded to the Shabbat, and together they shall redeem the world!"

רָשַׁם בְּדַת הָאֵל חֹק אֶל סְגָנָיו,
בּוֹ לַעֲרֹךְ לֶחֶם פָּנִים בְּפָנָיו.
עַל כֵּן לְהִתְעַנּוֹת בּוֹ עַל פִּי נְבוֹנָיו
אָסוּר, לְבַד מִיּוֹם כִּפּוּר עֲוֹנִי:

כִּי אֶשְׁמְרָה שַׁבָּת אֵל יִשְׁמְרֵנִי.
אוֹת הִיא לְעוֹלְמֵי עַד בֵּינוֹ וּבֵינִי:

הוּא יוֹם מְכֻבָּד הוּא יוֹם תַּעֲנוּגִים,
לֶחֶם וְיַיִן טוֹב בָּשָׂר וְדָגִים.
הַמִּתְאַבְּלִים בּוֹ אָחוֹר נְסוֹגִים,
כִּי יוֹם שְׂמָחוֹת הוּא וּתְשַׂמְּחֵנִי:

כִּי אֶשְׁמְרָה שַׁבָּת אֵל יִשְׁמְרֵנִי.
אוֹת הִיא לְעוֹלְמֵי עַד בֵּינוֹ וּבֵינִי:

מֵחֵל מְלָאכָה בּוֹ סוֹפוֹ לְהַכְרִית,
עַל כֵּן אֲכַבֵּס בּוֹ לִבִּי כְּבוֹרִית.
וְאֶתְפַּלְּלָה אֶל אֵל עַרְבִית וְשַׁחֲרִית,
מוּסָף וְגַם מִנְחָה הוּא יַעֲנֵנִי:

כִּי אֶשְׁמְרָה שַׁבָּת אֵל יִשְׁמְרֵנִי.
אוֹת הִיא לְעוֹלְמֵי עַד בֵּינוֹ וּבֵינִי:

He inscribed in the Godly law a decree for his priests
that on it they prepare Show Bread before Him.
Therefore it is forbidden to fast on it by order of His wise sages
Except for the day when my sin is atoned.

> If I safeguard Shabbat, God will safeguard me;
> It is a sign forever and ever between Him and me.

It is an honored day; it is a day of pleasures:
Bread and good wine, meat and fish.
Those who mourn — on it they must withdraw,
For it is a day of joys, and it will gladden me.

> If I safeguard Shabbat, God will safeguard me;
> It is a sign forever and ever between Him and me.

For performing desecrating work upon it one's end will be excision,
Therefore on it I shall cleanse my heart as if with soap.
I shall pray to God *Ma'ariv* and *Shaharit*, *Musaf* and *Minha*
And He will answer me.

> If I safeguard Shabbat, God will safeguard me;
> It is a sign forever and ever between Him and me.

דרור יקרא

דְּרוֹר יִקְרָא לְבֵן עִם בַּת, וְיִנְצָרְכֶם כְּמוֹ בָבַת.
נְעִים שִׁמְכֶם וְלֹא יֻשְׁבַּת, שְׁבוּ נוּחוּ בְּיוֹם שַׁבָּת:

דְּרוֹשׁ נָוִי וְאוּלָמִי, וְאוֹת יֶשַׁע עֲשֵׂה עִמִּי.
נְטַע שׂוֹרֵק בְּתוֹךְ כַּרְמִי, שְׁעֵה שַׁוְעַת בְּנֵי עַמִּי:

דְּרוֹךְ פּוּרָה בְּתוֹךְ בָּצְרָה, וְגַם בָּבֶל אֲשֶׁר גָּבְרָה.
נְתוֹץ צָרַי בְּאַף וְעֶבְרָה, שְׁמַע קוֹלִי בְּיוֹם אֶקְרָא:

אֱלֹהִים תֵּן בַּמִּדְבָּר הַר, הֲדַס שִׁטָּה בְּרוֹשׁ תִּדְהָר.
וְלַמַּזְהִיר וְלַנִּזְהָר, שְׁלוֹמִים תֵּן כְּמֵי נָהָר:

הֲדוֹךְ קָמַי אֵל קַנָּא בְּמוֹג לֵבָב וּבַמְּגִנָּה.
וְנַרְחִיב פֶּה וּנְמַלְאֶנָּה, לְשׁוֹנֵנוּ לְךָ רִנָּה:

דְּעֵה חָכְמָה לְנַפְשֶׁךָ, וְהִיא כֶתֶר לְרֹאשֶׁךָ.
נְצֹר מִצְוַת קְדוֹשֶׁךָ, שְׁמֹר שַׁבַּת קָדְשֶׁךָ:

***

DEROR YIKRA

The Torah institutes the cycle of the Jubilee fiftieth year, following seven Sabbatical years, in which every servant is freed, every debt rescinded, and every individual reinstated in his familial homestead. This Jubilee year is our representation of the political and economic

DEROR YIKRA

Freedom shall He proclaim for son and daughter,
And protect you like the apple of His eye.
Pleasant will be your reputation, never ceasing:
Rest and be content on the Shabbat day.

Seek My Temple and My Hall;
Perform a sign of salvation for me.
Plant a branch within my vineyard;
Turn to the cry of my people!

Tread the press in Botzra,
And also Babylon which overpowered.
Smash my foes with wrathful anger;
Hear my voice on the day I call.

O God, let bloom on the desert-like mountain
Myrtle, acacia, cypress and box tree.
To the exhorters and the scrupulous give peace
As flowing as a river's waters.

Crush my foes, O jealous God
With melting heart and grief.
May we open our mouth and fill it;
Our tongue sing Your joyful song.

Let your soul know wisdom,
Then it will be a crown on your head.
Observe the precepts of your Holy One —
Safeguard your holy Shabbat.

freedom — the societal well-being — that is synonymous with redemption. "And you shall proclaim freedom (*deror*) in the land for all of its inhabitants" (Lev. 25:10). Shabbat is our oasis in time, our portable paradise, our weekly Jubilee. ✦

שבת היום לה'

שַׁבָּת הַיּוֹם לַיְיָ, מְאֹד צַהֲלוּ בְּרִנּוּנִי,
וְגַם הַרְבּוּ מַעֲדַנַּי. אוֹתוֹ לִשְׁמוֹר כְּמִצְוַת יְיָ:
שַׁבָּת הַיּוֹם לַיְיָ

מֵעֲבוֹר דֶּרֶךְ וּגְבוּלִים, מֵעֲשׂוֹת הַיּוֹם פְּעָלִים
לֶאֱכוֹל וְלִשְׁתּוֹת בְּהִלּוּלִים. זֶה הַיּוֹם עָשָׂה יְיָ:
שַׁבָּת הַיּוֹם לַיְיָ

וְאִם תִּשְׁמְרֶנּוּ יָהּ יִנְצָרְךָ כְּבָבַת, אַתָּה וּבִנְךָ וְגַם הַבַּת.
וְקָרֵאתָ עֹנֶג לַשַּׁבָּת, אָז תִּתְעַנַּג עַל יְיָ:
שַׁבָּת הַיּוֹם לַיְיָ

אֱכוֹל מַשְׁמַנִּים וּמַעֲדַנִּים, וּמַטְעַמִּים הַרְבֵּה מִינִים,
אֱגוֹזֵי פֶרֶךְ וְרִמּוֹנִים. וְאָכַלְתָּ וְשָׂבָעְתָּ וּבֵרַכְתָּ אֶת יְיָ:
שַׁבָּת הַיּוֹם לַיְיָ

לַעֲרוֹךְ בְּשֻׁלְחָן לֶחֶם חֲמוּדוֹת, לַעֲשׂוֹת הַיּוֹם שָׁלֹשׁ סְעוּדוֹת.
אֶת הַשֵּׁם הַנִּכְבָּד לְבָרֵךְ וּלְהוֹדוֹת, שִׁקְדוּ וְשִׁמְרוּ וַעֲשׂוּ בָנַי:
שַׁבָּת הַיּוֹם לַיְיָ

SHABBAT HA-YOM LA-HASHEM
"Increase my delicacies... eat and drink while praising God" — A righteous convert once complained to me that her only critique of Judaism is that she is constantly "battling her bulge," since Jews celebrate a "Thanksgiving weekend" every Shabbat!

SHABBAT HA-YOM LA-HASHEM

Today is the Shabbat for Hashem.

Exult exceedingly with my joyous songs and increase my delicacies
To safeguard it like Hashem's command.
> Today is the Shabbat for Hashem.

Not to travel on roads nor overstep the boundaries, nor engage in labor on this day
But to eat and drink while praising God — This is the day that God created.
> Today is the Shabbat for Hashem.

Then, if you observe it, God will protect you like the apple of His eye —
You, your son, and daughter as well.
Proclaim the Shabbat as a pleasure — then you shall have pleasure with Hashem.
> Today is the Shabbat for Hashem.

Each rich foods and delicacies, and tasty morsels of all kinds;
Soft-shelled nuts and pomegranates; eat, be satisfied, and bless Hashem —
> Today is the Shabbat for Hashem.

To prepare on the table beloved bread, to make for the day three repasts.
The Glorious Name to bless and thank be zealous, observe and accomplish, my sons.
> Today is the Shabbat for Hashem.

The gastronomy of the three Shabbat meals is not for the sake of the stomach, but rather for the sake of heaven. The genius of Judaism is not to deny material pleasures, but rather to utilize them as a gateway for praising God, teaching Torah and sharing with the less fortunate.

סעודה שלישית

אתקינו סעודתא

אַתְקִינוּ סְעוּדָתָא דִמְהֵימְנוּתָא שְׁלֵמָתָא חֶדְוָתָא דְמַלְכָּא קַדִּישָׁא.
אַתְקִינוּ סְעוּדָתָא דְמַלְכָּא דָּא הִיא סְעוּדָתָא דַּחֲקַל תַּפּוּחִין קַדִּישִׁין
וּזְעֵיר אַנְפִּין וְעַתִּיקָא קַדִּישָׁא. אַתְיָן לְסַעֲדָא בַּהֲדֵהּ:

בְּנֵי הֵיכָלָא דִכְסִיפִין,

לְמֶחֱזֵי זִיו דִּזְעֵיר אַנְפִּין:

יְהוֹן הָכָא, בְּהַאי תַּכָּא, דְּבֵהּ מַלְכָּא בְּגִלּוּפִין:

צְבוּ לַחֲדָא, בְּהַאי וַעֲדָא, בְּגוֹ עִירִין וְכָל גַּדְפִין:

חֲדוּ הַשְׁתָּא, בְּהַאי שַׁעֲתָא, דְּבֵהּ רַעֲוָא וְלֵית זַעֲפִין:

קְרִיבוּ לִי, חֲזוּ חֵילִי, דְּלֵית דִּינִין דִּתְקִיפִין:

לְבַר נַטְלִין, וְלָא עָאלִין, הֲנֵי כַּלְבִּין דַּחֲצִיפִין:

וְהָא אַזְמִין, עַתִּיק יוֹמִין, לְמִנְחָה (לְמִצְחָא) עֲדֵי יְהוֹן חָלְפִין:

רְעוּ דִילֵהּ, דְּגַלֵּי לֵהּ, לְבַטָּלָא בְּכָל קְלִיפִין:

יְשַׁוֵּי לוֹן, בְּנוֹקְבֵיהוֹן, וְיִטַּמְרוּן בְּגוֹ כֵפִין:

אֲרֵי הַשְׁתָּא בְּמִנְחָתָא, בְּחֶדְוָתָא דִּזְעֵיר אַנְפִּין:

ATKINU SE'UDATA

Composed by the Holy Ari (R. Yitzhak Luria), 16th century Safed.

The third meal generally takes place as the Shabbat sun is setting and the Shabbat joy is about to give way to the weekday, workday frustrations and despair; it therefore always contains a note of sadness at the imminent departure of the Shabbat Queen. The story is told of a Hassidic Rebbe who would always share the third meal with his disciples and would

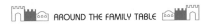

SHALOSH SE'UDOT (SE'UDAH SHELISHIT) THE "THIRD MEAL"

ATKINU SE'UDATA

I shall prepare the feast of perfect faith, the joy of the Holy King. Prepare the feast of the King! This is the feast of the Miniature Presence, the Ancient Holy One and th Field of Sacred Apples. Come to feast with it.

Members of the Sanctuary who yearn
to see the glow of the Miniature Presence,
May they be here at this table in which is inscribed the King in joy.
Long to be part of this assemblage among many-winged angels,
Be exultant now at this very time in which there is favor, with no anger.
Approach me, see my strength, when there are no powerful judgements;
Outside, let them remain, never to arise — those brazen dogs.
But I invite the Holy Ancient One at *Minha*,
the time when they fade away,
His favor — when revealed — to negate all impure shells.
Hay He place them in their nether holes and hide them among rocks.
I ask this now, at *Minha* time,
With the exultation of the Miniature Presence.

always empathize with the beginnings of despondency that they would feel with the setting sun. The Rebbe would look up to God with yearning and with beseeching: "Please tell me, please reveal to me, the secret. When will the Master Messiah come?" But, alas, there was never a Divine response.

One Shabbat, however, during the third meal, the Rebbe's eyes brightened and his face lit up. "I have the solution!" he shouted to his gathered disciples. "I know how to force the hand of God and bring down the Messiah! After all, the messianic period of redemption is known as the "day which is completely Shabbat'" the period when Shabbat never ends. We will simply continue this third meal; we will never recite the closing Havdalah prayers. As long as we retain the Shabbat eternally, the Messiah will have to come!"

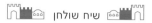
מזמור לדוד

מִזְמוֹר לְדָוִד יְיָ רֹעִי לֹא אֶחְסָר.
בִּנְאוֹת דֶּשֶׁא יַרְבִּיצֵנִי
עַל מֵי מְנֻחוֹת יְנַהֲלֵנִי.
נַפְשִׁי יְשׁוֹבֵב
יַנְחֵנִי בְמַעְגְּלֵי צֶדֶק לְמַעַן שְׁמוֹ.
גַּם כִּי אֵלֵךְ בְּגֵיא צַלְמָוֶת
לֹא אִירָא רָע כִּי אַתָּה עִמָּדִי
שִׁבְטְךָ וּמִשְׁעַנְתֶּךָ הֵמָּה יְנַחֲמֻנִי.
תַּעֲרֹךְ לְפָנַי שֻׁלְחָן נֶגֶד צֹרְרָי
דִּשַּׁנְתָּ בַשֶּׁמֶן רֹאשִׁי כּוֹסִי רְוָיָה.
אַךְ טוֹב וָחֶסֶד יִרְדְּפוּנִי כָּל יְמֵי חַיָּי
וְשַׁבְתִּי בְּבֵית יְיָ לְאֹרֶךְ יָמִים:

His disciples agreed that this was a marvelous idea. Outside the sun had set; the moon and stars were shining brightly, and everyone had begun their weekday chores. But at the Rebbe's table it was still Shabbat. His disciples kept singing and even dancing. They had the secret; the Shabbat would never end. The Messiah would have to come.

But then, one by one, the wives of the disciples began entering the room. They called out to their husbands, some quietly, others more insistently. The children needed to be put to bed, the clothes and dishes had to be washed, purchases had to be made for the coming week... It did not take long until the Rebbe was all alone, singing a solo Shabbat song. And then even his own *rebbitzen* came in, wondering what had happened, and insisting that he recite Havdalah so that the work week could begin. Reluctantly, with tears streaming down his cheeks at the failure of his revolution, he recited Havdalah. But then he heard the Divine response, God's answer to the agonizing question he had asked Shabbat after Shabbat: "The Messiah will

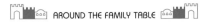
MIZMOR LE-DAVID

A song of David: Hashem is my Shepherd, I shall not lack.

In lush meadows He lays me down;

beside tranquil waters He leads me.

He restores my soul.

He leads me along paths of justice for His Name's sake.

Though I walk in the valley overshadowed by death,

I will fear no evil, for You are with me.

Your rod and Your staff, they comfort me.

You prepare a table before me in full view of my tormentors.

You anointed my head with oil, my cup overflows.

May only goodness and kindness pursue me all the days of my life,

and I shall dwell in the House of Hashem for the length of days.

come when the Jews really want to be redeemed. The Messiah will come when the Jews work on themselves and on the world to prepare the way and pave the road for redemption." And so the songs of the third meal are chanted soulfully in an attempt to experience the Holy King at the time of redemption, to dwell in the House of the Lord forever, and Israel's yearning to be protected by the Tabernacle of God's peace. ✦

MIZMOR LE-DAVID (Psalm 23)

"Your rod and Your staff, they comfort me" — Sometimes life seems good, like lush meadows near tranquil waters. Sometimes life is difficult, like a valley overshadowed by death. The world seems to relate to me at times with a punitive rod, and at times with a supporting staff. In every period I find comfort in the God Who guarantees ultimate redemption. ✦

ידיד נפש

יְדִיד נֶפֶשׁ אָב הָרַחֲמָן, מְשׁךְ עַבְדְּךָ אֶל רְצוֹנֶךָ.
יָרוּץ עַבְדְּךָ כְּמוֹ אַיָּל. יִשְׁתַּחֲוֶה אֶל מוּל הֲדָרֶךָ.
יֶעֱרַב לוֹ יְדִידוֹתֶיךָ
מִנֹּפֶת צוּף וְכָל טָעַם:

הָדוּר נָאֶה זִיו הָעוֹלָם, נַפְשִׁי חוֹלַת אַהֲבָתֶךָ.
אָנָּא אֵל נָא רְפָא נָא לָהּ, בְּהַרְאוֹת לָהּ נֹעַם זִיוֶךָ.
אָז תִּתְחַזֵּק וְתִתְרַפֵּא,
וְהָיְתָה לָהּ שִׂמְחַת עוֹלָם:

וָתִיק יֶהֱמוּ נָא רַחֲמֶיךָ,
וְחוּסָה נָּא עַל בֵּן אֲהוּבֶךָ.
כִּי זֶה כַּמָּה נִכְסֹף נִכְסַפְתִּי לִרְאוֹת בְּתִפְאֶרֶת עֻזֶּךָ.
אֵלֶּה חָמְדָה לִבִּי, וְחוּסָה נָּא וְאַל תִּתְעַלֵּם:

הִגָּלֵה נָא וּפְרֹשׁ חֲבִיבִי עָלַי,
אֶת סֻכַּת שְׁלוֹמֶךָ.
תָּאִיר אֶרֶץ מִכְּבוֹדֶךָ, נָגִילָה וְנִשְׂמְחָה בָּךְ.
מַהֵר אֱהֹב כִּי בָא מוֹעֵד, וְחָנֵּנוּ כִּימֵי עוֹלָם:

YEDID NEFESH
Composed by R. Elazar Azkari, 16th century Safed
"Beloved of the soul" — When Maimonides seeks to define the love we ought to feel for the
Divine, he uses the analogy of a lover and his beloved, "Whom he thinks of constantly, when

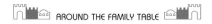
YEDID NEFESH

Beloved of the soul, Compassionate Father, draw Your servant to Your will;
Then Your servant will run like a hart to bow before Your majesty.
Your friendship will be sweeter to him
than the dripping of the honey-comb and any taste.

Majestic, Beautiful, Radiance of the universe: my soul is sick for Your love.
Please, O God, heal her now, by showing her the pleasantness
of Your radiance.
Then she will be strengthened and healed,
And she will be eternally joyful.

All-worthy One: may Your mercy be aroused,
and please take pity on the son of Your beloved,
because for so long I have yearned intensely to see the splendor
of Your strength.
Only these my heart desired, so please take pity and do not conceal Yourself.

Please be revealed and spread upon me, my Beloved,
The shelter of Your peace.
Illuminate the world with Your glory, that we may rejoice and be glad
with You.
Hasten, show love, for the time has come, and show us grace as
in days of old.

awake and when sleeping, when eating and when drinking, when in movement or at rest"
(Laws of Repentance, Chapter 10). This intense love is expressed in The Song of Songs, as well
as in this magnificent lovesong of Divine praise. ♦

גאט פון אברהם

גָּאט פוּן אַבְרָהָם אוּן פוּן יִצְחָק אוּן פוּן יַעֲקֹב, בֶּעהִיט דֵּיין לִיב פָאלְק יִשְׂרָאֵל פוּן
אַלֶעם בִּיזֶען אִין דֵּיינֶעם לוֹיב אַז דֶער לִיבֶּער שַׁבָּת קֹדֶשׁ גֵייט, אַז דִי וָואךְ אוּן דֶער
חֹדֶשׁ אוּן דֶער יָאר זָאל אוּנְז צוּא קוּמֶען צוּא אֱמוּנָה שְׁלֵמָה, צוּא אֱמוּנַת חֲכָמִים,
צוּא אַהֲבַת חֲבֵרִים, צוּא דְּבֵיקַת הַבּוֹרֵא בָּרוּךְ הוּא, מַאֲמִין צוּ זֵיין בִּשְׁלֹשׁ עֶשְׂרֵה
עִקָּרִים שֶׁלְּךָ וּבְגְאֻלָּה קְרוֹבָה בִּמְהֵרָה בְּיָמֵינוּ, וּבִתְחִיַּת הַמֵּתִים וּבִנְבוּאַת מֹשֶׁה רַבֵּנוּ
עָלָיו הַשָּׁלוֹם:

רִבּוֹנוֹ שֶׁל עוֹלָם, דוּ בִּיזְט דָאךְ הַנּוֹתֵן לַיָּעֵף כֹּחַ, גִיב דֵּיינֶע לִיבֶּע יוּדִישֶׁע קִינְדֶּערְלַאךְ
אוֹיךְ כֹּחַ דִּיךְ צוּא לוֹיבֶּען, אֵין נָאר דִּיךְ צוּא דִּינֶען אוּן קֵיין אַנְדֶּערִין חָלִילָה נִישְׁט.
אוּן אַז דִי וָואךְ אוּן דֶער חֹדֶשׁ אוּן דֶער יָאר זָאל אוּנְז קוּמֶען צוּא גֶעזוּנְד אוּן צוּא
מַזָּל אוּן צוּא בְּרָכָה וְהַצְלָחָה אוּן צוּא חֶסֶד אוּן צוּא בְּנֵי חַיֵּי אָרִיכֵי וּמְזוֹנֵי רְוִיחֵי
וְסִיַּעְתָּא דִשְׁמַיָּא לָנוּ וּלְכָל יִשְׂרָאֵל, וְנֹאמַר אָמֵן:

אֱלֹהֵי אַבְרָהָם אֱלֹהֵי יִצְחָק וֵאלֹהֵי יַעֲקֹב, שְׁמֹר וְהַצֵּל אֶת יִשְׂרָאֵל עַם
אֲהוּבֶךָ מִכָּל רָע. לְמַעַן תְּהִלָּתֶךָ, כַּאֲשֶׁר שַׁבַּת קֹדֶשׁ הָאֲהוּבָה יוֹצֵאת,
שֶׁהַשָּׁבוּעַ וְהַחֹדֶשׁ וְהַשָּׁנָה יָבוֹא לָנוּ לֶאֱמוּנָה שְׁלֵמָה, לֶאֱמוּנַת חֲכָמִים,
לְאַהֲבַת חֲבֵרִים, לִדְבֵקוּת הַבּוֹרֵא בָּרוּךְ הוּא, לְהַאֲמִין בִּשְׁלֹשׁ עֶשְׂרֵה
עִקָּרִים שֶׁלְּךָ וּבִגְאֻלָּה קְרוֹבָה בִּמְהֵרָה בְּיָמֵינוּ וּבִתְחִיַּת הַמֵּתִים
וּבִנְבוּאַת מֹשֶׁה רַבֵּנוּ עָלָיו הַשָּׁלוֹם:

רִבּוֹנוֹ שֶׁל עוֹלָם, אַתָּה הִנְּךָ הַנּוֹתֵן לַיָּעֵף כֹּחַ, תֵּן גַּם לִבְנֵי יִשְׂרָאֵל
אֲהוּבֶךָ כֹּחַ לְהוֹדוֹת לָךְ, וְרַק אוֹתְךָ לַעֲבֹד וְלֹא לְאַחֵר חָלִילָה.
וְשֶׁהַשָּׁבוּעַ וְהַחֹדֶשׁ וְהַשָּׁנָה יָבוֹא לָנוּ לִבְרִיאוּת וּלְמַזָּל טוֹב, לִבְרָכָה
וּלְהַצְלָחָה וּלְחֶסֶד וּלְבָנֵי, חַיֵּי אָרִיכֵי, מְזוֹנֵי רְוִיחֵי, וְסִיַּעְתָּא דִשְׁמַיָּא,
לָנוּ וּלְכָל יִשְׂרָאֵל, וְנֹאמַר אָמֵן:

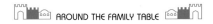

GOTT FUN AVROHOM

God of Abraham, of Isaac and of Jacob: Protect Your people, Israel, from all, in Your praise — as the beloved, holy Shabbat takes leave; that this week, month and year may arrive to bring perfect faith, faith in scholars; love of and attachment to good friends; attachment to the Creator, blessed be He, to have faith in Your Thirteen Principles, and in the complete and close Redemption, speedily in our days; in the Resurrection of the dead and in the prophecy of our teacher, Moses — peace be upon him.

Master of the universe: since You are the One Who gives strength to the exhausted — also give Your beloved Jewish children the strength to praise You, and to serve only You and no other. May this week arrive for kindness, for good fortune, for blessing, for success, for good health, for wealth and honor, and for children, life, and sustenance for us and for all Israel. Amen.

GOTT FUN AVROHOM

The Shabbat concludes with the Havdalah prayer. "Gott fun Avrohom" is a Yiddish equivalent, created by Jewish women in Europe, asking for a good, healthy and successful week. It takes the place of אתה חוננתנו for women who do not recite the evening prayer. ⚜

הבדלה

הִנֵּה אֵל יְשׁוּעָתִי אֶבְטַח וְלֹא אֶפְחָד, כִּי עָזִּי וְזִמְרָת יָהּ יְיָ וַיְהִי לִי
לִישׁוּעָה: וּשְׁאַבְתֶּם מַיִם בְּשָׂשׂוֹן מִמַּעַיְנֵי הַיְשׁוּעָה. לַיְיָ הַיְשׁוּעָה עַל
עַמְּךָ בִרְכָתֶךָ סֶּלָה. יְיָ צְבָאוֹת עִמָּנוּ מִשְׂגָּב לָנוּ אֱלֹהֵי יַעֲקֹב סֶלָה. יְיָ
צְבָאוֹת אַשְׁרֵי אָדָם בֹּטֵחַ בָּךְ. יְיָ הוֹשִׁיעָה הַמֶּלֶךְ יַעֲנֵנוּ בְיוֹם קָרְאֵנוּ.
לַיְּהוּדִים הָיְתָה אוֹרָה וְשִׂמְחָה וְשָׂשׂוֹן וִיקָר, כֵּן תִּהְיֶה לָּנוּ. כּוֹס
יְשׁוּעוֹת אֶשָּׂא וּבְשֵׁם יְיָ אֶקְרָא:

The blessing over the wine is recited now, but the wine is drunk only at the end of Havdalah:

סַבְרִי מָרָנָן וְרַבָּנָן וְרַבּוֹתַי
בָּרוּךְ אַתָּה יְיָ אֱלֹהֵינוּ מֶלֶךְ הָעוֹלָם, בּוֹרֵא פְּרִי הַגָּפֶן:

After the following blessing, smell the spices:

בָּרוּךְ אַתָּה יְיָ אֱלֹהֵינוּ מֶלֶךְ הָעוֹלָם, בּוֹרֵא מִינֵי בְשָׂמִים:

After the following blessing, hold the fingers up toward the flames:

בָּרוּךְ אַתָּה יְיָ אֱלֹהֵינוּ מֶלֶךְ הָעוֹלָם, בּוֹרֵא מְאוֹרֵי הָאֵשׁ:

בָּרוּךְ אַתָּה יְיָ אֱלֹהֵינוּ מֶלֶךְ הָעוֹלָם, הַמַּבְדִּיל בֵּין קֹדֶשׁ לְחֹל, בֵּין אוֹר
לְחשֶׁךְ, בֵּין יִשְׂרָאֵל לָעַמִּים, בֵּין יוֹם הַשְּׁבִיעִי לְשֵׁשֶׁת יְמֵי הַמַּעֲשֶׂה.
בָּרוּךְ אַתָּה יְיָ, הַמַּבְדִּיל בֵּין קֹדֶשׁ לְחֹל:

HAVDALAH

Since the "additional soul" granted to us on Shabbat departs during Havdalah, fragrant spices
are smelled to ease the sense of spiritual loss.

The Havdalah candle must be composed of at least two wicks joined together, symbolizing the
ultimate messianic unity that will merge darkness into light, evil into good, and will make every
day a Shabbat day.

HAVDALAH

Behold, God is my salvation, I will have trust and not be afraid. Indeed, the Lord is my strength and my song and He has become my salvation. You shall draw water with joy from the wells of salvation. Salvation belongs to the Lord; may Your blessing be upon Your people, Selah.

The Lord of Hosts is with us, the God of Jacob is a refuge for us, Selah. Lord of Hosts, happy is the man who trusts in You. Lord, save us; may the King answer us on the day we call. "The Jews had radiance and happiness, joy and honor" — so may it be for us. I will lift up the cup of salvation and call on the Name of the Lord.

The blessing over the wine is recited now, but the wine is drunk only at the end of Havdalah:

You are blessed, Lord our God, Sovereign of the universe, Creator of the fruit of the vine.

After the following blessing, smell the spices:

You are blessed, Lord our God, Sovereign of the universe, Creator of various kinds of spices.

After the following blessing, hold the fingers up toward the flames:

You are blessed, Lord our God, Sovereign of the universe, Creator of the lights of fire.

You are blessed, Lord our God, Sovereign of the universe, Who makes a distinction between sacred and mundane, between light and darkness, between Israel and the other nations, between the seventh day and the six working days. You are blessed, Lord, Who makes a distinction between the sacred and the mundane.

In 1975 I came to Israel for a special conference. I was still living in New York and had almost forgotten my dream of moving to Israel. Whenever I did visit the Holy Land, I would buy Hebrew books from Reb Shmuel, a bookseller who lived in Meah She'arim and whose book store was in his apartment. We got to know each other quite well, although he was a man of

המבדיל

הַמַּבְדִיל בֵּין קֹדֶשׁ לְחֹל, חַטֹּאתֵינוּ הוּא יִמְחֹל.
זַרְעֵנוּ וְכַסְפֵּנוּ יַרְבֶּה כַּחוֹל, וְכַכּוֹכָבִים בַּלָּיְלָה:

יוֹם פָּנָה כְּצֵל תֹּמֶר, אֶקְרָא לָאֵל עָלַי גּוֹמֵר.
אָמַר שׁוֹמֵר אָתָא בֹקֶר וְגַם לָיְלָה:

צִדְקָתְךָ כְּהַר תָּבוֹר עַל חֲטָאַי עָבוֹר תַּעֲבֹר.
כְּיוֹם אֶתְמוֹל כִּי יַעֲבֹר וְאַשְׁמוּרָה בַלָּיְלָה:

חָלְפָה עוֹנַת מִנְחָתִי מִי יִתֵּן מְנוּחָתִי.
יָגַעְתִּי בְאַנְחָתִי אַשְׂחֶה בְכָל לָיְלָה:

קוֹלִי בַּל יִנָּטָל, פְּתַח לִי שַׁעַר הַמְנֻטָּל.
שֶׁרֹאשִׁי נִמְלָא טָל קְוֻצּוֹתַי רְסִיסֵי לָיְלָה:

הֵעָתֵר נוֹרָא וְאָיוֹם, אֲשַׁוֵּעַ תְּנָה פִדְיוֹם.
בְּנֶשֶׁף בְּעֶרֶב יוֹם בְּאִישׁוֹן לָיְלָה:

קְרָאתִיךָ יָהּ הוֹשִׁיעֵנִי, אֹרַח חַיִּים תּוֹדִיעֵנִי.
מִדַּלּוּת תְּבַצְּעֵנִי מִיּוֹם וְעַד לָיְלָה:

few words. In fact, sometimes when he opened the door he would look at me and merely grunt. I learned to understand that he was in no way being disrespectful: he was merely indicating to me that he had taken upon himself a "fast of words" (*ta'anit dibbur*), a 24-hour period in which he would not speak. He believed — probably correctly — that we sin more with what comes out of our mouths than with what goes into them. If he was in fasting mode

HA-MAVDIL

He Who makes a distinction between the sacred and the mundane —
May He also pardon our sins.
May he make our children and our wealth proliferate like the sand,
and like the stars at night.

Twilight has arrived like the shade of a palm tree; I call to God Who
gives me everything.
The watchman says morning comes, but night, too.

Your righteousness is as great as Mount Tabor; please ignore,
disregard my sins.
May they be like yesterday — gone — like a watch in the night.

The time when I would bring offerings is long gone. If only I had rest!
I am so tired of sighing; I weep every night.

Do not allow my voice to be stifled; open the gate on high for me,
For my head is soaked with dew, my locks with the drops of the night.

Grant my prayer, Revered and Awesome One; I implore You, bring
redemption
At dusk, in the evening, in the dark of night.

I am calling You, God — save me; show me life's scheme.
Keep me from poverty, by day and by night.

and would give two grunts, it meant he had a very good book for me. Three grunts meant he
had a magnificent buy waiting for me, a very special acquisition of an especially rare volume at
a fairly good price. (continued on page 110)

טַהֵר טִנּוּף מַעֲשַׂי פֶּן יֹאמְרוּ מַכְעִיסָי.
אַיֵּה נָא אֱלוֹהַּ עֹשָׂי הַנּוֹתֵן זְמִירוֹת בַּלָּיְלָה:

נַחְנוּ בְּיָדְךָ כַּחֹמֶר, סְלַח נָא עַל קַל וָחֹמֶר.
יוֹם לְיוֹם יַבִּיעַ אֹמֶר וְלַיְלָה לְּלָיְלָה:

סעודת דוד המלך — מלוה מלכה

אַתְקִינוּ סְעוּדָתָא דִּמְהֵימְנוּתָא שְׁלֵמָתָא חֶדְוָתָא דְּמַלְכָּא קַדִּישָׁא.
אַתְקִינוּ סְעוּדָתָא דְּמַלְכָּא דָּא הִיא סְעוּדָתָא דְּדָוִד מַלְכָּא מְשִׁיחָא.
וְאַבְרָהָם יִצְחָק וְיַעֲקֹב אַתְיָן לְסַעֲדָא בַּהֲדֵהּ. דָּוִד מֶלֶךְ יִשְׂרָאֵל חַי
וְקַיָּם. סִמָּן טוֹב וּמַזָּל טוֹב יְהֵא לָנוּ וּלְכָל יִשְׂרָאֵל. אָמֵן:

אמר ה' ליעקב

אַל תִּירָא עַבְדִּי יַעֲקֹב:	אָמַר יְיָ לְיַעֲקֹב
אַל תִּירָא עַבְדִּי יַעֲקֹב:	בָּחַר יְיָ בְּיַעֲקֹב
אַל תִּירָא עַבְדִּי יַעֲקֹב:	גָּאַל יְיָ אֶת יַעֲקֹב
אַל תִּירָא עַבְדִּי יַעֲקֹב:	דָּרַךְ כּוֹכָב מִיַּעֲקֹב
אַל תִּירָא עַבְדִּי יַעֲקֹב:	הַבָּאִים יַשְׁרֵשׁ יַעֲקֹב
אַל תִּירָא עַבְדִּי יַעֲקֹב:	וְיֵרֶד מִיַּעֲקֹב
אַל תִּירָא עַבְדִּי יַעֲקֹב:	זָכֹר זֹאת לְיַעֲקֹב
אַל תִּירָא עַבְדִּי יַעֲקֹב:	חֶדְוַת יְשׁוּעוֹת יַעֲקֹב

Purify the defilement of my actions, lest those who incite me ask Where is the God Who made me, Who can inspire hymns in the night.

We are as clay in Your hand; please forgive our petty and our major sins.
Each day tells the story, and each night.

THE MEAL OF KING DAVID — USHERING OUT THE SHABBAT QUEEN

Prepare the feast of perfect faith, the joy of the Holy King. Prepare the feast of the King! This is the feast of David, the anointed king. Avraham, Isaac and Jacob — come feast with him. David, king of Israel, lives and endures. May a good sign and good fortune come to us and to all Israel. Amen.

AMAR HASHEM LE-YA'AKOV

Hashem said to Jacob	fear not, My servant Jacob.
Hashem chose Jacob	fear not, My servant Jacob.
Hashem will redeem Jacob	fear not, My servant Jacob.
A star will emerge from Jacob	fear not, My servant Jacob.
In time to come, Jacob will strike roots	fear not, My servant Jacob.
A ruler will arise from Jacob	fear not, My servant Jacob.
Remember this for Jacob's sake	fear not, My servant Jacob.
Delight will come with Jacob's salvation	fear not, My servant Jacob.

אַל תִּירָא עַבְדִּי יַעֲקֹב:	טוֹבוּ אוֹהָלֶיךָ יַעֲקֹב
אַל תִּירָא עַבְדִּי יַעֲקֹב:	יוֹרוּ מִשְׁפָּטֶיךָ לְיַעֲקֹב
אַל תִּירָא עַבְדִּי יַעֲקֹב:	כִּי לֹא נַחַשׁ בְּיַעֲקֹב
אַל תִּירָא עַבְדִּי יַעֲקֹב:	לֹא הִבִּיט אָוֶן בְּיַעֲקֹב
אַל תִּירָא עַבְדִּי יַעֲקֹב:	מִי מָנָה עֲפַר יַעֲקֹב
אַל תִּירָא עַבְדִּי יַעֲקֹב:	נִשְׁבַּע יְיָ לְיַעֲקֹב
אַל תִּירָא עַבְדִּי יַעֲקֹב:	סְלַח נָא לַעֲוֹן יַעֲקֹב
אַל תִּירָא עַבְדִּי יַעֲקֹב:	עַתָּה הָשֵׁב שְׁבוּת יַעֲקֹב
אַל תִּירָא עַבְדִּי יַעֲקֹב:	פְּדֵה יְיָ אֶת יַעֲקֹב
אַל תִּירָא עַבְדִּי יַעֲקֹב:	צַוֵּה יְשׁוּעוֹת יַעֲקֹב
אַל תִּירָא עַבְדִּי יַעֲקֹב:	קוֹל קוֹל יַעֲקֹב
אַל תִּירָא עַבְדִּי יַעֲקֹב:	רַנִּי וְשִׂמְחִי לְיַעֲקֹב
אַל תִּירָא עַבְדִּי יַעֲקֹב:	שָׁב יְיָ אֶת שְׁבוּת יַעֲקֹב
אַל תִּירָא עַבְדִּי יַעֲקֹב:	תִּתֵּן אֱמֶת לְיַעֲקֹב

This time, when I knocked on the door, he was extremely verbose and affable; he asked after my health and that of my family, and vividly described a number of books he suggested that I buy. When I asked what had caused his especially good humor, he looked at me incredulously: "Don't you know? Haven't you heard? The Messiah is in Jerusalem!"

I consider myself a rationalist, a disciple of Rav Soloveitchik, a student of Maimonides. I took my purchase and went on my way.

Nevertheless, I was disturbed — and even strangely excited. I decided to go back to the Western Wall for the afternoon and evening prayers. A day later, when Shabbat arrived, I made certain to be at the Western Wall for every prayer. After all, I told myself, if indeed the Messiah is in Jerusalem, he would probably be at the Western Wall.

Shabbat passed uneventfully, and even on the Saturday night news there was no announcement of the Messiah. Early Sunday morning, on my way to the airport, even though it was before dawn, I couldn't resist visiting my friend Reb Shmuel. He opened the door still in

Your tents are goodly, Jacob	fear not, My servant Jacob.
They shall teach Your ordinances to Jacob	fear not, My servant Jacob.
For there is no sorcery in Jacob	fear not, My servant Jacob.
He perceives no wrong in Jacob	fear not, My servant Jacob.
Who can count the dust of Jacob?	fear not, My servant Jacob.
Hashem swore to Jacob	fear not, My servant Jacob.
Please forgive the sin of Jacob	fear not, My servant Jacob.
Bring back, now, the captivity of Jacob	fear not, My servant Jacob.
God will redeem Jacob	fear not, My servant Jacob.
Command salvations for Jacob	fear not, My servant Jacob.
The voice is Jacob's voice	fear not, My servant Jacob.
Sing in gladness for Jacob	fear not, My servant Jacob.
Hashem will have returned the pride of Jacob	fear not, My servant Jacob.
Make the prophecies come true for Jacob	fear not, My servant Jacob.

his night clothes, asking as to whether there was a book I had forgotten to purchase. I explained that before I left for New York I wanted to understand what he had meant when he said the Messiah was in Jerusalem; I had waited and waited and no one came....

He took my hand in his and looked deeply into my eyes. "You make a great mistake, Rabbi Riskin," he said to me. "You think that we are waiting for the Messiah. In reality, the Messiah is waiting for us; the Messiah is waiting for you." I have since come to believe that indeed the Messiah is in Jerusalem, waiting to reveal himself. But he cannot do so until all the Jews come to Jerusalem, until all the Jews keep at least one Shabbat as it is supposed to be kept in Jerusalem. Our efforts must be directed to paving the way for a better world of peace and harmony, a world which is truly entirely Shabbat. ֍

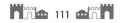

אליהו הנביא

אֵלִיָּהוּ הַנָּבִיא, אֵלִיָּהוּ הַתִּשְׁבִּי, אֵלִיָּהוּ הַגִּלְעָדִי.
בִּמְהֵרָה יָבֹא אֵלֵינוּ עִם מָשִׁיחַ בֶּן דָּוִד.

אִישׁ **אֲשֶׁר** קִנֵּא לְשֵׁם הָאֵל.
אִישׁ **בִּשַּׂר** שָׁלוֹם עַל יַד יְקוּתִיאֵל.
אִישׁ **גָּשׁ** וַיְכַפֵּר עַל בְּנֵי יִשְׂרָאֵל:
אֵלִיָּהוּ הַנָּבִיא, אֵלִיָּהוּ הַתִּשְׁבִּי, אֵלִיָּהוּ הַגִּלְעָדִי.
בִּמְהֵרָה יָבֹא אֵלֵינוּ עִם מָשִׁיחַ בֶּן דָּוִד.

אִישׁ **דֹּ**רוֹת שְׁנֵים עָשָׂר רָאוּ עֵינָיו.
אִישׁ **הַ**נִּקְרָא בַּעַל שֵׂעָר בְּסִימָנָיו.
אִישׁ **וְ**אֵזוֹר עוֹר אָזוּר בְּמָתְנָיו:
אֵלִיָּהוּ הַנָּבִיא, אֵלִיָּהוּ הַתִּשְׁבִּי, אֵלִיָּהוּ הַגִּלְעָדִי.
בִּמְהֵרָה יָבֹא אֵלֵינוּ עִם מָשִׁיחַ בֶּן דָּוִד.

אִישׁ **זָ**עַף עַל עוֹבְדֵי חַמָּנִים.
אִישׁ **חָ**שׁ וְנִשְׁבַּע מִהְיוֹת גִּשְׁמֵי מְעוֹנִים.
אִישׁ **טַ**ל וּמָטָר עָצַר שָׁלֹשׁ שָׁנִים:
אֵלִיָּהוּ הַנָּבִיא, אֵלִיָּהוּ הַתִּשְׁבִּי, אֵלִיָּהוּ הַגִּלְעָדִי.
בִּמְהֵרָה יָבֹא אֵלֵינוּ עִם מָשִׁיחַ בֶּן דָּוִד.

❧

ELIYAHU HA-NAVI
The Passover Seder is dedicated to parents and children: "You shall tell your children... (*ve-higadeta, haggadah*). The Shabbat and Festivals are dedicated to familial continuity and

ELIYAHU HA-NAVI

Elijah the prophet, Elijah the Tishbi, Elijah the Gil'adi —
May he quickly come to us with Messiah, the son of David.

The man who was zealous in defense of God's Name;
The man who was promised peace by the symbol of hope in God;
The man who approached sinners and atoned for Israel;
> Elijah the prophet, Elijah the Tishbi, Elijah the Gil'adi —
> May he quickly come to us with Messiah, the son of David.

The man whose eyes saw twelve generations;
The man called "hairy one" because of his appearance;
The man with a leather belt girding his loins;
> Elijah the prophet, Elijah the Tishbi, Elijah the Gil'adi —
> May he quickly come to us with Messiah, the son of David.

The man who raged against worshippers of the sun;
The man who rushed and swore there would be no rain from heaven;
The man who withheld dew and rain three years;
> Elijah the prophet, Elijah the Tishbi, Elijah the Gil'adi —
> May he quickly come to us with Messiah, the son of David.

togetherness amidst songs of praise to Hashem and Torah study. Elijah the prophet, herald of our ultimate redemption, has as his supreme task "restoring the hearts of the parents to the children, and the hearts of the children to the parents". Our greatest challenge is to achieve the family unity which is the only authentic harbinger of world unity. ✿

אִישׁ **יָ**צָא לִמְצוֹא לְנַפְשׁוֹ נַחַת.
אִישׁ **כִּ**לְכְּלוּהוּ הָעוֹרְבִים וְלֹא מֵת לַשַּׁחַת.
אִישׁ **לְ**מַעֲנוֹ נִתְבָּרְכוּ כַּד וְצַפַּחַת:
אֵלִיָּהוּ הַנָּבִיא, אֵלִיָּהוּ הַתִּשְׁבִּי, אֵלִיָּהוּ הַגִּלְעָדִי.
בִּמְהֵרָה יָבֹא אֵלֵינוּ עִם מָשִׁיחַ בֶּן דָּוִד.

אִישׁ **מ**וּסָרָיו הִקְשִׁיבוּ כְּמֵהִים.
אִישׁ **נַ**עֲנָה בָּאֵשׁ מִשְּׁמֵי גְבוֹהִים.
אִישׁ **שָׂ**חוּ אַחֲרָיו יְיָ הוּא הָאֱלֹהִים:
אֵלִיָּהוּ הַנָּבִיא, אֵלִיָּהוּ הַתִּשְׁבִּי, אֵלִיָּהוּ הַגִּלְעָדִי.
בִּמְהֵרָה יָבֹא אֵלֵינוּ עִם מָשִׁיחַ בֶּן דָּוִד.

אִישׁ **עָ**תִיד לְהִשְׁתַּלֵּחַ מִשְּׁמֵי עֲרָבוֹת.
אִישׁ **פָּ**קִיד עַל כָּל בְּשׂוֹרוֹת טוֹבוֹת.
אִישׁ **צִ**יר נֶאֱמָן לְהָשִׁיב לֵב בָּנִים עַל אָבוֹת:
אֵלִיָּהוּ הַנָּבִיא, אֵלִיָּהוּ הַתִּשְׁבִּי, אֵלִיָּהוּ הַגִּלְעָדִי.
בִּמְהֵרָה יָבֹא אֵלֵינוּ עִם מָשִׁיחַ בֶּן דָּוִד.

אִישׁ **קָ**רָא קַנֹּא קִנֵּאתִי לַייָ בְּתִפְאָרָה.
אִישׁ **רָ**כַב עַל סוּסֵי אֵשׁ וְעָלָה בַּסְּעָרָה.
אִישׁ **שֶׁ**לֹּא טָעַם טַעַם מִיתָה וּקְבוּרָה:
אֵלִיָּהוּ הַנָּבִיא, אֵלִיָּהוּ הַתִּשְׁבִּי, אֵלִיָּהוּ הַגִּלְעָדִי.
בִּמְהֵרָה יָבֹא אֵלֵינוּ עִם מָשִׁיחַ בֶּן דָּוִד.

The man who left to find himself tranquility;
The man nourished by ravens not to die for the grave;
The man on whose behalf the jug and jar were blessed;
    Elijah the prophet, Elijah the Tishbi, Elijah the Gil'adi —
    May he quickly come to us with Messiah, the son of David.

The man whose admonitions attracted those longing for God;
The man whom fire answered from the high heavens;
The man after whom they said, "Hashem is God!"
    Elijah the prophet, Elijah the Tishbi, Elijah the Gil'adi —
    May he quickly come to us with Messiah, the son of David.

The man destined to be sent from the heavens;
The man appointed over all good tidings;
The man who is the trusty agent to return children's hearts to
their parents;
    Elijah the prophet, Elijah the Tishbi, Elijah the Gil'adi —
    May he quickly come to us with Messiah, the son of David.

The man who proclaimed in splendor, "I acted zealously
for Hashem!"
The man who rode fiery horses in a stormy wind;
The man who never felt the taste of death and burial;
    Elijah the prophet, Elijah the Tishbi, Elijah the Gil'adi —
    May he quickly come to us with Messiah, the son of David.

אִישׁ **תִּ**שְׁבִּי עַל שְׁמוֹ נִקְרָא.
תַּצְלִיחֵנוּ עַל יָדוֹ בַּתּוֹרָה.
תַּשְׁמִיעֵנוּ מִפִּיו בְּשׂוֹרָה טוֹבָה בִּמְהֵרָה.
תּוֹצִיאֵנוּ מֵאֲפֵלָה לְאוֹרָה:
אֵלִיָּהוּ הַנָּבִיא, אֵלִיָּהוּ הַתִּשְׁבִּי, אֵלִיָּהוּ הַגִּלְעָדִי.
בִּמְהֵרָה יָבֹא אֵלֵינוּ עִם מָשִׁיחַ בֶּן דָּוִד.

תִּשְׁבִּי תַּצִּילֵנוּ מִפִּי אֲרָיוֹת.
תְּבַשְּׂרֵנוּ בְּשׂוֹרוֹת טוֹבוֹת בְּמוֹצָאֵי שַׁבָּתוֹת.
תְּשַׂמְּחֵנוּ בָּנִים עַל אָבוֹת:
אֵלִיָּהוּ הַנָּבִיא, אֵלִיָּהוּ הַתִּשְׁבִּי, אֵלִיָּהוּ הַגִּלְעָדִי.
בִּמְהֵרָה יָבֹא אֵלֵינוּ עִם מָשִׁיחַ בֶּן דָּוִד.

כַּכָּתוּב הִנֵּה אָנֹכִי שֹׁלֵחַ לָכֶם אֶת אֵלִיָּה הַנָּבִיא
לִפְנֵי בּוֹא יוֹם יְיָ הַגָּדוֹל וְהַנּוֹרָא.
וְהֵשִׁיב לֵב אָבוֹת עַל בָּנִים וְלֵב בָּנִים עַל אֲבוֹתָם:
אֵלִיָּהוּ הַנָּבִיא, אֵלִיָּהוּ הַתִּשְׁבִּי, אֵלִיָּהוּ הַגִּלְעָדִי.
בִּמְהֵרָה יָבֹא אֵלֵינוּ עִם מָשִׁיחַ בֶּן דָּוִד.

אַשְׁרֵי מִי שֶׁרָאָה פָּנָיו בַּחֲלוֹם.
אַשְׁרֵי מִי שֶׁנָּתַן לוֹ שָׁלוֹם. וְהֶחֱזִיר לוֹ שָׁלוֹם.
יְיָ יְבָרֵךְ אֶת עַמּוֹ בַשָּׁלוֹם:
אֵלִיָּהוּ הַנָּבִיא, אֵלִיָּהוּ הַתִּשְׁבִּי, אֵלִיָּהוּ הַגִּלְעָדִי.
בִּמְהֵרָה יָבֹא אֵלֵינוּ עִם מָשִׁיחַ בֶּן דָּוִד.

The man called "Tishbi" in addition to his name;
Make our Torah study successful through him.
Let us hear speedily from his mouth the good tidings;
May he remove us from darkness to light.

> Elijah the prophet, Elijah the Tishbi, Elijah the Gil'adi —
> May he quickly come to us with Messiah, the son of David.

The man, Tishbi — may he rescue us from the lion's mouth;
May he herald good tidings for us;
May he gladden children together with parents at the departure
of Shabbat.

> Elijah the prophet, Elijah the Tishbi, Elijah the Gil'adi —
> May he quickly come to us with Messiah, the son of David.

As it is written, "Behold! I send you Elijah the prophet,
Before the great and awesome day of Hashem comes.
And he shall return the hearts of parents to children, and
of children to parents."

> Elijah the prophet, Elijah the Tishbi, Elijah the Gil'adi —
> May he quickly come to us with Messiah, the son of David.

Fortunate is he who has seen his face in a dream,
Fortunate is he who greeted him with "Peace" and to whom
he responded, "Peace."
May Hashem bless his people with peace.

> Elijah the prophet, Elijah the Tishbi, Elijah the Gil'adi —
> May he quickly come to us with Messiah, the son of David.

FESTIVALS

עירוב תבשילין

בָּרוּךְ אַתָּה יְיָ אֱלֹהֵינוּ מֶלֶךְ הָעוֹלָם אֲשֶׁר קִדְּשָׁנוּ בְּמִצְוֹתָיו וְצִוָּנוּ עַל מִצְוַת עֵרוּב:

בְּעֵרוּב הַזֶּה יְהֵא מֻתָּר לָנוּ לֶאֱפוֹת וּלְבַשֵּׁל וּלְהַטְמִין וּלְהַדְלִיק נֵר, וְלַעֲשׂוֹת כָּל צָרְכֵינוּ מִיּוֹם טוֹב לְשַׁבָּת, וּלְכָל יִשְׂרָאֵל הַדָּרִים בָּעִיר הַזֹּאת:

סדר הדלקת נרות לחג

On the Festivals we first recite the blessing(s) and then kindle the lights. If the Festival falls on a Friday evening, the regular procedure for Erev Shabbat is followed.

בָּרוּךְ אַתָּה יְיָ אֱלֹהֵינוּ מֶלֶךְ הָעוֹלָם, אֲשֶׁר קִדְּשָׁנוּ בְּמִצְוֹתָיו וְצִוָּנוּ לְהַדְלִיק נֵר שֶׁל (שַׁבָּת וְשֶׁל) יוֹם טוֹב:

Omit on the last evening (in the Diaspora, on the last two evenings) of Pesach:

בָּרוּךְ אַתָּה יְיָ אֱלֹהֵינוּ מֶלֶךְ הָעוֹלָם, שֶׁהֶחֱיָנוּ וְקִיְּמָנוּ וְהִגִּיעָנוּ לַזְּמַן הַזֶּה:

ERUV TAVSHILIN

The *Eruv Tavshilin* ceremony is performed before the onset of a festival which begins on Thursday evening (on Wednesday evening for Rosh Ha-Shanah, and in the Diaspora whenever the first day of the Festival falls on Wednesday evening), in order to allow for the

FESTIVALS

ERUV TAVSHILIN

You are blessed, Lord our God, Sovereign of the world, Who made us holy with His commandments and commanded us concerning the *Eruv*.

By means of this *eruv* may it become permissible for us to bake, to cook and to heat up food, to transfer a fire, and to prepare on the festival all that is needed for Shabbat — for us and for all the people of this city.

CANDLE LIGHTING FOR FESTIVALS

On the Festivals we first recite the blessing(s) and then kindle the lights. If the Festival falls on a Friday evening, the regular procedure for Erev Shabbat is followed.

You are blessed, Lord our God, Sovereign of the world, Who made us holy with His commandments and commanded us to kindle lights for (Shabbat and for) the Festival.

Omit on the last evening (in the Diaspora, on the last two evenings) of Pesach:

You are blessed, Lord our God, Sovereign of the world, Who has kept us alive and sustained us and enabled us to reach this occasion.

preparation of food for Shabbat. A hallah or a matzah and another cooked food are set aside for one of the Shabbat meals and we recite the following blessing and declaration, by means of which we demonstrate that we will not be preparing on the Festival for Shabbat, but merely adding to what we already began to prepare for Shabbat prior to the onset of the Festival. ✒

סדר הדלקת נרות לליל יום כפור

The lights should be lit after the pre-Yom Kippur meal *(Se'udah Mafseket)* has been eaten, and at least 30 minutes before sunset.

בָּרוּךְ אַתָּה יְיָ אֱלֹהֵינוּ מֶלֶךְ הָעוֹלָם, אֲשֶׁר קִדְּשָׁנוּ בְּמִצְוֹתָיו וְצִוָּנוּ לְהַדְלִיק נֵר שֶׁל (שַׁבָּת וְשֶׁל) יוֹם הַכִּפּוּרִים:

בָּרוּךְ אַתָּה יְיָ אֱלֹהֵינוּ מֶלֶךְ הָעוֹלָם, שֶׁהֶחֱיָנוּ וְקִיְּמָנוּ וְהִגִּיעָנוּ לַזְּמַן הַזֶּה:

After kindling the Yom Kippur candles, the following prayer is recited.

יְהִי רָצוֹן מִלְּפָנֶיךָ יְיָ אֱלֹהַי וֵאלֹהֵי אֲבוֹתַי, שֶׁיִּבָּנֶה בֵּית הַמִּקְדָּשׁ בִּמְהֵרָה בְיָמֵינוּ, וְתֵן חֶלְקֵנוּ בְּתוֹרָתֶךָ. וְשָׁם נַעֲבָדְךָ בְּיִרְאָה כִּימֵי עוֹלָם וּכְשָׁנִים קַדְמוֹנִיּוֹת.

יְהִי רָצוֹן מִלְּפָנֶיךָ יְיָ אֱלֹהַי וֵאלֹהֵי אֲבוֹתַי, שֶׁתְּחוֹנֵן אוֹתִי (וְאֶת אִישִׁי) וְאֶת כָּל קְרוֹבַי, וְתִתֶּן לָנוּ וּלְכָל יִשְׂרָאֵל חַיִּים טוֹבִים וַאֲרוּכִים. וְתִזְכְּרֵנוּ בְּזִכְרוֹן טוֹבָה וּבְרָכָה, וְתִפְקְדֵנוּ בִּפְקֻדַּת יְשׁוּעָה וְרַחֲמִים, וּתְשַׁכֵּן שְׁכִינָתְךָ בֵּינֵנוּ, וְזַכֵּנוּ לְגַדֵּל בָּנִים וּבְנֵי בָנִים חֲכָמִים וּנְבוֹנִים, אוֹהֲבֵי יְיָ, יִרְאֵי אֱלֹהִים, אַנְשֵׁי אֱמֶת, זֶרַע קֹדֶשׁ, בַּייָ דְּבֵקִים וּמְאִירִים אֶת הָעוֹלָם בַּתּוֹרָה וּבְמַעֲשִׂים טוֹבִים וּבְכָל מְלֶאכֶת עֲבוֹדַת הַבּוֹרֵא. אָנָּא, שְׁמַע אֶת תְּחִנָּתִי בִּזְכוּת שָׂרָה, רִבְקָה, רָחֵל וְלֵאָה אִמּוֹתֵינוּ. וְהָאֵר נֵרֵנוּ שֶׁלֹּא יִכְבֶּה לְעוֹלָם וָעֶד, וְהָאֵר פָּנֶיךָ וְנִוָּשֵׁעָה. אָמֵן:

YOM KIPPUR EVE

Our Sages teach that if one festively dines and drinks on the day before Yom Kippur, he/she is considered as having fasted for two days — probably because the fast on Yom Kippur is not an expression of sadness and mourning, as it is on Tish'a B'Av, but rather a testimony to human discipline and potential spirituality. Hence the Hassidic Sage Rav Levi Yitzhak of Berditchev used

CANDLE LIGHTING FOR YOM KIPPUR EVE

The lights should be lit after the pre-Yom Kippur meal (Se'udah Mafseket) has been eaten, and at least 30 minutes before sunset.

You are blessed, Lord our God, Sovereign of the world, Who made us holy with His commandments and commanded us to kindle lights for (Shabbat and for) Yom Kippur.

You are blessed, Lord our God, Sovereign of the world, Who has kept us alive and sustained us and enabled us to reach this occasion.

After kindling the Yom Kippur candles, the following prayer is recited.

May it be Your will, Lord our God and God of our fathers, that the Temple should be rebuilt soon in our time, and grant our involvement with Your Torah. And there we will serve You reverently as in days gone by, in olden times.

May it be Your will, Lord my God and God of my fathers, to be gracious to me (and to my husband/and children) and to all my family, crowning our home with the feeling of Your Divine presence dwelling among us. Make me worthy to raise learned children and grandchildren who will enlighten the world with Torah and kindness, and ensure that the glow of our lives will never be dimmed. Show us the light of Your countenance and we will be saved. Please hear my beseechings in the merit of Sarah, Rebecca, Rachel and Leah our matriarchs, and send Your tabernacle of peace to our home, our nation and our world. Amen.

to say that even if we had not been commanded to fast, he would not eat on Tish'a B'Av because of his sadness over the destruction of the Temple, and he would not eat on Yom Kippur because of his joy over his proximity to the Divine. Hence the meal before the Yom Kippur fast, known as the *Se'udah Mafseket*, is usually graced with two hallot as on a regular Festival, includes dipping the hallah in honey for a sweet year, and is either preceded by or followed with a special blessing for children and grandchildren. ✦

ברכת הילדים לליל יום כפור

The parents (either only one, each separately, or both together, depending on custom) place their hands upon the head of each child in turn and bless him/her.

For a son:

יְשִׂמְךָ אֱלֹהִים כְּאֶפְרַיִם וְכִמְנַשֶּׁה. יְבָרֶכְךָ יְיָ וְיִשְׁמְרֶךָ. יָאֵר יְיָ פָּנָיו אֵלֶיךָ וִיחֻנֶּךָּ. יִשָּׂא יְיָ פָּנָיו אֵלֶיךָ וְיָשֵׂם לְךָ שָׁלוֹם:

יְהִי רָצוֹן מִלְּפְנֵי אָבִינוּ שֶׁבַּשָּׁמַיִם שֶׁיִּתֵּן בְּלִבְּךָ אַהֲבָתוֹ וְיִרְאָתוֹ. וְתִהְיֶה יִרְאַת יְיָ עַל פָּנֶיךָ כָּל יְמֵי חַיֶּיךָ שֶׁלֹּא תֶחֱטָא. וּתְהִי חֶשְׁקְךָ בַּתּוֹרָה וּבַמִּצְוֹת עֵינֶיךָ לְנֹכַח יַבִּיטוּ. פִּיךָ יְדַבֵּר חָכְמוֹת וְלִבְּךָ יֶהְגֶּה אֵימוֹת. יָדֶיךָ יִהְיוּ עוֹסְקוֹת בְּמִצְוֹת. רַגְלֶיךָ יָרוּצוּ לַעֲשׂוֹת רְצוֹן אָבִיךָ שֶׁבַּשָּׁמַיִם. יִתֵּן לְךָ בָּנִים וּבָנוֹת צַדִּיקִים וְצִדְקָנִיּוֹת עוֹסְקִים בַּתּוֹרָה וּבַמִּצְוֹת כָּל יְמֵיהֶם, וִיהִי מְקוֹרְךָ בָּרוּךְ, וְיַזְמִין לְךָ פַּרְנָסָתְךָ בְּהֶתֵּר וּבְנַחַת וּבְרֶוַח מִתַּחַת יָדוֹ הָרְחָבָה. וְלֹא עַל יְדֵי מַתְּנַת בָּשָׂר וָדָם. כְּדֵי שֶׁתִּהְיֶה פָּנוּי לַעֲבוֹדַת יְיָ. וְתִכָּתֵב וְתֵחָתֵם לְחַיִּים טוֹבִים וַאֲרֻכִים בְּתוֹךְ כָּל צַדִּיקֵי יִשְׂרָאֵל, אָמֵן:

For a daughter:

יְשִׂמֵךְ אֱלֹהִים כְּשָׂרָה רִבְקָה רָחֵל וְלֵאָה. יְבָרֶכֵךְ יְיָ וְיִשְׁמְרֵךְ. יָאֵר יְיָ פָּנָיו אֵלַיִךְ וִיחֻנֵּךְ. יִשָּׂא יְיָ פָּנָיו אֵלַיִךְ וְיָשֵׂם לָךְ שָׁלוֹם.

יְהִי רָצוֹן מִלְּפְנֵי אָבִינוּ שֶׁבַּשָּׁמַיִם שֶׁיִּתֵּן בְּלִבֵּךְ אַהֲבָתוֹ וְיִרְאָתוֹ. וְתִהְיֶה יִרְאַת יְיָ עַל פָּנַיִךְ כָּל יָמַיִךְ שֶׁלֹּא תֶחֱטָאִי וּתְהִי חֶשְׁקֵךְ בַּתּוֹרָה וּבַמִּצְוֹת. עֵינַיִךְ לְנֹכַח יַבִּיטוּ. פִּיךְ יְדַבֵּר חָכְמוֹת וְלִבֵּךְ יֶהְגֶּה אֵימוֹת. יָדַיִךְ יַעַסְקוּ בְּמִצְוֹת. רַגְלַיִךְ יָרוּצוּ לַעֲשׂוֹת רְצוֹן אָבִיךְ שֶׁבַּשָּׁמַיִם. יִתֵּן לָךְ בָּנִים וּבָנוֹת צַדִּיקִים וְצִדְקָנִיּוֹת עוֹסְקִים בַּתּוֹרָה וּבַמִּצְוֹת כָּל יְמֵיהֶם, וִיהִי אִישֵׁךְ בָּרוּךְ. וְיַזְמִין לָךְ פַּרְנָסָתֵךְ בְּהֶתֵּר וּבְנַחַת וּבְרֶוַח מִתַּחַת יָדוֹ הָרְחָבָה. וְלֹא עַל יְדֵי מַתְּנַת בָּשָׂר וָדָם. וְתִכָּתְבִי וְתֵחָתְמִי לְחַיִּים טוֹבִים וַאֲרֻכִים בְּתוֹךְ כָּל צַדִּיקֵי יִשְׂרָאֵל, אָמֵן:

BLESSING FOR THE CHILDREN ON YOM KIPPUR EVE

The parents (either only one, each separately, or both together, depending on custom) place their hands upon the head of each child in turn and bless him/her.

For a son:

May God make you like Efraim and like Menashe.

For a daughter:

May God make you like Sarah, Rebecca, Rachel and Leah.

For both, continue:

May God bless you and watch over you;
May God shine His countenance upon you and give you grace;
May God turn His face to you and give you peace.

May it be the will of our Parent in Heaven that He place love and awe of God in your heart, that reverence for the Divine Name be implanted within you all of your life so that you do not sin; may your greatest delight be in Torah and the commandments, may your eyes always look straight ahead, may your mouth speak wisdom, may your heart express reverence, may your hands be occupied with commandments, and may your legs run to do the will of your Parent in Heaven. May the Almighty grant you righteous sons and daughters who will be involved in Torah and the commandments all the days of their lives; may your spouse be blessed. May the Almighty provide you with honest, easy and comfortable sustenance from His open hand, but not from human gifts, so that you will have the free time to devote to the service of the Lord. May you be written and sealed for a good and long life among all the righteous of Israel, Amen.

קידוש לליל ראש השנה

On Shabbat, begin with the following introduction:

(וַיַּרְא אֱלֹהִים אֶת כָּל אֲשֶׁר עָשָׂה וְהִנֵּה טוֹב מְאֹד) וַיְהִי עֶרֶב וַיְהִי בֹקֶר, יוֹם הַשִּׁשִּׁי. וַיְכֻלּוּ הַשָּׁמַיִם וְהָאָרֶץ וְכָל צְבָאָם וַיְכַל אֱלֹהִים בַּיּוֹם הַשְּׁבִיעִי מְלַאכְתּוֹ אֲשֶׁר עָשָׂה. וַיִּשְׁבֹּת בַּיּוֹם הַשְּׁבִיעִי מִכָּל מְלַאכְתּוֹ אֲשֶׁר עָשָׂה, וַיְבָרֶךְ אֱלֹהִים אֶת יוֹם הַשְּׁבִיעִי וַיְקַדֵּשׁ אֹתוֹ כִּי בוֹ שָׁבַת מִכָּל מְלַאכְתּוֹ אֲשֶׁר בָּרָא אֱלֹהִים לַעֲשׂוֹת.

בָּרוּךְ אַתָּה יְיָ אֱלֹהֵינוּ מֶלֶךְ הָעוֹלָם, בּוֹרֵא פְּרִי הַגָּפֶן.

On Shabbat, add the words in parentheses:

בָּרוּךְ אַתָּה יְיָ, אֱלֹהֵינוּ מֶלֶךְ הָעוֹלָם, אֲשֶׁר בָּחַר בָּנוּ מִכָּל־עָם וְרוֹמְמָנוּ מִכָּל־לָשׁוֹן, וְקִדְּשָׁנוּ בְּמִצְוֹתָיו, וַתִּתֶּן לָנוּ יְיָ אֱלֹהֵינוּ בְּאַהֲבָה. (אֶת יוֹם הַשַּׁבָּת הַזֶּה וְ) אֶת יוֹם הַזִּכָּרוֹן הַזֶּה, יוֹם (זִכְרוֹן) תְּרוּעָה (בְּאַהֲבָה) מִקְרָא קֹדֶשׁ, זֵכֶר לִיצִיאַת מִצְרָיִם. כִּי בָנוּ בָחַרְתָּ וְאוֹתָנוּ קִדַּשְׁתָּ מִכָּל הָעַמִּים, וּדְבָרְךָ אֱמֶת וְקַיָּם לָעַד. בָּרוּךְ אַתָּה יְיָ, מֶלֶךְ עַל כָּל הָאָרֶץ, מְקַדֵּשׁ (הַשַּׁבָּת וְ)יִשְׂרָאֵל וְיוֹם הַזִּכָּרוֹן:

On Saturday night add:

בָּרוּךְ אַתָּה יְיָ אֱלֹהֵינוּ מֶלֶךְ הָעוֹלָם, בּוֹרֵא מְאוֹרֵי הָאֵשׁ: בָּרוּךְ אַתָּה יְיָ אֱלֹהֵינוּ מֶלֶךְ הָעוֹלָם, הַמַּבְדִּיל בֵּין קֹדֶשׁ לְחֹל, בֵּין אוֹר לְחֹשֶׁךְ, בֵּין יִשְׂרָאֵל לָעַמִּים, בֵּין יוֹם הַשְּׁבִיעִי לְשֵׁשֶׁת יְמֵי הַמַּעֲשֶׂה, בֵּין קְדֻשַּׁת שַׁבָּת לִקְדֻשַּׁת יוֹם טוֹב הִבְדַּלְתָּ, וְאֶת יוֹם הַשְּׁבִיעִי מִשֵּׁשֶׁת יְמֵי הַמַּעֲשֶׂה קִדַּשְׁתָּ. הִבְדַּלְתָּ וְקִדַּשְׁתָּ אֶת עַמְּךָ יִשְׂרָאֵל בִּקְדֻשָּׁתֶךָ. בָּרוּךְ אַתָּה יְיָ, הַמַּבְדִּיל בֵּין קֹדֶשׁ לְקֹדֶשׁ:

On both evenings of Rosh Ha-Shanah, continue here:

בָּרוּךְ אַתָּה יְיָ אֱלֹהֵינוּ מֶלֶךְ הָעוֹלָם, שֶׁהֶחֱיָנוּ וְקִיְּמָנוּ וְהִגִּיעָנוּ לַזְּמַן הַזֶּה:

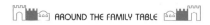

KIDDUSH FOR ROSH HA-SHANAH EVENING

On Shabbat, begin with the following introduction:

And God saw everything that He had made and behold it was very good. And it was evening and it was morning, the sixth day. So the heavens and earth were finished, with all their complement. Thus on the seventh day, God had completed His work which He had undertaken, and He rested on the seventh day from all His work which He had been doing. Then God blessed the seventh day and made it holy, because on it He rested from all His creative work, which God had brought into being to fulfill its purpose.

You are blessed, Lord our God, Sovereign of the world, Creator of the fruit of the vine.

On Shabbat, add the words in parentheses:

You are blessed, Lord our God, Sovereign of the world, who chose us out of all the nations, and exalted us above all peoples, and made us holy with His commandments. You gave us, Lord our God, with love, this (Shabbat day and this) Day of Remembrance, a day for (mentioning) blowing the *shofar*, a sacred assembly marking the Exodus from Egypt. For — out of all the nations — You chose us and made us holy, and Your word is true and reliable forever. You are blessed, Lord, the King of the whole earth Who sanctifies (Shabbat,) Israel and the Day of Remembrance.

On Saturday night, add:

You are blessed, Lord our God, Sovereign of the world, Creator of the lights of fire. You are blessed, Lord our God, Sovereign of the world, Who makes a distinction between sacred and secular, between light and darkness, between Israel and the other nations, between the seventh day and the six working days. You made a distinction between the holiness of Shabbat and the holiness of a festival, just as You made the seventh day holier than the six working days. You have set levels of holiness for Your people, Israel, through Your sanctity. You are blessed, Lord, Who sets different levels of holiness.

On both evenings of Rosh Ha-Shanah, continue here:

You are blessed, Lord our God, Sovereign of the world, Who has kept us alive and sustained us and enabled us to reach this occasion.

⋅◦❀◦⋅

KIDDUSH FOR ROSH HA-SHANAH EVENING
Since there is a halakhic question as to whether the second night of Rosh Ha-Shanah permits the blessing of *"shehehiyanu"* ("...Who has kept us alive...") (continued on page 128)

סימני ליל ראש השנה

After Kiddush, and before washing for hallah, the leader makes a blessing over each type of fruit and vegetable, eats and then dispenses that food to the celebrants around the table and explains the symbolism of each:

בָּרוּךְ אַתָּה יְיָ אֱלֹהֵינוּ מֶלֶךְ הָעוֹלָם, בּוֹרֵא פְּרִי הָעֵץ.

(This blessing is recited only once, over the first type of fruit that is consumed, since the other fruits are included in the original blessing.)

a. Date

יְהִי רָצוֹן מִלְּפָנֶיךָ יְיָ אֱלֹהֵינוּ וֵאלֹהֵי אֲבוֹתֵינוּ, שֶׁיִּתַּמּוּ שׂוֹנְאֵינוּ וְאוֹיְבֵינוּ.

b. Pomegranate

יְהִי רָצוֹן מִלְּפָנֶיךָ יְיָ אֱלֹהֵינוּ וֵאלֹהֵי אֲבוֹתֵינוּ, שֶׁיִּרְבּוּ זְכֻיּוֹתֵינוּ כְּרִמּוֹן.

(The Talmudic Sages maintained that the average pomegranate had 613 seeds.)

c. Apple sweetened with honey

יְהִי רָצוֹן מִלְּפָנֶיךָ יְיָ אֱלֹהֵינוּ וֵאלֹהֵי אֲבוֹתֵינוּ, שֶׁתְּחַדֵּשׁ עָלֵינוּ שָׁנָה טוֹבָה וּמְתֻקָה.

בָּרוּךְ אַתָּה יְיָ אֱלֹהֵינוּ מֶלֶךְ הָעוֹלָם, בּוֹרֵא פְּרִי הָאֲדָמָה.

d. Gourd (pumpkin, squash)

יְהִי רָצוֹן מִלְּפָנֶיךָ יְיָ אֱלֹהֵינוּ וֵאלֹהֵי אֲבוֹתֵינוּ, שֶׁתִּקְרַע רוֹעַ גְּזַר דִּינֵנוּ.

e. Beets

יְהִי רָצוֹן מִלְּפָנֶיךָ יְיָ אֱלֹהֵינוּ וֵאלֹהֵי אֲבוֹתֵינוּ, שֶׁיִּסְתַּלְּקוּ אוֹיְבֵינוּ וּמַשְׂטִינֵינוּ.

f. Leeks

יְהִי רָצוֹן מִלְּפָנֶיךָ יְיָ אֱלֹהֵינוּ וֵאלֹהֵי אֲבוֹתֵינוּ, שֶׁיִּכָּרְתוּ שׂוֹנְאֵינוּ.

SEDER ROSH HA-SHANAH

After Kiddush, and before washing for hallah, the leader makes a blessing over each type of fruit and vegetable, eats and then dispenses that food to the celebrants around the table and explains the symbolism of each:

You are blessed, Lord our God, Sovereign of the world, Who creates fruit from the trees.

(This blessing is recited only once, over the first type of fruit that is consumed, since the other fruits are included in the original blessing.)

a. Date

May it be Your will, Lord our God and God of our fathers, that our enemies and those who hate us, cease to be (or "become pure", the Hebrew תם (*'tam'*) means 'end', 'complete' or 'pure'.)

b. Pomegranate (The Talmudic Sages maintained that the average pomegranate had 613 seeds.)

May it be Your will, Lord our God and God of our forbears, that our merits increase like (the seeds of) a pomegranate.

c. Apple sweetened with honey

May it be Your will, our God and God of our forbears, that You renew for us a good and sweet year.

You are blessed, Lord our God, Sovereign of the world, Who creates the fruit of the earth.

d. Gourd (pumpkin, squash) ("kara" ; קרע — in Hebrew means 'tear').

May it be Your will, Lord our God and God of our forbears, that the evil decree of our judgment be torn asunder.

e. Beets (The Hebrew סלק — "selek" — means 'remove'.)

May it be Your will, Lord our God and God of our forbears, that our enemies be swept away.

f. Leeks ("karet" — כרת — means 'cut off'.)

May it be Your will, Lord our God and God of our forbears, that all of our enemies be cut off.

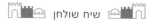
קידוש ליום ראש השנה

On Shabbat begin with the following introduction:

(וְשָׁמְרוּ בְנֵי יִשְׂרָאֵל אֶת הַשַּׁבָּת לַעֲשׂוֹת אֶת הַשַּׁבָּת לְדֹרֹתָם בְּרִית
עוֹלָם. בֵּינִי וּבֵין בְּנֵי יִשְׂרָאֵל אוֹת הִיא לְעוֹלָם, כִּי שֵׁשֶׁת יָמִים עָשָׂה יְיָ
אֶת הַשָּׁמַיִם וְאֶת הָאָרֶץ, וּבַיּוֹם הַשְּׁבִיעִי שָׁבַת וַיִּנָּפַשׁ:)

תִּקְעוּ בַחֹדֶשׁ שׁוֹפָר בַּכֶּסֶה לְיוֹם חַגֵּנוּ:
כִּי חֹק לְיִשְׂרָאֵל הוּא מִשְׁפָּט לֵאלֹהֵי יַעֲקֹב:

סַבְרִי מָרָנָן וְרַבָּנָן וְרַבּוֹתַי
בָּרוּךְ אַתָּה יְיָ אֱלֹהֵינוּ מֶלֶךְ הָעוֹלָם, בּוֹרֵא פְּרִי הַגָּפֶן:

because perhaps both days are really to be seen as one long day — it is proper to have fruit
out on the table which the person reciting Kiddush had not yet eaten that season, or to have
him wear a new garment for the *"shehehiyanu"* blessing on the *second* night.

Following Kiddush, there is a custom to eat a piece of apple dipped in honey, expressing the
wish that the New Year should be a sweet one.

After Kiddush on the eve of Rosh Ha-Shanah and before the ritual washing of the hands in
order to partake of the two round hallot (symbolizing the cycle of life), it is customary for the
leader to partake of and dispense to the celebrants various fruits, vegetables and foods
whose names symbolize our New Year wishes. Our Sages teach that especially on Rosh Ha-
Shanah, symbols take on real significance (*"simana milta hee"*). The best procedure is to make
the blessing over each category of food, taste each food after its proper blessing, explain the
symbolism of each individually, dispensing each in turn to all of the celebrants immediately
after expressing each New Year wish associated with that particular food.

During the meal itself, it is appropriate to the spirit of the Festival to continue with the
symbolism — and even to improvise. The hallah for the *ha-motzi* blessing is dipped in honey,

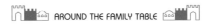
KIDDUSH FOR ROSH HA-SHANAH MORNINGS

On Shabbat begin with the following introduction:

(The children of Israel should keep Shabbat, observing Shabbat throughout their generations, as an everlasting covenant. It is a sign between Me and the children of Israel for all time, that in six days the Lord made the heavens and the earth, and that on the seventh day He was finished and He rested.)

Blow the *Shofar* in that month, at the full moon for our festive day. For it is a statute of Israel, an ordinance of the God of Jacob.

You are blessed, Lord our God, Sovereign of the world, Creator of the fruit of the vine.

the head of a fish and head of a lamb are often served, accompanied by the declaration: "May it be God's will that we be the head and not the tail."

(At my own table we suffice with a picture of a fish-head and a lamb-head rather than the real thing.)

And it is customary to serve *tzimmes* (a mixture of sweetened carrots and prunes) with the main dish, expressing the wish: "May it be Your will... that we multiply (in Yiddish the word for carrots is *'meren',* which means 'to multiply,' 'to become more') and that our (evil) decree be torn asunder" (in Hebrew the word for carrot is *'gezer' —* גזר, as in *'gezerah' —* גזר — decree). My wife usually adds kiwis ("For your salvation do I await [קִוִּיתִי *kiviti*!] — O God), onions (*'botzal'* בצל in Hebrew, as in "In the shadow (*'be-tzel'* בצל of Your wings please shelter us"), olives ("May your children be as numerous as olive plantings around your table" — Psalms 128) and a mixture of raisins and celery ("May the year bring a "raise in salary").... ✤

שִׂמְחָה לְאַרְצֶךָ וְשָׂשׂוֹן לְעִירֶךָ,
וּצְמִיחַת קֶרֶן לְדָוִד עַבְדֶּךָ,
וַעֲרִיכַת נֵר לְבֶן יִשַׁי מְשִׁיחֶךָ.

אַחַת שָׁאַלְתִּי מֵאֵת יְיָ
אוֹתָהּ אֲבַקֵּשׁ,
שִׁבְתִּי בְּבֵית יְיָ כָּל יְמֵי חַיַּי
לַחֲזוֹת בְּנֹעַם יְיָ וּלְבַקֵּר בְּהֵיכָלוֹ.

וַהֲבִיאוֹתִים אֶל הַר קָדְשִׁי
וְשִׂמַּחְתִּים בְּבֵית תְּפִלָּתִי,
עוֹלוֹתֵיהֶם וְזִבְחֵיהֶם
לְרָצוֹן עַל מִזְבְּחִי,
כִּי בֵיתִי בֵּית תְּפִלָּה יִקָּרֵא
לְכָל הָעַמִּים.

הֲבֵן יַקִּיר לִי אֶפְרַיִם
אִם יֶלֶד שַׁעֲשׁוּעִים,
כִּי מִדֵּי דַבְּרִי בּוֹ זָכֹר אֶזְכְּרֶנּוּ עוֹד
עַל כֵּן הָמוּ מֵעַי לוֹ
רַחֵם אֲרַחֲמֶנּוּ נְאֻם יְיָ.

קְחוּ עִמָּכֶם דְּבָרִים וְשׁוּבוּ אֶל יְיָ
אִמְרוּ אֵלָיו כָּל תִּשָּׂא עָוֹן וְקַח טוֹב
וּנְשַׁלְּמָה פָרִים שְׂפָתֵינוּ:

וְכָל מַאֲמִינִים שֶׁהוּא חַי וְקַיָּם
הַטּוֹב וּמֵטִיב לָרָעִים וְלַטּוֹבִים.

אַתָּה זוֹכֵר מַעֲשֵׂה עוֹלָם
וּפוֹקֵד כָּל יְצוּרֵי קֶדֶם,
לְפָנֶיךָ נִגְלוּ כָּל תַּעֲלוּמוֹת
וַהֲמוֹן נִסְתָּרוֹת שֶׁמִּבְּרֵאשִׁית.

וַהֲבִיאֵנוּ לְשָׁלוֹם
מֵאַרְבַּע כַּנְפוֹת הָאָרֶץ.
וְתוֹלִיכֵנוּ קוֹמְמִיּוּת לְאַרְצֵנוּ.
כִּי אֵל פּוֹעֵל יְשׁוּעוֹת אָתָּה.
וּבָנוּ בָחַרְתָּ מִכָּל עַם וְלָשׁוֹן
וְקֵרַבְתָּנוּ מַלְכֵּנוּ
לְשִׁמְךָ הַגָּדוֹל סֶלָה בֶּאֱמֶת
לְהוֹדוֹת לְךָ וּלְיַחֶדְךָ בְּאַהֲבָה:

חֲמֹל עַל מַעֲשֶׂיךָ
וְתִשְׂמַח בְּמַעֲשֶׂיךָ,
וְיֹאמְרוּ לְךָ חוֹסֶיךָ בְּצַדֶּקְךָ עֲמוּסֶיךָ.
תִּקְדַּשׁ אָדוֹן עַל כָּל מַעֲשֶׂיךָ
כִּי מַקְדִּישֶׁךָ בִּקְדֻשָּׁתְךָ קִדַּשְׁתָּ,
נָאֶה לְקָדוֹשׁ פְּאֵר מִקְּדוֹשִׁים.

SONGS FOR ROSH HA-SHANAH

כָּל הָעוֹלָם כֻּלּוֹ
גֶּשֶׁר צַר מְאֹד.
וְהָעִקָּר לֹא לְפַחֵד כְּלָל.

לֵב טָהוֹר בְּרָא לִי אֱלֹהִים
וְרוּחַ נָכוֹן חַדֵּשׁ בְּקִרְבִּי.
אַל תַּשְׁלִיכֵנִי מִלְּפָנֶיךָ
וְרוּחַ קָדְשְׁךָ אַל תִּקַּח מִמֶּנִּי.

שְׂאוּ שְׁעָרִים רָאשֵׁיכֶם
וְהִנָּשְׂאוּ פִּתְחֵי עוֹלָם
וְיָבוֹא מֶלֶךְ הַכָּבוֹד.
מִי הוּא זֶה מֶלֶךְ הַכָּבוֹד
יְיָ צְבָאוֹת הוּא מֶלֶךְ הַכָּבוֹד סֶלָה.

וְקָרֵב פְּזוּרֵינוּ מִבֵּין הַגּוֹיִם,
וּנְפוּצוֹתֵינוּ כַּנֵּס מִיַּרְכְּתֵי אָרֶץ.

אַדִּיר אַדִּירֵנוּ יְיָ אֲדֹנֵינוּ
מָה אַדִּיר שִׁמְךָ בְּכָל הָאָרֶץ.
וְהָיָה יְיָ לְמֶלֶךְ עַל כָּל הָאָרֶץ.
בַּיּוֹם הַהוּא יִהְיֶה יְיָ אֶחָד
וּשְׁמוֹ אֶחָד:

אָבִינוּ מַלְכֵּנוּ. חָנֵּנוּ וַעֲנֵנוּ
כִּי אֵין בָּנוּ מַעֲשִׂים
עֲשֵׂה עִמָּנוּ צְדָקָה וָחֶסֶד וְהוֹשִׁיעֵנוּ:

וְעָלוּ מוֹשִׁיעִים בְּהַר צִיּוֹן
לִשְׁפֹּט אֶת הַר עֵשָׂו.
וְהָיְתָה לַיְיָ הַמְּלוּכָה:

וְהָיָה יְיָ לְמֶלֶךְ עַל כָּל הָאָרֶץ.
בַּיּוֹם הַהוּא יִהְיֶה יְיָ אֶחָד
וּשְׁמוֹ אֶחָד:

אַב הָרַחֲמִים.
הֵיטִיבָה בִרְצוֹנְךָ אֶת צִיּוֹן.
תִּבְנֶה חוֹמוֹת יְרוּשָׁלָיִם:

כִּי בְךָ לְבַד בָּטָחְנוּ.
מֶלֶךְ אֵל רָם וְנִשָּׂא
אֲדוֹן עוֹלָמִים:

הוֹרֵנִי יְיָ דַּרְכֶּךָ
וּנְחֵנִי בְּאֹרַח מִישׁוֹר
לְמַעַן שׁוֹרְרָי:
לוּלֵא הֶאֱמַנְתִּי
לִרְאוֹת בְּטוּב יְיָ
בְּאֶרֶץ חַיִּים:

קידוש לליל שלוש רגלים

On Shabbat add this introduction:

(וַיַּרְא אֱלֹהִים אֶת כָּל אֲשֶׁר עָשָׂה וְהִנֵּה טוֹב מְאֹד) וַיְהִי עֶרֶב וַיְהִי בֹקֶר, יוֹם הַשִּׁשִּׁי. וַיְכֻלּוּ הַשָּׁמַיִם וְהָאָרֶץ וְכָל צְבָאָם. וַיְכַל אֱלֹהִים בַּיּוֹם הַשְּׁבִיעִי מְלַאכְתּוֹ אֲשֶׁר עָשָׂה. וַיִּשְׁבֹּת בַּיּוֹם הַשְּׁבִיעִי מִכָּל מְלַאכְתּוֹ אֲשֶׁר עָשָׂה, וַיְבָרֶךְ אֱלֹהִים אֶת יוֹם הַשְּׁבִיעִי וַיְקַדֵּשׁ אֹתוֹ כִּי בוֹ שָׁבַת מִכָּל מְלַאכְתּוֹ אֲשֶׁר בָּרָא אֱלֹהִים לַעֲשׂוֹת.

סַבְרִי מָרָנָן וְרַבָּנָן וְרַבּוֹתַי
בָּרוּךְ אַתָּה יְיָ אֱלֹהֵינוּ מֶלֶךְ הָעוֹלָם, בּוֹרֵא פְּרִי הַגָּפֶן:

On Shabbat add the words in parentheses:

בָּרוּךְ אַתָּה יְיָ אֱלֹהֵינוּ מֶלֶךְ הָעוֹלָם, אֲשֶׁר בָּחַר בָּנוּ מִכָּל עָם וְרוֹמְמָנוּ מִכָּל לָשׁוֹן וְקִדְּשָׁנוּ בְּמִצְוֹתָיו, וַתִּתֶּן לָנוּ יְיָ אֱלֹהֵינוּ בְּאַהֲבָה (שַׁבָּתוֹת לִמְנוּחָה וּ)מוֹעֲדִים לְשִׂמְחָה, חַגִּים וּזְמַנִּים לְשָׂשׂוֹן, אֶת יוֹם (הַשַּׁבָּת הַזֶּה וְאֶת יוֹם)

חַג הַמַּצּוֹת הַזֶּה, זְמַן חֵרוּתֵנוּ / חַג הַשָּׁבֻעוֹת הַזֶּה, זְמַן מַתַּן תּוֹרָתֵנוּ / חַג הַסֻּכּוֹת הַזֶּה, זְמַן שִׂמְחָתֵנוּ / שְׁמִינִי חַג הָעֲצֶרֶת הַזֶּה, זְמַן שִׂמְחָתֵנוּ

(בְּאַהֲבָה) מִקְרָא קֹדֶשׁ, זֵכֶר לִיצִיאַת מִצְרָיִם. כִּי בָנוּ בָחַרְתָּ וְאוֹתָנוּ קִדַּשְׁתָּ מִכָּל הָעַמִּים, (וְשַׁבָּת) וּמוֹעֲדֵי קָדְשֶׁךָ (בְּאַהֲבָה וּבְרָצוֹן) בְּשִׂמְחָה וּבְשָׂשׂוֹן הִנְחַלְתָּנוּ. בָּרוּךְ אַתָּה יְיָ, מְקַדֵּשׁ (הַשַּׁבָּת וְ)יִשְׂרָאֵל וְהַזְּמַנִּים:

KIDDUSH FOR FESTIVAL EVENINGS

Unlike Shabbat, whose major motif is God (as the Torah teaches in the Decalogue, "The Shabbat is for the Lord your God", and as the Friday evening Amidah prayer opens: "You have sanctified the Shabbat day for Your Name") and focuses our commitment to the God of creation and freedom, the major motif of the Festivals is the uniqueness and eternity of the Jewish people. Each Festival emphasizes another aspect of our mission to the world: Pesach with its message of universal freedom, Shavuot with its message of the responsibility which must come with being free, and Sukkot with the promise of redemption under the sheltering

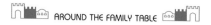

KIDDUSH FOR FESTIVAL EVENINGS

On Shabbat add this introduction:

And God saw everything that He had made and behold it was very good. And it was evening and it was morning, the sixth day. So the heavens and earth were finished, with all their complement. Thus on the seventh day, God had completed His work which He had undertaken, and He rested on the seventh day from all His work which He had been doing. Then God blessed the seventh day and made it holy, because on it He rested from all His creative work, which God had brought into being to fulfill its purpose.

You are blessed, Lord our God, Sovereign of the world, creator of the fruit of the vine.

On Shabbat add the words in parentheses:

You are blessed, Lord our God, Sovereign of the world, who chose us out of all the nations, and exalted us above all peoples, and made us holy with His commandments. You gave us, Lord our God, with love, (Shabbat for rest and) set times for joy, festivals and holidays for happiness: this (Shabbat and this) Festival day of

Pesach / Shavuot / Sukkot / Shemini Atzeret

(with love), a sacred assembly marking the Exodus from Egypt. For — out of all the nations — You chose us and made us holy, and you gave us Your holy (Shabbat and) Festival (in love and favor) for joy and for happiness, as our heritage. You are blessed, Lord, Who sanctifies (Shabbat), Israel and the holidays.

Tabernacle of God's peace. Rosh Ha-Shanah highlights the Jewish challenge to perfect the world under the kingship of God, and Yom Kippur gives us a taste of personal and national redemption in its emphasis on the atonement service performed in the Holy Temple in Jerusalem, where "God's house will become a house of prayer for all nations." Indeed, every Festival Amidah prayer highlights the words, "You have sanctified us from among all nations, and have lifted us above all tongues...". Most of all, if the Shabbat focuses our attention upon the God Who created the world, the Festivals orientate us towards an appreciation of the Jewish nation, its function in history and in the world as well as its eternal covenant with God. ◆

On Saturday night add:

בָּרוּךְ אַתָּה יְיָ אֱלֹהֵינוּ מֶלֶךְ הָעוֹלָם, בּוֹרֵא מְאוֹרֵי הָאֵשׁ:

בָּרוּךְ אַתָּהיְיָ אֱלֹהֵינוּ מֶלֶךְ הָעוֹלָם, הַמַּבְדִּיל בֵּין קֹדֶשׁ לְחֹל, בֵּין אוֹר לְחשֶׁךְ, בֵּין יִשְׂרָאֵל לָעַמִּים, בֵּין יוֹם הַשְּׁבִיעִי לְשֵׁשֶׁת יְמֵי הַמַּעֲשֶׂה, בֵּין קְדֻשַּׁת שַׁבָּת לִקְדֻשַּׁת יוֹם טוֹב הִבְדַּלְתָּ, וְאֶת יוֹם הַשְּׁבִיעִי מִשֵּׁשֶׁת יְמֵי הַמַּעֲשֶׂה קִדַּשְׁתָּ. הִבְדַּלְתָּ וְקִדַּשְׁתָּ אֶת עַמְּךָ יִשְׂרָאֵל בִּקְדֻשָּׁתֶךָ. בָּרוּךְ אַתָּה יְיָ, הַמַּבְדִּיל בֵּין קֹדֶשׁ לְקֹדֶשׁ:

Omit the following on the last evening (in the Diaspora, the last two evenings) of Pesach:

בָּרוּךְ אַתָּה יְיָ אֱלֹהֵינוּ מֶלֶךְ הָעוֹלָם, שֶׁהֶחֱיָנוּ וְקִיְּמָנוּ וְהִגִּיעָנוּ לַזְּמַן הַזֶּה:

In the Sukkah, add: (On the first evening of Sukkot only, recite this blessing before the preceding one.)

בָּרוּךְ אַתָּה יְיָ אֱלֹהֵינוּ מֶלֶךְ הָעוֹלָם, אֲשֶׁר קִדְּשָׁנוּ בְּמִצְוֹתָיו וְצִוָּנוּ לֵישֵׁב בַּסֻּכָּה:

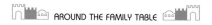
On Saturday night add:

You are blessed, Lord our God, Sovereign of the world,
Creator of the lights of fire.

You are blessed, Lord our God, Sovereign of the world, Who makes a distinction between sacred and secular, between light and darkness, between Israel and the other nations, between the seventh day and the six working days. You made a distinction between the holiness of Shabbat and the holiness of a festival, just as You made the seventh day holier than the six working days. You have set levels of holiness for Your people, Israel, through Your sanctity. You are blessed, Lord, Who sets different levels of holiness.

Omit the following on the last evening (in the Diaspora, the last two evenings) of Pesach:

You are blessed, Lord our God, Sovereign of the world, Who has kept us alive and sustained us and enabled us to reach this occasion.

In the Sukkah, add: (On the first evening of Sukkot only, recite this blessing before the preceding one.)

You are blessed, Lord our God, Sovereign of the world, Who made us holy with His commandments and commanded us to live in the sukkah.

אושפיזין

As we enter the sukkah each evening of the Festival, the leader declares before (or together with) all of the assembled:

יְהִי רָצוֹן מִלְּפָנֶיךָ יְהוָה אֱלֹהַי וֵאלֹהֵי אֲבוֹתַי שֶׁתַּשְׁרֶה שְׁכִינָתְךָ בֵּינֵינוּ וְתִפְרוֹס עָלֵינוּ סֻכַּת שְׁלוֹמֶךָ, וְתַקִּיף אוֹתָנוּ מִזִּיו כְּבוֹדֶךָ הַקָּדוֹשׁ וְהַטָּהוֹר כְּמוֹ שֶׁכָּתוּב בַּסֻּכָּה תֵּשְׁבוּ שִׁבְעַת יָמִים כָּל הָאֶזְרָח בְּיִשְׂרָאֵל יֵשְׁבוּ בַּסֻּכֹּת. לְמַעַן יֵדְעוּ דֹרֹתֵיכֶם כִּי בַסֻּכּוֹת הוֹשַׁבְתִּי אֶת בְּנֵי יִשְׂרָאֵל בְּהוֹצִיאִי אוֹתָם מֵאֶרֶץ מִצְרָיִם.

Before eating, the following greeting of special biblical guests is recited (and there are those who greet female biblical guests as well).

עוּלוּ אוּשְׁפִּיזִין עִלָּאִין קַדִּישִׁין, עוּלוּ אַבָּהָן עִלָּאִין קַדִּישִׁין. תִּיבוּ תִּיבוּ אוּשְׁפִּיזִין עִלָּאִין קַדִּישִׁין תִּיבוּ תִּיבוּ אוּשְׁפִּיזִין דִּמְהֵימְנוּתָא. זַכָּאָה חֶלְקָנָא, זַכָּאָה חוּלְקֵיהוֹן דְּיִשְׂרָאֵל, דִּכְתִיב, כִּי חֵלֶק יְיָ עַמּוֹ יַעֲקֹב חֶבֶל נַחֲלָתוֹ.

אֲזַמִּין לִסְעֻדָתִי אוּשְׁפִּיזִין עִלָּאִין אַבְרָהָם יִצְחָק וְיַעֲקֹב מֹשֶׁה אַהֲרֹן יוֹסֵף וְדָוִד. (שָׂרָה, רִבְקָה, לֵאָה וְרָחֵל, מִרְיָם, דְּבוֹרָה וְרוּת.)

On the first day, say:

בְּמָטוּ מִנָּךְ אַבְרָהָם אוּשְׁפִּיזִי עִלָּאִי דְּתִתְּבַ עִמִּי וְעִמָּךְ כָּל אוּשְׁפִּיזֵי עִלָּאֵי יִצְחָק יַעֲקֹב מֹשֶׁה אַהֲרֹן יוֹסֵף וְדָוִד. (בְּמָטוּ מִנָּךְ שָׂרָה אוּשְׁפִּיזִי עִלָּאֵי בַּהֲדֵי אוּשְׁפִּיזִין עִלָּאִין רִבְקָה, לֵאָה, רָחֵל, מִרְיָם, דְּבוֹרָה וְרוּת.)

USHPIZIN

There is a difference of opinion as to whether the sukkah (tabernacle) represents the temporary huts of Jewish wanderings in the desert and throughout our Exile, or the Divine clouds of glory that emanated from God and protected us in the desert. I might suggest that in the Diaspora the sukkah symbolizes the huts of Jewish exile, whereas in Israel we are privileged to feel the Divine shelter of ultimate protection.

USHPIZIN

As we enter the sukkah each evening of the Festival, the leader declares before (or together with) all of the assembled:

May it be Your will, Lord my God and God of my forbears, that You rest Your Divine presence among us, and spread over us the tabernacle of Your peace, and envelop us with the dazzling light of the holiness and purity of Your glory. As it is written in Your Torah: "You shall dwell in booths for seven days — every citizen of Israel shall dwell in booths; in order that your future generations shall know that I enabled the children of Israel to dwell in booths when I took them out of the land of Egypt." (Lev. 23:42, 43)

Before eating, the following greeting of special biblical guests is recited (and there are those who greet female biblical guests as well).

Enter exalted, holy guests; enter, exalted and holy forbears,
Return, return, exalted, holy guests,
Return, return, faithful guests.
Fortunate is our lot, fortunate is the lot of Israel
As it is written, "For the lot of God is His nation,
Jacob is the portion of His inheritance" (Deut. 32:9)

I invite to my meal the exalted guests
Abraham, Isaac and Jacob, Moses, Aaron, Joseph and David
(Sarah, Rebecca, Leah and Rachel, Miriam, Deborah and Ruth).

On the first day, say:

Would it please you, Abraham, exalted guests, to sit with me
And with you will be all the exalted guests,
Isaac and Jacob, Moses, Aaron, Joseph and David.
(Would it please you, Sarah, exalted guest, together with the exalted guests
Rebecca, Leah, Rachel, Miriam, Deborah and Ruth)

The Holy Zohar, building upon the fact that the Festival of Sukkot falls only five days after Yom Kippur — the day in which God's forgiveness was demonstrated by our having received the second Tablets of the Law, the renewed marriage contract between God and Israel — maintains that the sukkah ought then be seen as God's Tabernacle-home, into which He brings His bride (Israel). Hence the Festival of Sukkot lasts seven days, paralleling the seven

On the second day:

בְּמָטוּ מִנָּךְ יִצְחָק אוּשְׁפִּיזִי עִלָּאֵי דְתֵתֵב עִמִּי וְעִמָּךְ כָּל אוּשְׁפִּיזֵי עִלָּאֵי אַבְרָהָם יַעֲקֹב מֹשֶׁה אַהֲרֹן יוֹסֵף וְדָוִד.

(בְּמָטוּ מִנָּךְ רִבְקָה עִלָּאֵי בַּהֲדֵי אוּשְׁפִּיזִין עִלָּאִין שָׂרָה, לֵאָה, רָחֵל, מִרְיָם, דְּבוֹרָה וְרוּת.)

On the third day:

בְּמָטוּ מִנָּךְ יַעֲקֹב אוּשְׁפִּיזִי עִלָּאֵי דְתֵתֵב עִמִּי וְעִמָּךְ כָּל אוּשְׁפִּיזֵי עִלָּאֵי אַבְרָהָם יִצְחָק מֹשֶׁה אַהֲרֹן יוֹסֵף וְדָוִד.

(בְּמָטוּ מִנָּךְ לֵאָה אוּשְׁפִּיזִי עִלָּאֵי בַּהֲדֵי אוּשְׁפִּיזִין עִלָּאִין שָׂרָה, רִבְקָה, רָחֵל, מִרְיָם, דְּבוֹרָה וְרוּת.)

On the fourth day:

בְּמָטוּ מִנָּךְ מֹשֶׁה אוּשְׁפִּיזִי עִלָּאֵי דְתֵתֵב עִמִּי וְעִמָּךְ כָּל אוּשְׁפִּיזֵי עִלָּאֵי אַבְרָהָם יִצְחָק יַעֲקֹב אַהֲרֹן יוֹסֵף וְדָוִד.

(בְּמָטוּ מִנָּךְ רָחֵל אוּשְׁפִּיזִי עִלָּאֵי בַּהֲדֵי אוּשְׁפִּיזִין עִלָּאִין שָׂרָה, רִבְקָה, לֵאָה, מִרְיָם, דְּבוֹרָה וְרוּת.)

On the fifth day:

בְּמָטוּ מִנָּךְ אַהֲרֹן אוּשְׁפִּיזִי עִלָּאֵי דְתֵתֵב עִמִּי וְעִמָּךְ כָּל אוּשְׁפִּיזֵי עִלָּאֵי אַבְרָהָם יִצְחָק יַעֲקֹב מֹשֶׁה יוֹסֵף וְדָוִד.

(בְּמָטוּ מִנָּךְ מִרְיָם אוּשְׁפִּיזִי עִלָּאֵי בַּהֲדֵי אוּשְׁפִּיזִין עִלָּאִין שָׂרָה, רִבְקָה, לֵאָה, רָחֵל, דְּבוֹרָה וְרוּת.)

celebratory days of a wedding feast. Since the wedding feast must have "new faces" (*panim hadashot*) in order for the nuptial blessings to be intoned (since all who attended the wedding have already heard them), there is a new guest for each day of Sukkot: Abraham, Isaac, Jacob, Moses, Aaron, Joseph and David. (There is a new parallel custom to invite seven worthy women guests as well: Sarah, Rebecca, Leah, Rachel, Miriam, Deborah and Ruth.) There is yet another symbolism to the sukkah. We have just concluded Yom Kippur — our day

On the second day:

Would it please you, Isaac, exalted guest, to sit with me
And with you will be all the exalted guests —
Abraham, Jacob, Moses, Aaron, Joseph and David.
(Would it please you, Rebecca, exalted guest, together with the exalted guests Sarah, Leah, Rachel, Miriam, Deborah and Ruth).

On the third day:

Would it please you, Jacob, exalted guest, to sit with me
And with you will be all the exalted guests —
Abraham, Isaac, Moses, Aaron, Joseph and David.
(Would it please you, Leah, exalted guest, together with the exalted guests Sarah, Rebecca, Rachel, Miriam, Deborah and Ruth).

On the fourth day:

Would it please you, Moses, exalted guest, to sit with me
And with you will be all the exalted guests —
Abraham, Isaac, Jacob, Aaron, Joseph and David.
(Would it please you, Rachel, exalted guest, together with the exalted guests Sarah, Rebecca, Leah, Miriam, Deborah and Ruth).

On the fifth day:

Would it please you, Aaron, exalted guest, to sit with me
And with you will be all the exalted guests —
Abraham, Isaac, Jacob, Moses, Joseph and David.
(Would it please you, Miriam, exalted guest, together with the exalted guests Sarah, Rebecca, Leah, Rachel, Deborah and Ruth).

of forgiveness and the climax of the Ten Days of Repentance. What greater expression of repentance can we offer than by establishing a new residence ("starting anew") — but this time in accordance with the precise directions of the Torah. In effect, this is the ultimate significance of the sukkah, the kind of house that God orders us to build. It is the very antithesis of a massive or ornate structure; it is adorned with the lush vegetation of Israel, it enables us to see the stars through openings in the roof which link us to nature without and to the

On the sixth day:

בְּמָטוּ מִנָּךְ יוֹסֵף אוּשְׁפִּיזִי עִלָּאֵי דְּתֵתֵב עִמִּי וְעִמָּךְ כָּל אוּשְׁפִּיזֵי עִלָּאֵי אַבְרָהָם יִצְחָק יַעֲקֹב מֹשֶׁה אַהֲרֹן וְדָוִד.

(בְּמָטוּ מִנָּךְ דְּבוֹרָה אוּשְׁפִּיזִי עִלָּאֵי בַּהֲדֵי אוּשְׁפִּיזִין עִלָּאִין שָׂרָה, רִבְקָה, לֵאָה, רָחֵל, מִרְיָם וְרוּת.)

On the seventh day:

בְּמָטוּ מִנָּךְ דָּוִד אוּשְׁפִּיזִי עִלָּאֵי דְּתֵתֵב עִמִּי וְעִמָּךְ כָּל אוּשְׁפִּיזֵי עִלָּאֵי אַבְרָהָם יִצְחָק יַעֲקֹב מֹשֶׁה אַהֲרֹן וְיוֹסֵף.

(בְּמָטוּ מִנָּךְ רוּת אוּשְׁפִּיזִי עִלָּאֵי בַּהֲדֵי אוּשְׁפִּיזִין עִלָּאִין שָׂרָה, רִבְקָה, לֵאָה, רָחֵל, מִרְיָם וּדְבוֹרָה.)

Afterwards, continue with Kiddush (page 132).

On Hoshanah Rabbah (the seventh day of the Sukkot Festival), after eating the second meal in the Sukkah, we take leave of the Sukkah with the following prayer:

יְהִי רָצוֹן מִלְּפָנֶיךָ יְיָ אֱלֹהֵינוּ וֵאלֹהֵי אֲבוֹתֵינוּ כְּשֵׁם שֶׁקִּיַּמְתִּי וְיָשַׁבְתִּי בְּסוּכָּה זוֹ כֵּן אֶזְכֶּה לְשָׁנָה הַבָּאָה לֵישֵׁב בְּסוּכָּה שֶׁל לִוְיָתָן:

On Shemini Atzeret — Simhat Torah we make Kiddush and enjoy our Festival meals in the house, not in the sukkah. In the Diaspora, however, the major custom cited in the Talmud is that on the first of these two latter Festival days יָתְבִי יָתְבִינָן וּבָרוּכֵי לֹא מְבָרְכִינָן: one should recite Kiddush and eat in the sukkah, but without the blessing on "dwelling in the sukkah" — לֵישֵׁב בְּסֻכָּה.

supernal realms above, and it is bound with the strong bonds of familial togetherness. Indeed, the message of love emanating from a sukkah home is reminiscent of the Talmudic dictum: "When the love is strong, two people can live in a room the size of the tip of a sword; when the love is not strong, a bed of sixty miles is not large enough" (Sanhedrin 7a). And which guests

On the sixth day:

Would it please you, Joseph, exalted guest, to sit with me
And with you will be all the exalted guests —
Abraham, Isaac, Jacob, Moses, Aaron, and David.
(Would it please you, Deborah, exalted guest, together with the exalted
guests Sarah, Rebecca, Leah, Rachel, Miriam and Ruth).

On the seventh day:

Would it please you, David, exalted guest, to sit with me
And with you will be all the exalted guests —
Abraham, Isaac, Jacob, Moses, Aaron and Joseph.
(Would it please you, Ruth, exalted guest, together with the exalted guests
Sarah, Rebecca, Leah, Rachel, Miriam and Deborah).

Afterwards, continue with Kiddush (page 132).

On Hoshanah Rabbah (the seventh day of the Sukkot Festival), after eating the second meal in
the Sukkah, we take leave of the Sukkah with the following prayer:

Just as we merited the fulfillment of the commandment to dwell in the
sukkah, so may we merit to dwell in the sukkah made of the great fish,
Leviathan, in the period of the complete redemption, speedily and in our time.

On Shemini Atzeret — Simhat Torah we make Kiddush and enjoy our festival meals in the
house, not in the sukkah. In the Diaspora, however, the major custom cited in the Talmud is
that on the first of these two latter Festival days יתבי יתבינן וברכני לא ברכינן: one should
recite Kiddush and eat in the sukkah, but without the blessing on "dwelling in the sukkah" —
לישב בסוכה.

would God suggest that we bring into this house? Given the fact that guests always influence
the regular residents in some way — sometimes even taking over — we are urged to invite
into our sukkah the heroes and heroines of the Torah, with the hope that we will convince them
to remain with us long after the Sukkot Festival has passed.

SPECIAL SONGS FOR SUKKOT

א סוכה'לע אַ קליינע, פון ברעטעלעך געמיינע
האב איך מיר אַ סוכה'לע געמאכט.
צוגעדעק דעם דאך מיט אַ ביסעלע סכך
זיץ איך מיר אין סוכה'לע באנאכט.

א ווינט א קאלטן בלאזט דורך די שפאלטן
און די ליכטעלעך זיי לעשן זיך פיל
עס איז מיר אַ חידוש ווי איך מאך מיר קידוש
און די ליכטעלעך זיי ברענען גאנץ שטיל.

צום ערשטן געריכט מיט א בלאסן געזיכט
קומט מיר מיין טעכטערל אריין
זי שטעלט זיך אַוועק און זאגט מיט שרעק:
טאטעלע די סוכה פאלט באלד איין.

זיי נישט קיין נאר, האב ניט קיין צער
זאל דיר די סוכה ניט טאן באנג
עס איז שוין גאר באלד צוויי טויזנט יאר
אין די סוכה'לע זי שטייט נאך גאנץ לאנג.

הִנֵּה אֵל יְשׁוּעָתִי אֶבְטַח וְלֹא אֶפְחָד,
כִּי עָזִּי וְזִמְרָת יָהּ יְיָ וַיְהִי לִי לִישׁוּעָה.
וּשְׁאַבְתֶּם מַיִם בְּשָׂשׂוֹן מִמַּעַיְנֵי הַיְשׁוּעָה.
לַיְיָ הַיְשׁוּעָה עַל עַמְּךָ בִרְכָתֶךָ סֶּלָה.

SONGS FOR SUKKOT

A Sukkah'le

A small sukkah, from slats of a tree
Such a sukkah did I make for me.
I added a little bit of *"sekhakh"* to the ceiling
And I sat in the small sukkah in the evening.

A cold wind through the cracks made me shiver
And the Festival candle-lights began to flicker
As I recited Kiddush I was amazed at the fact
That the glowing candles still remained intact.

My young daughter brought in the first course
With a pale face and a voice trembling and hoarse
She stood next to me, and said with much fear,
"Tattele, the sukkah is about to collapse and disappear!"

"Don't be a fool, relax and unwind,
Don't let the sukkah upset your mind.
Almost two thousand years of exile have already passed
And look how our small sukkah has managed to last!"

כִּי בְשִׂמְחָה תֵצֵאוּ וּבְשָׁלוֹם תּוּבָלוּן.
הֶהָרִים וְהַגְּבָעוֹת יִפְצְחוּ לִפְנֵיכֶם רִנָּה.
וְכָל עֲצֵי הַשָּׂדֶה יִמְחֲאוּ כָף.

כֹּה אָמַר יְיָ מָצָא חֵן בַּמִּדְבָּר
עַם שְׂרִידֵי חָרֶב הָלוֹךְ לְהַרְגִּיעוֹ יִשְׂרָאֵל.

SONGS FOR SHAVUOT

אֲשֶׁר בָּרָא שָׂשׂוֹן וְשִׂמְחָה,
חָתָן וְכַלָּה,
גִּילָה, רִנָּה, דִּיצָה וְחֶדְוָה,
אַהֲבָה וְאַחֲוָה, שָׁלוֹם וְרֵעוּת.
מְהֵרָה ה׳ אֱלֹהֵינוּ,
יִשָּׁמַע בְּעָרֵי יְהוּדָה
וּבְחוּצוֹת יְרוּשָׁלַיִם,
קוֹל שָׂשׂוֹן וְקוֹל שִׂמְחָה,
קוֹל חָתָן וְקוֹל כַּלָּה.

וְהָאֵר עֵינֵינוּ בְּתוֹרָתֶךָ
וְדַבֵּק לִבֵּנוּ בְּמִצְוֹתֶיךָ,
וְיַחֵד לְבָבֵנוּ לְאַהֲבָה וּלְיִרְאָה
אֶת שְׁמֶךָ, שֶׁלֹּא נֵבוֹשׁ וְלֹא נִכָּשֵׁל
לְעוֹלָם וָעֶד.

כַּד יָתְבִין יִשְׂרָאֵל
וְעָסְקִין בְּשִׂמְחַת הַתּוֹרָה
קוּדְשָׁא בְּרִיךְ הוּא אוֹמֵר
לְפַמַּלְיָא דִּילֵיהּ
חֲזוּ חֲזוּ בָּנֵי בָּנֵי
בְּנֵי חֲבִיבִי
דְּהֵם מִשְׁתַּכְּחִין בְּצָרָה דִּילְהוֹן
וְעָסְקִין בְּחֶדְוָה דִּילֵיהּ.

יָשִׂישׂ עָלַיִךְ אֱלֹהָיִךְ
כִּמְשׂוֹשׂ חָתָן עַל כַּלָּה.

כִּי הֵם חַיֵּינוּ וְאֹרֶךְ יָמֵינוּ
וּבָהֶם נֶהְגֶּה יוֹמָם וָלָיְלָה.

בִּלְבָבִי מִשְׁכָּן אֶבְנֶה לַהֲדַר כְּבוֹדוֹ,
וּלְמִשְׁכָּן מִזְבֵּחַ אָשִׂים
לְקַרְנֵי הוֹדוֹ.
וּלְנֵר תָּמִיד אֶקַּח לִי
אֶת אֵשׁ הָעֲקֵדָה,
וּלְקָרְבָּן אַקְרִיב לוֹ
אֶת נַפְשִׁי הַיְחִידָה.

כִּי מִצִּיּוֹן תֵּצֵא תוֹרָה,
וּדְבַר יְיָ מִירוּשָׁלַיִם.

תּוֹרַת יְיָ תְּמִימָה מְשִׁיבַת נָפֶשׁ.
עֵדוּת יְיָ נֶאֱמָנָה מַחְכִּימַת פֶּתִי.

כֵּיצַד מְרַקְּדִין לִפְנֵי הַכַּלָּה?
כַּלָּה נָאָה וַחֲסוּדָה.

וַיְהִי בִישֻׁרוּן מֶלֶךְ בְּהִתְאַסֵּף
רָאשֵׁי עָם, יַחַד שִׁבְטֵי יִשְׂרָאֵל.

SONGS FOR ALL FESTIVALS

אַחֵינוּ כָּל בֵּית יִשְׂרָאֵל,
הַנְּתוּנִים בַּצָּרָה וּבַשִּׁבְיָה,
הָעוֹמְדִים בֵּין בַּיָּם וּבֵין בַּיַּבָּשָׁה,
הַמָּקוֹם יְרַחֵם עֲלֵיהֶם
וְיוֹצִיאֵם מִצָּרָה לִרְוָחָה
וּמֵאֲפֵלָה לְאוֹרָה
וּמִשִּׁעְבּוּד לִגְאֻלָּה
הַשְׁתָּא בַּעֲגָלָא וּבִזְמַן קָרִיב,
וְנֹאמַר אָמֵן.

הַמַּלְאָךְ הַגּוֹאֵל אוֹתִי מִכָּל רָע,
יְבָרֵךְ אֶת הַנְּעָרִים
וְיִקָּרֵא בָהֶם שְׁמִי
וְשֵׁם אֲבֹתַי אַבְרָהָם וְיִצְחָק,
וְיִדְגּוּ לָרֹב בְּקֶרֶב הָאָרֶץ.

אָנָּא בְּכֹחַ גְּדֻלַּת יְמִינְךָ
תַּתִּיר צְרוּרָה,
קַבֵּל רִנַּת עַמְּךָ
שַׂגְּבֵנוּ טַהֲרֵנוּ נוֹרָא.

הַלְלוּ אֶת יְיָ כָּל גּוֹיִם.
שַׁבְּחוּהוּ כָּל הָאֻמִּים:
כִּי גָבַר עָלֵינוּ חַסְדּוֹ.
וֶאֱמֶת יְיָ לְעוֹלָם. הַלְלוּיָהּ.

אֲנִי מַאֲמִין בֶּאֱמוּנָה שְׁלֵמָה
בְּבִיאַת הַמָּשִׁיחַ.
וְאַף עַל פִּי שֶׁיִּתְמַהְמֵהַּ,
עִם כָּל זֶה אֲחַכֶּה לוֹ
בְּכָל יוֹם שֶׁיָּבוֹא.

בָּרוּךְ אֱלֹהֵינוּ שֶׁבְּרָאָנוּ לִכְבוֹדוֹ,
וְהִבְדִּילָנוּ מִן הַתּוֹעִים,
וְנָתַן לָנוּ תּוֹרַת אֱמֶת,
וְחַיֵּי עוֹלָם נָטַע בְּתוֹכֵנוּ.

יִשְׂרָאֵל בְּטַח בַּיְיָ.
עֶזְרָם וּמָגִנָּם הוּא.

פִּתְחוּ לִי שַׁעֲרֵי צֶדֶק.
אָבֹא בָם אוֹדֶה יָהּ:
זֶה הַשַּׁעַר לַיְיָ.
צַדִּיקִים יָבֹאוּ בוֹ.

אֵלֶּה בָרֶכֶב וְאֵלֶּה בַסּוּסִים.
וַאֲנַחְנוּ בְּשֵׁם יְיָ נַזְכִּיר.

בָּרוּךְ הַמָּקוֹם בָּרוּךְ הוּא,
בָּרוּךְ שֶׁנָּתַן תּוֹרָה לְעַמּוֹ יִשְׂרָאֵל,
בָּרוּךְ הוּא.

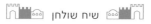
"Oyfn Pripetchik"

At the fireplace a little fire burns;
in the room it's hot
And the Rebbe teaches
little children
The aleph-bet.

Look, darling children,
remember dear ones
what you're learning now.
Say once again, and then another
time, "Komets-alef: awe!"

Learn children, with great desire
I want you to be wise.
Whomever learns Hebrew best
Shall receive a prize.

When darling children
you grow in years,
You yourselves will surmise
That in these letters lie many years
And many weeping cries.

My dear ones
You will tire from an exile
That makes your spirit wilt.
Draw your strength from these
letters; they will inspire until the third
Temple is built.

אויפן פריפעטשיק

אויפן פריפעטשיק ברענט אַ פֿײַערל,
און אין שטוב איז הייס.
און דער רבי לערנט
קלײנע קינדערלעך
דעם אָלֶף-בֵית.

זעט-זשע, קינדערלעך,
געדענקט-זשע, טײַערע,
וואָס איר לערנט דאָ.
זאָגט-זשע נאָך אַ מאָל
און טאָקע נאָך אַ מאָל: קמץ-אָלֶף: אָ!

לערנט קינדער מיט גרויסע חשק
אזוי זאָג איך אײך און
ועֶר סוועֶט גיכער פֿון אײך קײנען עברי
דער באקמט א פֿון.   זעט-זשע, קינדערלעך...

אז איר וועט קינדער, עלטער ווערן,
וועט איר אלײן פֿארשטײן
וויפֿל אין די אותיות
ליגן טרערן,
און ווי פֿיל געווײן.   זעט-זשע, קינדערלעך...

אז איר וועט קינדער,
דעם גלות שלעפֿן,
אויסגעמושעט זײַן,
זאלט איר פֿון די אותיות
כוח שעפֿן
קוקט אין זי אריין.   זעט-זשע, קינדערלעך...

KIDDUSH FOR FESTIVAL MORNINGS

קידוש ליום שלש רגלים

On Shabbat begin with the following introduction:

The children of Israel should keep Shabbat, observing Shabbat throughout their generations, as an everlasting covenant. ⟩
It is a sign between Me and the children of Israel for all time, that in six days the Lord made the heavens and the earth, and that on the seventh day He was finished and He rested.

וְשָׁמְרוּ בְנֵי יִשְׂרָאֵל אֶת הַשַּׁבָּת לַעֲשׂוֹת אֶת הַשַּׁבָּת לְדֹרֹתָם בְּרִית עוֹלָם. בֵּינִי וּבֵין בְּנֵי יִשְׂרָאֵל אוֹת הִיא לְעוֹלָם, כִּי שֵׁשֶׁת יָמִים עָשָׂה יְיָ אֶת הַשָּׁמַיִם וְאֶת הָאָרֶץ, וּבַיּוֹם הַשְּׁבִיעִי שָׁבַת וַיִּנָּפַשׁ:

These are the set times of the Lord, sacred assemblies, which you shall proclaim in their appointed seasons.

אֵלֶּה מוֹעֲדֵי יְיָ מִקְרָאֵי קֹדֶשׁ אֲשֶׁר תִּקְרְאוּ אֹתָם בְּמוֹעֲדָם:

So Moses told the children of Israel about the set times of the Lord.

וַיְדַבֵּר מֹשֶׁה אֶת מוֹעֲדֵי יְיָ אֶל בְּנֵי יִשְׂרָאֵל:

סַבְרִי מָרָנָן וְרַבָּנָן וְרַבּוֹתַי

You are blessed, Lord our God, Sovereign of the world, Creator of the fruit of the vine.

בָּרוּךְ אַתָּה יְיָ אֱלֹהֵינוּ מֶלֶךְ הָעוֹלָם, בּוֹרֵא פְּרִי הַגָּפֶן:

In the sukkah add:

You are blessed, Lord our God, Sovereign of the world, Who made us holy with His commandments and commanded us to live in the sukkah.

In the sukkah add:

בָּרוּךְ אַתָּה יְיָ אֱלֹהֵינוּ מֶלֶךְ הָעוֹלָם, אֲשֶׁר קִדְּשָׁנוּ בְּמִצְוֹתָיו וְצִוָּנוּ לֵישֵׁב בַּסֻּכָּה:

HANNUKAH EVENINGS

The great victory of the Judeans, led by the band of Priest-Maccabees, the followers of Judah the Hammer (*makav* means hammer; some say the term "Maccabee" comes from the Hebrew verse, *"Mi Kamokha B'Eilim Y-HVH"* — "Who is like You among the mighty, O God"), over the Greek-Syrians took place on the 25th day of Kislev, 164 BCE. The Jews purified the Holy Temple and kindled the Menorah. Tradition records that they found a cruse of ritually pure oil sufficient to last only for one day, and it would take eight days to acquire new pure oil. Nevertheless, they immediately lit the Menorah, and the one cruse of oil lasted for eight days. Hence we light our menorahs for eight days.

The Talmud ordains that the primary place to commemorate the miracle of Hannukah is in the home ("Each individual kindles the light in his home", B.T. Shabbat 21b), where the menorah (or *"hannukiah"*) is to be kindled.

I believe the emphasis is on the home because the initial conflict leading to the military battle was an internal one, a civil war between the more traditional Jews who insisted on the sanctity of Jerusalem, and the Hellenist Jews who wished to turn Jerusalem into a Greek city-state replete with Olympic Games. When the Hellenist Judean leaders saw that they were losing the battle, they brought in the Greek-Syrians to help them. (See "The Greeks and the Jews," Victor Tcherikover.) Since it is the home which must be the bulwark against foreign influences undermining Jewish traditions, we kindle our menorahs at home. The major custom is that every member of the household lights, women as well as men.

I always remind the celebrants every Hannukah that Rav Moshe Besdin maintained that the greatest hero of the Festival is not Judah the Maccabee, but rather the anonymous High Priest who — in the midst of the initial defeat of the Judeans and the defilement of the Temple — put away a cruse of pure oil for the time when the Temple would be rededicated. His was the faith which kept Israel courageous and committed even during the most difficult years of exile and persecution!

It is customary — but not mandatory — to have special Hannukah meals with potato "latkes" and jelly donuts (*sufganiot*) baked and/or fried in oil as a reminder of the miracle of the oil, to give Hannukah *gelt* ('money' in Yiddish), to the children and grandchildren, and to play games with a *dreidel* (a four-sided spinning top) — in my family we play for chocolate chips. The *dreidel* suggests that life and its fortunes are a matter of chance, but the letters inscribed on it — *nun* (Yiddish: *nem'* — take the pot), *gimmel* (Yiddish: *gantz* — take it all), *heh* (Yiddish: *halb* — take half) and *peh* (Hebrew: *para* — put in, pay) standing for the phrase *'nes gadol hayah poh'* — a great miracle happened here; in the Diaspora the last letter is *shin* (Yiddish: *shtehl* — put in), for *sham*, 'there' — bear testimony to the truth that behind the seeming happenstance, all significant historical events are directed by the undisclosed "finger" of the Divine. In the words of Rabbi A.Y.H. Kook, history is *hester kah*, the unfolding of the plan of God. This parallels the word Purim, 'lots', which is the name of the other rabbinically ordained holiday, whose Megillah story-text — while devoid of God's name — points to a "behind-the-scenes" Divine direction.

HALAKHIC DIRECTIONS FOR THE LIGHTING

The *hannukiah* is to be kindled preferably at the entrance to one's home, opposite the doorway lintel upon which the mezuzah is affixed, so that the individual entering the home is surrounded by mitzvot, or on the window sill facing the outside, in order to proclaim and publicize the miracle.

It is preferable to use olive oil rather than wax candles — although the ritual is properly executed with wax candles as well — and the way to demonstrate the most respect for the commandment is by having everyone kindle his/her own hannukiah, with each reciting his/her own blessings in the presence of all other family members and guests.

The candles ought be lit immediately at sunset, but may be lit by latecomers into the night as long as there are still people on the streets or other household members present with whom to share the miracle.

The wicks, or candles, are to be placed at the right end of the *hannukiah* — one on the first night, two on the second, and so on, until eight on the last night — filling in the *hannukiah* from right to left (as we write Hebrew script). The "newest" wick or candle, to the left of the wick kindled the previous night, is the first to be lit each evening. An extra candle, called the *shamash*, is used to kindle the other wicks or candles, and has its own additional place in the *hannukiah*.

סדר הדלקת נר חנוכה

Before lighting, each individual recites over his/her hannukiah:

בָּרוּךְ אַתָּה יְיָ אֱלֹהֵינוּ מֶלֶךְ הָעוֹלָם אֲשֶׁר קִדְּשָׁנוּ בְּמִצְוֹתָיו וְצִוָּנוּ
לְהַדְלִיק נֵר (שֶׁל) חֲנֻכָּה.
בָּרוּךְ אַתָּה יְיָ אֱלֹהֵינוּ מֶלֶךְ הָעוֹלָם שֶׁעָשָׂה נִסִּים לַאֲבוֹתֵינוּ בַּיָּמִים
הָהֵם בַּזְּמַן הַזֶּה.

On the first night only, add:

בָּרוּךְ אַתָּה יְיָ אֱלֹהֵינוּ מֶלֶךְ הָעוֹלָם שֶׁהֶחֱיָנוּ וְקִיְּמָנוּ וְהִגִּיעָנוּ לַזְּמַן הַזֶּה.

After lighting the candles, the entire assemblage may sing or recite together:

הַנֵּרוֹת הַלָּלוּ אָנוּ מַדְלִיקִין עַל הַנִּסִּים וְעַל הַנִּפְלָאוֹת וְעַל הַתְּשׁוּעוֹת
וְעַל הַמִּלְחָמוֹת. שֶׁעָשִׂיתָ לַאֲבוֹתֵינוּ בַּיָּמִים הָהֵם בַּזְּמַן הַזֶּה. עַל יְדֵי
כֹּהֲנֶיךָ הַקְּדוֹשִׁים. וְכָל שְׁמוֹנַת יְמֵי חֲנֻכָּה הַנֵּרוֹת הַלָּלוּ קֹדֶשׁ הֵם. וְאֵין
לָנוּ רְשׁוּת לְהִשְׁתַּמֵּשׁ בָּהֶם. אֶלָּא לִרְאוֹתָם בִּלְבָד. כְּדֵי לְהוֹדוֹת וּלְהַלֵּל
לְשִׁמְךָ הַגָּדוֹל עַל נִסֶּיךָ וְעַל נִפְלְאוֹתֶיךָ וְעַל יְשׁוּעָתֶךָ.

מעוז צור

מָעוֹז צוּר יְשׁוּעָתִי לְךָ נָאֶה לְשַׁבֵּחַ. תִּכּוֹן בֵּית תְּפִלָּתִי וְשָׁם תּוֹדָה נְזַבֵּחַ. לְעֵת
תָּכִין מַטְבֵּחַ מִצָּר הַמְנַבֵּחַ. אָז אֶגְמוֹר בְּשִׁיר מִזְמוֹר חֲנֻכַּת הַמִּזְבֵּחַ.

רָעוֹת שָׂבְעָה נַפְשִׁי בְּיָגוֹן כֹּחִי כָּלָה. חַיַּי מֵרְרוּ בְקֹשִׁי בְּשִׁעְבּוּד מַלְכוּת עֶגְלָה.
וּבְיָדוֹ הַגְּדוֹלָה הוֹצִיא אֶת הַסְּגֻלָּה. חֵיל פַּרְעֹה וְכָל זַרְעוֹ יָרְדוּ כְאֶבֶן בִּמְצוּלָה.

THE BLESSING OVER THE HANNUKAH CANDLES

In our tradition, we do not merely commemorate significant moments of our past, we attempt
to relive them. The *hannukiah* before us becomes transformed into the Temple Menorah; that
is why it is forbidden for us to derive benefit from such a sacred object. Hence I believe that the
preferred language of the blessing is להדליק נר חנוכה — the actual Hannukah Menorah wick —
rather than להדליק נר של חנוכה the candle of the festival of Hannukah. ♦

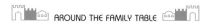
KINDLING THE HANNUKAH LIGHTS

Before lighting, each individual recites over his/her hannukiah:

You are blessed, Lord our God, Sovereign of the world, Who made us holy with His commandments and commanded us to kindle Hannukah lights. You are blessed, Lord our God, Sovereign of the world, Who performed miracles for our ancestors in those days on this occasion.

On the first night only, add:

You are blessed, Lord our God, Sovereign of the world, Who has kept us alive and sustained us and enabled us to reach this occasion.

After lighting the candles, the entire assemblage may sing or recite together:

These lights which we kindle are for the miracles, the wonders, the victories and the wars which You brought about in those days on this occasion, through the agency of Your holy priests. These lights are sacred all the eight days of Hannukah, and we may not use them in any way — we may only look at them — with the purpose of giving thanks and praise to Your great name for Your miracles, Your salvation and Your wonders.

MAOZ TZUR

O mighty stronghold of my salvation, to praise You is a delight. Restore my House of Prayer and there we will bring a thanksgiving offering. When You will have prepared the slaughter for the blaspheming foe, then I shall complete with a song of hymn the dedication of the Altar.

My soul had been sated with troubles, my strength had been consumed with grief. They had embittered my life with hardship, with the calf-like kingdom's bondage. But with His great power He brought forth the treasured ones, Pharaoh's army and all his offspring went down like a stone into the deep.

MAOZ TZUR

13th century German-Jewish *piyut* (liturgical poem) written by an anonymous Mordekhai (as seen by the acrosticon). The first stanza gives praise to our Rock of Salvation, requesting the rebuilding of the Holy Temple and the destruction of our enemies. The next stanzas delineate our rescue from Egypt, Babylon, Haman, and the Greek-Syrians respectively, and the final stanza petitions for the ultimate redemption. ✦

דְּבִיר קָדְשׁוֹ הֱבִיאַנִי וְגַם שָׁם לֹא שָׁקַטְתִּי. וּבָא נוֹגֵשׂ וְהִגְלַנִי. כִּי זָרִים עֲבַדְתִּי. וְיַיִן
רַעַל מָסַכְתִּי כִּמְעַט שֶׁעָבַרְתִּי. קֵץ בָּבֶל זְרֻבָּבֶל. לְקֵץ שִׁבְעִים נוֹשַׁעְתִּי.

כְּרוֹת קוֹמַת בְּרוֹשׁ בִּקֵּשׁ אֲגָגִי בֶּן הַמְּדָתָא. וְנִהְיָתָה לּוֹ לְפַח וּלְמוֹקֵשׁ וְגַאֲוָתוֹ
נִשְׁבָּתָה. רֹאשׁ יְמִינִי נִשֵּׂאתָ. וְאוֹיֵב שְׁמוֹ מָחִיתָ. רֹב בָּנָיו וְקִנְיָנָיו עַל הָעֵץ תָּלִיתָ.

יְוָנִים נִקְבְּצוּ עָלַי אֲזַי בִּימֵי חַשְׁמַנִּים. וּפָרְצוּ חוֹמוֹת מִגְדָּלַי וְטִמְּאוּ כָּל הַשְּׁמָנִים.
וּמִנּוֹתַר קַנְקַנִּים נַעֲשָׂה נֵס לַשּׁוֹשַׁנִּים. בְּנֵי בִינָה יְמֵי שְׁמוֹנָה קָבְעוּ שִׁיר וּרְנָנִים.

חֲשׂוֹף זְרוֹעַ קָדְשֶׁךָ וְקָרֵב קֵץ הַיְשׁוּעָה. נְקֹם נִקְמַת דַּם עֲבָדֶיךָ מֵאֻמָּה הָרְשָׁעָה. כִּי
אָרְכָה לָנוּ הַשָּׁעָה. וְאֵין קֵץ לִימֵי הָרָעָה. דְּחֵה אַדְמוֹן בְּצֵל צַלְמוֹן הָקֵם לָנוּ רוֹעֶה
שִׁבְעָה:

סְבִיבוֹן, סֹב, סֹב, סֹב!
חֲנֻכָּה הוּא חַג טוֹב.
חֲנֻכָּה הוּא חַג טוֹב.
סְבִיבוֹן, סֹב, סֹב, סֹב!
סֹב נָא, סֹב, כֹּה וָכֹה, נֵס גָּדוֹל הָיָה פֹּה.
סֹב נָא, סֹב, כֹּה וָכֹה, נֵס גָּדוֹל הָיָה פֹּה!

* * *

בָּאנוּ חֹשֶׁךְ לְגָרֵשׁ.
בְּיָדֵינוּ אוֹר וָאֵשׁ.
כָּל אֶחָד הוּא אוֹר קָטָן,
וְכֻלָּנוּ – אוֹר אֵיתָן.
סוּרָה חֹשֶׁךְ, הָלְאָה שְׁחוֹר!
סוּרָה מִפְּנֵי הָאוֹר!

יְמֵי הַחֲנֻכָּה, חֲנֻכַּת מִקְדָּשֵׁנוּ.
גִּיל וְשִׂמְחָה מְמַלְּאִים אֶת לִבֵּנוּ.
לַיְלָה וָיוֹם סְבִיבוֹנֵנוּ יִסֹּב.
סֻפְגָּנִיּוֹת נֹאכַל בָּם לָרֹב.
הָאִירוּ, הַדְלִיקוּ, נֵרוֹת חֲנֻכָּה רַבִּים!
עַל הַנִּסִּים וְעַל הַנִּפְלָאוֹת,
אֲשֶׁר חוֹלְלוּ הַמַּכַּבִּים.
עַל הַנִּסִּים וְעַל הַנִּפְלָאוֹת,
אֲשֶׁר עָשָׂה ה' לַמַּכַּבִּים.

* * *

עַל הַנִּסִּים וְעַל הַפֻּרְקָן
וְעַל הַגְּבוּרוֹת וְעַל הַתְּשׁוּעוֹת
וְעַל הַמִּלְחָמוֹת שֶׁעָשִׂיתָ לַאֲבוֹתֵינוּ
בַּיָּמִים הָהֵם בַּזְּמַן הַזֶּה.

To the holy abode of His word He brought me. But there, too, I had no rest. And an oppressor came and exiled me. For I had served aliens, and had drunk benumbing wine. Scarcely had I departed, at Babylon's end Zerubabel came. At the end of seventy years I was saved.

To sever the towering cypress sought the Aggagite, son of Hamdata, but it became a snare and a stumbling block to him, and his arrogance was stilled. The head of the Benjamin tribe You lifted, and the enemy, his name You obliterated — his numerous progeny — his possessions — on the gallows You hanged.

Greeks gathered against me then in Hasmonean days. They breached the walls of my towers and they defiled all the oils; and from the one remnant of the flasks a miracle was wrought for the roses. Men of insight — eight days established for song and jubilation.

Bare Your holy arm and hasten the end for salvation. Avenge the vengeance of Your servants' blood from the wicked nation. For the triumph is too long delayed for us, and there is no end to days of evil. Repel the Red One in the nethermost shadow and establish for us the seven shepherds.

נֵר לִי, נֵר לִי, נֵר לִי דַּקִיק.
בַּחֲנֻכָּה נֵרִי אַדְלִיק.
בַּחֲנֻכָּה נֵרִי יָאִיר,
בַּחֲנֻכָּה שִׁירִים אָשִׁיר.

* * *

חֲנֻכָּה, חֲנֻכָּה, חַג יָפֶה כָּל כָּךְ.
אוֹר חָבִיב מִסָּבִיב, גִּיל לְיֶלֶד רַךְ.
חֲנֻכָּה, חֲנֻכָּה סְבִיבוֹן סֹב סֹב.
סֹב סֹב סֹב, סֹב סֹב סֹב,
מַה נָּעִים וָטוֹב.

מִי יְמַלֵּל גְּבוּרוֹת יִשְׂרָאֵל,
אוֹתָן מִי יִמְנֶה?
הֵן בְּכָל דּוֹר
יָקוּם הַגִּבּוֹר, גּוֹאֵל הָעָם.
שְׁמַע, בַּיָּמִים הָהֵם בַּזְּמַן הַזֶּה,
מַכַּבִּי מוֹשִׁיעַ וּפוֹדֶה.
וּבְיָמֵינוּ כָּל עַם יִשְׂרָאֵל
יִתְאַחֵד יָקוּם וְיִגָּאֵל.

ליל יום העצמאות

Upon returning home from the synagogue on the eve of Yom Ha-Atzma'ut, the family celebrants gather around the set table and chant together the "Song of Ascents," *Shir Ha-Ma'alot*.

שִׁיר הַמַּעֲלוֹת בְּשׁוּב יְיָ אֶת שִׁיבַת צִיּוֹן הָיִינוּ כְּחֹלְמִים. אָז יִמָּלֵא
שְׂחוֹק פִּינוּ וּלְשׁוֹנֵנוּ רִנָּה. אָז יֹאמְרוּ בַגּוֹיִם הִגְדִּיל יְיָ לַעֲשׂוֹת עִם אֵלֶּה,
הִגְדִּיל יְיָ לַעֲשׂוֹת עִמָּנוּ הָיִינוּ שְׂמֵחִים. שׁוּבָה יְיָ אֶת שְׁבִיתֵנוּ כַּאֲפִיקִים
בַּנֶּגֶב. הַזֹּרְעִים בְּדִמְעָה בְּרִנָּה יִקְצֹרוּ. הָלוֹךְ יֵלֵךְ וּבָכֹה נֹשֵׂא מֶשֶׁךְ הַזָּרַע.
בֹּא יָבֹא בְרִנָּה נֹשֵׂא אֲלֻמֹּתָיו:

תְּהִלַּת יְיָ יְדַבֶּר פִּי וִיבָרֵךְ כָּל־בָּשָׂר שֵׁם קָדְשׁוֹ לְעוֹלָם וָעֶד. וַאֲנַחְנוּ נְבָרֵךְ
יָהּ מֵעַתָּה וְעַד־עוֹלָם הַלְלוּיָהּ. הוֹדוּ לַייָ כִּי טוֹב כִּי לְעוֹלָם חַסְדּוֹ: מִי
יְמַלֵּל גְּבוּרוֹת יְיָ יַשְׁמִיעַ כָּל תְּהִלָּתוֹ:

The leader reads the following two verses (Deut. 26: 9-10) which conclude the declaration at the bringing of the first fruits to the holy Temple on Shavuot, verses which were deleted from the Passover Seder service, but which are certainly applicable to Yom Ha-Atzma'ut (this was cleverly suggested by Rav Yoel Bin Nun).

וַיְבִיאֵנוּ אֶל הַמָּקוֹם הַזֶּה וַיִּתֶּן לָנוּ אֶת הָאָרֶץ הַזֹּאת אֶרֶץ זָבַת חָלָב וּדְבָשׁ.
וְעַתָּה הִנֵּה הֵבֵאתִי אֶת רֵאשִׁית פְּרִי הָאֲדָמָה אֲשֶׁר נָתַתָּה לִּי יְיָ וְהִנַּחְתּוֹ לִפְנֵי
יְיָ אֱלֹהֶיךָ וְהִשְׁתַּחֲוִיתָ לִפְנֵי יְיָ אֱלֹהֶיךָ:

The leader chants Ezekiel chapter 37, verses 1-14, the prophecy of the "dry bones," miraculously depicting the rebirth of Israel from the ashes of Auschwitz to the Knesset of Israel.

הָיְתָה עָלַי יַד יְיָ וַיּוֹצִאֵנִי בְרוּחַ יְיָ וַיְנִיחֵנִי בְּתוֹךְ הַבִּקְעָה וְהִיא מְלֵאָה עֲצָמוֹת.
וְהֶעֱבִירַנִי עֲלֵיהֶם סָבִיב סָבִיב וְהִנֵּה רַבּוֹת מְאֹד עַל פְּנֵי הַבִּקְעָה וְהִנֵּה יְבֵשׁוֹת מְאֹד.
וַיֹּאמֶר אֵלַי בֶּן אָדָם הֲתִחְיֶינָה הָעֲצָמוֹת הָאֵלֶּה וָאֹמַר אֲדֹנָי יְהוִה אַתָּה יָדָעְתָּ. וַיֹּאמֶר

YOM HA-ATZMA'UT

On Shabbat and Festivals, as well as family life-cycle celebrations, it is customary to recite Psalm 126, "A Song of Ascents", as the introduction to the Grace After Meals. Both this song and the Grace as a whole, deal with the subject of redemption, and there are many who customarily sing this song to the tune of Ha-Tikvah. When we return to Zion, the psalmist tells

LEIL YOM HA-ATZMA'UT

Upon returning home from the synagogue on the eve of Yom Ha-Atzma'ut, the family celebrants gather around the set table and chant together the "Song of Ascents," Shir Ha-Ma'alot.

A Song of Ascents. When the Lord brought back the captivity of Zion, we were like people in a dream. At that time our mouth was filled with laughter and our tongue with joy; at that time it was said among the nations, "The Lord has done great things for them." The Lord had done great things for us; we were happy. Return our captivity, Lord, like dried-up streams in the Negev. Those who sow in tears will reap with joy. He who walks, weeping, as he trails the seed along will return with joy, carrying his sheaves.

Let my mouth declare God's praise, and let all flesh bless His holy name for all time. As for us, we will bless the Lord from now on and forever more — halleluyah. Give thanks to God for He is good, for His kindness is everlasting. Who can describe the mighty deeds of the Lord, or utter all of His praise?

The leader reads the following two verses (Deut. 26: 9-10) which conclude the declaration at the bringing of the first fruits to the holy Temple on Shavuot, verses which were deleted from the Passover Seder service, but which are certainly applicable to Yom Ha-Atzma'ut (this was cleverly suggested by Rav Yoel Bin Nun).

And he brought us to this place and gave us this land, a land flowing with milk and honey. And now, behold, I have brought the first fruits of the land, which You, O Lord, have given me, and you shall set it before the Lord your God and worship before the Lord your God.

The leader chants Ezekiel chapter 37, verses 1-14, the prophecy of the "dry bones," miraculously depicting the rebirth of Israel from the ashes of Auschwitz to the Knesset of Israel.

The hand of the Lord was upon me, and carried me out in the wind of the Lord, and set me down in the midst of the valley which was full of bones, And He led me around among them; and, behold, there were very many in the open valley; and,

us, we will be like dreamers, and the great dream of Zionism was realized because the pioneers continued to dream even when they were awake! And it was a dream which repeated itself, giving the dreamers no rest. We must continue to dream this dream of Zion, which — although it is beginning to be realized — can never achieve its goal unless "nation will not lift up sword against nation and humanity will not learn war any more." ✦

אֵלֶי הַנָּבֵא עַל הָעֲצָמוֹת הָאֵלֶּה וְאָמַרְתָּ אֲלֵיהֶם הָעֲצָמוֹת הַיְבֵשׁוֹת שִׁמְעוּ דְּבַר יְיָ. כֹּה אָמַר אֲדֹנָי יֱהוִה לָעֲצָמוֹת הָאֵלֶּה הִנֵּה אֲנִי מֵבִיא בָכֶם רוּחַ וִחְיִיתֶם. וְנָתַתִּי עֲלֵיכֶם גִּדִים וְהַעֲלֵתִי עֲלֵיכֶם בָּשָׂר וְקָרַמְתִּי עֲלֵיכֶם עוֹר וְנָתַתִּי בָכֶם רוּחַ וִחְיִיתֶם וִידַעְתֶּם כִּי אֲנִי יְיָ. וְנִבֵּאתִי כַּאֲשֶׁר צֻוֵּיתִי וַיְהִי קוֹל כְּהִנָּבְאִי וְהִנֵּה רַעַשׁ וַתִּקְרְבוּ עֲצָמוֹת עֶצֶם אֶל עַצְמוֹ. וְרָאִיתִי וְהִנֵּה עֲלֵיהֶם גִּדִים וּבָשָׂר עָלָה וַיִּקְרַם עֲלֵיהֶם עוֹר מִלְמַעְלָה וְרוּחַ אֵין בָּהֶם. וַיֹּאמֶר אֵלַי הִנָּבֵא אֶל הָרוּחַ הִנָּבֵא בֶן אָדָם וְאָמַרְתָּ אֶל הָרוּחַ כֹּה אָמַר אֲדֹנָי יֱהוִה מֵאַרְבַּע רוּחוֹת בֹּאִי הָרוּחַ וּפְחִי בַּהֲרוּגִים הָאֵלֶּה וְיִחְיוּ. וְהִנַּבֵּאתִי כַּאֲשֶׁר צִוָּנִי וַתָּבוֹא בָהֶם הָרוּחַ וַיִּחְיוּ וַיַּעַמְדוּ עַל רַגְלֵיהֶם חַיִל גָּדוֹל מְאֹד מְאֹד. וַיֹּאמֶר אֵלַי בֶּן אָדָם הָעֲצָמוֹת הָאֵלֶּה כָּל בֵּית יִשְׂרָאֵל הֵמָּה הִנֵּה אֹמְרִים יָבְשׁוּ עַצְמוֹתֵינוּ וְאָבְדָה תִקְוָתֵנוּ נִגְזַרְנוּ לָנוּ. לָכֵן הִנָּבֵא וְאָמַרְתָּ אֲלֵיהֶם כֹּה אָמַר אֲדֹנָי יֱהוִה הִנֵּה אֲנִי פֹתֵחַ אֶת קִבְרוֹתֵיכֶם וְהַעֲלֵיתִי אֶתְכֶם מִקִּבְרוֹתֵיכֶם עַמִּי וְהֵבֵאתִי אֶתְכֶם אֶל אַדְמַת יִשְׂרָאֵל. וִידַעְתֶּם כִּי אֲנִי יְיָ בְּפִתְחִי אֶת קִבְרוֹתֵיכֶם וּבְהַעֲלוֹתִי אֶתְכֶם מִקִּבְרוֹתֵיכֶם עַמִּי: וְנָתַתִּי רוּחִי בָכֶם וִחְיִיתֶם וְהִנַּחְתִּי אֶתְכֶם עַל אַדְמַתְכֶם וִידַעְתֶּם כִּי אֲנִי יְיָ דִּבַּרְתִּי וְעָשִׂיתִי נְאֻם יְיָ:

All assembled rise to sing *Ha-Tikvah*, and recite the blessing over wine.

התקוה

כָּל עוֹד בַּלֵּבָב פְּנִימָה נֶפֶשׁ יְהוּדִי הוֹמִיָּה.
וּלְפַאֲתֵי מִזְרָח קָדִימָה עַיִן לְצִיּוֹן צוֹפִיָּה.
עוֹד לֹא אָבְדָה תִקְוָתֵנוּ הַתִּקְוָה שְׁנוֹת אַלְפַּיִם
לִהְיוֹת עַם חָפְשִׁי בְּאַרְצֵנוּ, אֶרֶץ צִיּוֹן יְרוּשָׁלַיִם.

בָּרוּךְ אַתָּה יְיָ אֱלֹהֵינוּ מֶלֶךְ הָעוֹלָם, בּוֹרֵא פְּרִי הַגָּפֶן.

Then comes the ritual washing of the hands, as the leader recites the Ha-Motzi blessing over three pittahs: one representing the renewed State of Israel, the second representing the liberation of Jerusalem, and the third for our ultimate redemption, the redemption of the world. A beautiful custom is to center the meal around typical Israeli foods like hummous, falafel and eggplant, as well as distinctive foods of the various communities that comprise Israeli society: hilba and kubana (Yemenite), gondi (Persian), kubeh and "cigars" (Moroccan), gefilte fish and kneidlakh (Russian, East European), franks or pizza (American — but pizza only if it is a dairy meal!). Songs of Eretz Yisrael would be the appropriate Zemirot (see pp. 208-216).

behold, they were very dry. And He said to me, Son of man, can these bones live? And I answered, O Lord God, you know. And He said to me, Prophesy over these bones, and say to them, O you dry bones, hear the word of the Lord. Thus says the Lord God to these bones; Behold, I will cause breath to enter into you, and you shall live; And I will lay sinews upon you, and will bring up flesh upon you, and cover you with skin, and put breath in you, and you shall live; and you shall know that I am the Lord. And I prophesied as I was commanded; and as I prophesied, there was a noise, and behold a shaking, and the bones came together, bone to its bone. And as I beheld, behold, the sinews and the flesh came up upon them, and the skin covered them above; but there was no breath in them. And He said to me, Prophesy to the breath, prophesy, son of man, and say to the breath, Thus says the Lord God: Come from the four winds, O breath, and breathe upon these slain, that they may live. And I prophesied as He commanded me, and the breath came into them, and they lived, and stood up upon their feet, a very large army. Then He said to me, son of man, these bones are the whole house of Israel; behold, they say, Our bones are dried, and our hope is lost; we are clean cut off. Therefore prophesy and say to them, Thus says the Lord God: Behold, O my people, I will open your graves, and cause you to come up out of your graves, and bring you into the land of Israel. And you shall know that I am the Lord, when I have opened your graves, O my people, and brought you up from your graves, And I shall put my spirit in you, and you shall live, and I shall place you in your land; then shall you know that I, the Lord, have spoken it, and performed it, says the Lord.

All assembled rise to sing Ha-Tikvah and recite the blessing over wine.

HA-TIKVAH

As long as, deep in the heart, the soul of a Jew yearns
And towards the East, an eye looks to Zion.

Our hope is not yet lost, the hope of two thousand years
To be a free people in our land, the land of Zion and Jerusalem.

You are blessed, Lord our God, Sovereign of the world, Who creates the fruit of the vine.

Chapter 37 of the prophet Ezekiel is the prophecy of the Dry Bones, in which God shows the prophet a flat plain with scatters of dry bones and guarantees that He will ultimately cover them with sinews, flesh and skin as well as with renewed spirit. The parallelism between the close to 2,000 years of Jewish exile culminating in the horrors of the Holocaust and the skeletal "musselmen" having become transformed into the proud Israeli sabra in our generation is a most fitting theme for the Israeli Independence Day celebration. ✦

TU B'SHVAT

The 15th day of the Hebrew month of Shevat is established as the New Year for trees — specifically with regard to the rules of tithing and *orlah* — because the very beginning of the blossoming of the fruit on the tree is on that date (Mishna Rosh HaShanah 1:1). The Sages of the Talmud also tell us that the majority of the rains have passed by the 15th day of Shevat. Indeed, one can usually begin to see the white foliage of the almond tree, which is generally the first tree to blossom in Israel. From this perspective, Tu B'Shevat signals the beginning of spring — at least from the very optimistic world-view that sees a foretaste of spring even in the midst of winter.

Since the fruits of Israel represent the very bedrock of the sanctity of Israel as expressed by the Torah — witness the lyric words, "Since the Lord your God is bringing you to a good land; a land with rivulets of water and deep wellsprings emerging from the plains and the mountains, a land of wheat and barley, of grapes, figs and pomegranates, a land of olive oil and date honey, a land whose bread you will not eat in poverty and which lacks nothing, a land whose stones are iron and from whose mountains copper is quarried" (Deut. 8:7-9) — and since the spring is our classical symbol for the beginning of redemption (Song of Songs), Tu B'Shevat became a day of yearning for Jewish sovereignty in the Land of Israel and messianic redemption, especially in 16th century Safed (following the Spanish Inquisition and Expulsion), and in the various Diaspora communities.

Since the Torah also declares that "the human being is like a tree of the field" (Deut. 20:19), the eating of fruits served as a repair (*tikkun*) of the

sin of eating of the fruit of knowledge as well as a means of linking the individual to the God of all life.

For these reasons, the religious community of 16th century Safed — most prominently Rav Haim Vital, chief disciple of the Holy Ari — originated a "seder" for Tu B'Shevat (see page 160), which has become especially popular since the creation of the modern State of Israel.

The "seder" for Tu B'Shevat features four cups of wine drunk by all of the celebrants, with the blessing over wine to be made only before drinking the first cup. The first cup is to be white wine, the second mostly white with an added mixture of red, the third mostly red with a small amount of white, and the fourth completely red. The symbolism of the movement from white to red wine is a reflection of the movement of nature from the white foliage of the almond tree at the first signs of spring to the red anemones that dot the Judean landscape towards the end of summer; it is likewise a reflection of the change of the white, wintry sky to the red spring/summer sky. Both symbolic explanations express yearning for the transformation from winter to spring, from death of nature to rebirth of nature, from servitude to redemption.

TU B'SHEVAT SEDER

THE FIRST CUP OF WINE (white)

בָּרוּךְ אַתָּה יְיָ אֱלֹהֵינוּ מֶלֶךְ הָעוֹלָם, בּוֹרֵא פְּרִי הַגָּפֶן.

You are blessed, Lord our God, Sovereign of the world,
Who creates the fruit of the vine.

After drinking some wine, the celebrants partake of fruits. The first category of fruits to be eaten are those which have neither a peel nor an inedible pip, and are therefore considered to emanate from the most ethereal and spiritual of worlds — the world of Divine creation (*Beriah*) closest to the Divine source. There are nine fruits in this category from which several or all may be served at this stage in the *seder*: grapes, figs, apples, citrons, pears, quinces, strawberries, carobs, and persimmons. Begin with the blessing over grapes —

בָּרוּךְ אַתָּה יְיָ אֱלֹהֵינוּ מֶלֶךְ הָעוֹלָם, בּוֹרֵא פְּרִי הָעֵץ.

You are blessed, Lord our God, Sovereign of the world,
Who creates the fruit of the tree.

and have in mind all of the fruits that will be eaten until the Grace After Meals is recited.

THE SECOND CUP OF WINE (mostly white with a little admixture of red)

The category of fruits eaten with this cup of wine includes those that have no peel, but do have a hard pit which is not edible. These are considered to emanate from the second-level world, the world of formation (*Yetzirah*) — the cosmos that we see when we look up at the heavens: olives, dates, cherries, apricots, plums, peaches.

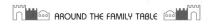
THE THIRD CUP OF WINE (mostly red, with a little admixture of white)

The celebrants now partake of the third category of fruits — those with an inedible peel, considered to emanate from our present-day world of activity; the world and earth of the regular agricultural and nutritional aspects of our lives (*Asiyah*): pomegranates, nuts, walnuts, almonds, chestnuts, peanuts, pistachio, pine nuts and bananas. (For bananas, recite the blessing:

בָּרוּךְ אַתָּה יְיָ אֱלֹהֵינוּ מֶלֶךְ הָעוֹלָם, בּוֹרֵא פְּרִי הָאֲדָמָה.

You are blessed, Lord our God, Sovereign of the world,
Who creates the fruit of the earth.)

The movement of the fruit brings us from the highest celestial spheres to the world in which we live, expressing our wish to bring the highest of spiritual realms into our world of matter and materialism, to bring God from heaven to earth, to redeem the physical world below by uniting it with the spiritual world from above.

THE FOURTH CUP OF WINE (completely red, symbolizing spring/summer and the joy of salvation)

Conclude with the blessing after wine and fruits on page 36.

One may now perform the regular ritual washing of the hands, and enjoy a festive meal.

נישואין, קדושין ושבע ברכות בשבעת ימי משתה

BETROTHAL, MARRIAGE AND THE SEVEN DAYS OF NUPTIAL JOY

THE BIBLICAL VIEW OF MARRIAGE

Immediately following the creation of man (Adam), the Almighty declares: "It is not good that man should be alone: I will make a help-counterpart for him" (Genesis 2:18). This statement contains first a recognition of man's existential loneliness and then an attempt to mitigate it through the institution of marriage. Woman's description as a help-counterpart signifies that she is not to be viewed as a mere aid and blind amen-sayer, but also as an "opposite view" (*kenegdo*), an alter ego, who will provide her husband with the companionship and intense relationship they each desperately require.

The Bible continues to record how God caused a deep sleep to descend upon Adam and how He formed Eve from Adam's side. (This Hebrew *tsela* is usually translated as rib — but the Bible also uses the same word to mean "side" with respect to the Sanctuary. The Midrash teaches that the first human being was androgynous with the male and female sides joined together as Siamese twins).

This symbolic picture intensifies the notion that man and woman were meant to be united from the very beginning of creation; that each comprises but half of the whole which they combine to make. Therefore does Adam declare: "This time (she) is bone of my bone, flesh of my flesh" (Genesis 2:23).

The biblical picture is concluded with the ringing affirmation: "Therefore shall a man leave his mother and father, and cleave unto his wife, and they shall be one flesh" (Genesis 2:24). Once the individual achieves mature independence from his parents and finds a mate with whom he establishes a lasting relationship of mutual commitment, they together help realize the purpose of creation by means of the physical unity of the sexual relationship. Rashi (1040-1105), the biblical commentator par excellence, adds that the child who is the product of this union combines the characteristics of each of his two parents in his one flesh. Thus our prayer for the unity of the world becomes microcosmically fulfilled in the biblical command of marriage and family.

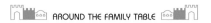

PREPARATIONS FOR THE WEDDING DAY

Mikvah

A bride who is *halakhically* able to immerse herself in a Mikvah, ought to do so within four days prior to her wedding night. From time immemorial, water has been a symbol of cleansing purity and rebirth. Ritual immersion in the Mikvah (a gathering of rain or well water) expresses to the woman the sanctity of her body as well as the life potential which is renewed once again within her at the conclusion of her monthly cycle. This immersion in the Mikvah is continued following each menstrual cycle after the wedding and is a necessary prelude for the resumption of sexual activity. There is a beautiful custom for the groom to ritually immerse himself in the Mikvah on the Friday before his wedding and to continue this practice each Friday thereafter.

Aufruf (lit.: to be called up), Shabbat Hatan and Shabbat Kallah

The groom should receive an *aliyah* to the Torah (customarily *maftir*) on the Sabbath prior to the wedding, so that he can formally thank God for the extra commandments which he will soon be privileged to perform as a married man. Among Ashkenazi Jews, the Sabbath prior to the wedding has become a special occasion of rejoicing and words of Torah for the groom and his friends and more recently for the bride and her friends in a separate Shabbat Kallah. The Sefardim celebrate all together on the Sabbath following the wedding.

Wedding Day Fast

It is customary for both bride and groom to fast from sunrise until the wedding ceremony when the couple drink a sip of wine. Since the wedding begins a new chapter in their lives, the fast serves as an atonement for past misdeeds and as a symbol of a kind of rebirth for the future. It is understood that the fast is suspended on the Sabbath, holidays and *Rosh Chodesh*

(Beginning of the New Month). Both bride and groom should also recite the *al chet* (confessional) following the afternoon (*Minha*) *amidah* prayer (as it is recited in Minha on the afternoon before Yom Kippur).

Chussen's Tish (lit.: Bridegroom's Table), *Shulhan Hatan*

Prior to the wedding ceremony, it is customary for the groom together with his father, father-in-law, rabbis, close relatives and friends to preside over a table replete with drinks (both hard and soft) and cake, and enlivened by song and dance. At this time he customarily begins a *d'var Torah* (thought from the Scriptures and Talmud in some way related to marriage) which is generally interrupted by the singing of his comrades (so as not to embarrass those bridegrooms incapable of presenting a learned discourse). The afternoon (Minha) and/or evening prayers (Maariv) are recited by the assemblage. In many instances there is now a *Kallah's Tisch* or Shulhan Kallah for the bride, her close family and friends in an adjoining room.

The Ketubah

The Ketubah, or marriage document, is then filled out by the rabbi. This contract, at least two-thousand years old and written in the ancient Aramaic, is a unilateral agreement in which the groom obligates himself to serve, cherish, support and sustain his bride in truth, as well as to provide her with a sum of money (sufficient for her to sustain herself for from five to eight years) in the eventuality of divorce or death. This was the original Hebraic alimony and life insurance policy, and expresses the idea that a declaration of love must have concomitant moral and financial responsibility. The groom accepts upon himself the obligations of the Ketubah by accepting an object (generally a handkerchief) from the rabbi in the presence of two male, religiously observant witnesses (who may not be related to bride, groom, or each other) in accordance with the Talmudic law of acquisition. The rabbi acts on behalf of the bride and the witnesses sign the marriage document. There is now an important practice to add a special pre-nuptial contract in which the groom obligates himself to pay a significant sum of money each day if his

wife is ever kept from being free to re-marry due to his obstinacy. This continues the tradition of the Ketubah's protection of the woman.

Badeken (lit.: to veil or cover in Yiddish; to investigate in Hebrew)

The groom, flanked on either side by father and father-in-law, escorted by musicians and dancing guests, is led to the seated bride who has been receiving the female guests and is flanked on either side by mother and mother-in-law. He places the veil over his bride's eyes as the rabbi declares: "Our sister, be thou the mother of myriads" (Genesis 24:60), words spoken to Rebecca as she was about to marry Isaac. This custom provides the groom with the opportunity of seeing that he is marrying the right bride, unlike the patriarch Jacob who was given the heavily veiled Leah instead of his beloved Rachel and was therefore deceived. The veil also symbolizes the married state, after which the bride is not to appear publicly with uncovered hair as a sign of modesty and commitment to her husband. The sacred Zohar adds that the Hebrew *bdk* has the same letters as the word *dbk*, to cleave, which connotes spiritual and emotional attachment. In effect, the groom is acting out and announcing the fact that although his initial attraction to the bride may have been physical — he is covering her face as a sign that he presently loves her heart and soul, her inner being, which is a far deeper commitment. The father of the bride then blesses his daughter, as often does the mother of the bride, as well as the parents of the groom:

> May God make you like Sarah, Rebeccah, Rachel and Leah
>
> May the Lord bless you and keep you.
>
> May the Lord make his countenance to shine upon you
>   and be gracious to you;
>
> May the Lord smile upon you and grant you peace. (Numbers 6:24-26)

INTRODUCTORY INTERPRETATIONS OF THE WEDDING CEREMONY

Processional

The groom and his parents, followed by the bride accompanied by her parents, are then led to the *huppah* (nuptial canopy), which symbolizes the new home about to be created in Israel. (According to some more Hassidic customs, the groom is led to the *huppah* by his father and father-in-law, and the bride by her mother and mother-in-law). According to some customs, this *huppah* is in the form of a *tallit* (prayer shawl), which is draped over the bride and groom. It is customary for the *huppah* to be "under the roof of heaven," as a further expression of divine protection. The groom's party precedes his entry and the bride's party precedes her entry much as courtiers who herald the coming of a king and queen. Each member of the processional marches to the accompaniment of an appropriately chosen Hebrew melody, with special blessings chanted by the cantor for the groom and bride respectively as each enters the *huppah* (see page 170).

It is customary in some families for the groom to wear a *kittel* (white robe) as a symbol of purity and rebirth, just as he wears one on Yom Kippur and during the Passover Seder. When the bride joins the groom, she encircles him seven times (with her train upheld by her mother and mother-in-law), symbolizing that he is now the center of her existence and that she is obligated to honor him even as he expresses his obligation to honor her in the Ketubah. The real source for this custom is a verse in Jeremiah (31:21) "...God has created a novelty on earth, that the woman will surround the man," which means that in the Messianic Age of Redemption, the woman will be more dominant. The entire marriage ceremony is replete with references to a more perfect time and faith in the future, a time when "there will yet be heard in the cities of Judea and great streets of Jerusalem, only the sounds of rejoicing and happiness, the sounds of bride and groom...". Seven is the symbolic number of completion and fulfillment and serves as a reminder of the seven traits of betrothal between God and Israel. Since the Revelation at Sinai was the primary expression of that betrothal with the Divine, and since Sinai was ablaze with fire, the parents march down with lit candles, saying:

I will betroth you to Myself forever;
I will betroth you to Myself in righteousness and justice and loving
   kindness and compassion;
I will betroth you to Myself in faithfulness, and you shall know the Lord."
(Hosea 2:21,22)

Kiddushin or *Erusin* (lit.: sanctification or betrothal) (see page 170)

There are two blessings of sanctification recited over a goblet of wine by the officiating rabbi (*Mesader Kiddushin*), the first being the blessing for wine itself as a symbol of joyous celebration, and the second giving praise to God for forbidding certain relationships and sanctifying us by means of the permitted relationships between bride and groom after the wedding. Both groom and bride partake of wine from the same goblet. The groom then declares:

"Behold, you are sanctified unto me with this ring in accordance with the laws of Moses and of Israel." (see page 172)

He then places a plain ring (any precious stone is forbidden in order to banish vain and materialistic thoughts from the betrothal relationship) upon the forefinger of the bride's right hand in the presence of two valid witnesses.

Reading the Ketubah

Our present-day marriage ceremony actually consists of what had previously been two ceremonies, separated by a twelve-month interval. The betrothal or sanctification merely resulted in mutual obligation. The celebration of the actual *huppah* and the establishment of a united home did not take place until one year later. By the eleventh century the betrothal and marriage ceremonies were celebrated at the same time, but were nevertheless kept distinct by reading the Ketubah between them and using a separate wine goblet for each set of blessings.

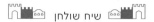
Nisuin (lit.: elevation)

This is the actual marital ceremony or the "lifting" of the bride into the new household. Many grooms wrap a new *tallit* (prayer shawl) around themselves (and their brides) immediately before the recitation of the seven blessings, as a symbol of their being protected by the tradition of the 613 commandments symbolized by the fringes. The groom makes the blessing over the *tallit* as well as the *Shekhiyanu* blessing for a new garment, as well as a new wife and a new relationship. The ceremony is marked by seven blessings in which we praise God for creating man not only in a physical sense with a circumscribed existence, but also in a spiritual sense which transcends time and spans all of Jewish existence. He has roots which go back to the primordial Garden of Eden and a destiny which is linked forward with the redemption of Israel and the world. The couple, filled with thanksgiving for the love and fellowship they feel for each other, take their place in the great chain of Jewish being and pray that their personal joy be transformed into universal celebration of peace. If the bride wishes to give her groom a ring as a gift of her love, she may do so at this point, reciting any words or Scriptural verse she chooses. She may declare, "My beloved is to me and I am to him" (Song of Songs 2:15) or "Place me as a seal upon your heart, as a seal upon your arm..., sparks of fire is the passionate flame of God" (Song of Songs 8:6).

The Breaking of a Glass

Because we understand the fragility of all physical relationships, because there is no moment of joy without its memory of sadness, because despite personal happiness we live in the midst of universal tragedy, and because we mourn the destruction of the Holy Temple (70 CE) which was responsible for a Diaspora of persecution and pogroms, culminating in the Holocaust and our past and present struggles with enemy Arab countries, the conclusion of the public wedding ceremony is the groom's breaking of a glass (preferably a wine goblet). In the words of Rebbe Nahman of Bretzlev, "In a world not yet redeemed, the only whole person is one with a broken heart." There is even

a custom in some places to put some ashes on the groom's forehead. The groom (as well as the assemblage) recites or sings the following excerpt from Psalm 137 prior to his stepping on the glass with his right foot:

> "If I forget thee, O Jerusalem,
> May my right hand forget its cunning
> May my tongue cleave to the roof of my mouth
> If I do not remember thee,
> If I do not hold Jerusalem above my greatest joy."

In Jerusalem the custom is to break the glass after the ceremony of betrothal and before the reading of the Ketubah, so that the marriage ceremony concludes on the high note of redemption rather than on the sadness of destruction.

Yihud (lit.: unity)

Marriage in the Jewish tradition is both a group responsibility and a personal fellowship. Immediately following the public ceremony, the couple retires to a private room where they have the opportunity to express their emotions to each other and to eat their first meal together as husband and wife. They are guarded from disturbance for at least seven minutes by two witnesses standing outside, and the fact that they are alone together for this length of time symbolizes the consummation of the marriage and establishes the permanence of their union.

The Wedding Ceremony

When the groom reaches the *huppah*, the *hazzan* sings:

בָּרוּךְ הַבָּא, מִי אַדִּיר עַל הַכֹּל, מִי בָרוּךְ עַל הַכֹּל, מִי גָדוֹל עַל הַכֹּל, מִי דָגוּל עַל
הַכֹּל, הוּא יְבָרֵךְ אֶת הֶחָתָן וְאֶת הַכַּלָּה.

As the bride approaches, the groom should take a step or two forward in greeting. She then
circles the groom, according to the custom, and the *hazzan* sings:

בְּרוּכָה הַבָּאָה, מִי בֶן שִׂיחַ שׁוֹשַׁן חוֹחִים, אַהֲבַת כַּלָּה מְשׂוֹשׂ דּוֹדִים. הוּא יְבָרֵךְ
אֶת הֶחָתָן וְאֶת הַכַּלָּה.

The Rabbi officiating at the ceremony raises the wine cup and recites:

בָּרוּךְ אַתָּה יְיָ אֱלֹהֵינוּ מֶלֶךְ הָעוֹלָם, בּוֹרֵא פְּרִי הַגָּפֶן:

בָּרוּךְ אַתָּה יְיָ אֱלֹהֵינוּ מֶלֶךְ הָעוֹלָם, אֲשֶׁר קִדְּשָׁנוּ בְּמִצְוֹתָיו וְצִוָּנוּ עַל
הָעֲרָיוֹת, וְאָסַר לָנוּ אֶת הָאֲרוּסוֹת, וְהִתִּיר לָנוּ אֶת הַנְּשׂוּאוֹת לָנוּ עַל
יְדֵי חֻפָּה וְקִדּוּשִׁין. בָּרוּךְ אַתָּה יְיָ, מְקַדֵּשׁ עַמּוֹ יִשְׂרָאֵל עַל יְדֵי חֻפָּה
וְקִדּוּשִׁין:

❧ ⚬✦❀✦⚬ ❧

WEDDING

Following the wedding feast itself, as well as for the seven days following, at any meal
attended by the newlyweds together with at least a quorum of ten adult males, at least one
of whom was not present at the wedding (except on Shabbat; the Shabbat itself counts as
such a "new face") there is a special addition to the *zimun* of the Grace After Meals as well as
the recitation of the seven nuptial blessings at the conclusion of the Grace (the very same
blessings that had been recited under the *huppah*). For this *zimun* two goblets of wine are
filled and a third goblet left empty. The leader takes one wine goblet in his right hand and
introduces the *zimun*.

The special introduction to the special nuptial *zimun* makes the magnificent point that a
celebration of marriage always takes place within the abode of the Divine. Judaism does not
ask us to be celibate; much the opposite, the unity between husband and wife is an expression

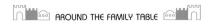

The Wedding Ceremony

When the groom reaches the *huppah*, the *hazzan* sings:

Blessed is he who arrives! He Who is supremely blessed, He Who is supremely great, may He bless the bridegroom and the bride.

As the bride approaches, the groom should take a step or two forward in greeting. She then circles the groom, according to the custom, and the *hazzan* sings:

Blessed is she who arrives! He who understands the speech of the rose and the thorns, the love of a bride, the joy of the beloved, may He bless the bridegroom and the bride.

The Rabbi officiating at the ceremony raises the wine cup and recites:

You are blessed, Lord our God, Sovereign of the world, Creator of the fruit of the vine.

You are blessed, Lord our God, Sovereign of the world, Who made us holy with His commandments and commanded us concerning the prohibited relationships; Who forbade us those betrothed but permitted us those whom we marry by means of the chuppah and the wedding ceremony. You are blessed, Lord, Who makes His people Israel holy through the huppah and the wedding ceremony.

of the biblical command, "You shall love your friend as yourself", and "Hear O Israel, the Lord our God, the Lord is One." Just as He is One, so do we become one with the other through the sanctification of marriage. Indeed, the very Hebrew term for "engagement" is *kiddushin* — sanctity — and one of the most lyrical books of the Bible, the Song of Songs, is at one and the same time a love song between Shlomo and Shulamit, a lover and his beloved, as well as between God and Israel. This motif takes on an additional dimension when we realize that every marriage means the creation of a new family and bears testimony to the eternal continuity of the Jewish people, the nation of the covenant with the Divine. The custom in Jerusalem is for the groom to now recite "If I forget thee O Jerusalem" and break a glass. Outside of Jerusalem, the marriage contract (*ketubah*) is now read, and the glass is broken — symbolizing the destruction of the holy Temple — only after the last of the seven nuptial blessings.

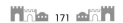

The bridegroom and the bride sip from the wine. The groom then recites the following and places the wedding ring on the forefinger of the right hand of the bride, in the presence of two witnesses:

הֲרֵי אַתְּ מְקֻדֶּשֶׁת לִי בְּטַבַּעַת זוֹ כְּדַת מֹשֶׁה וְיִשְׂרָאֵל:

The *ketubah* is read and the bridegroom presents it to the bride. The seven nuptial blessings are then recited.

שבע ברכות

Under the *huppah*: a second cup is filled with wine and the Seven Blessings are recited, the first one being בורא פרי הגפן.

After *Birkat Ha-Mazon*, the second cup is now held aloft during the recitation of the Seven Blessings, of which בורא פרי הגפן is recited last. It is customary to honor various participants with one of these blessings, passing the goblet of wine in turn to each of those reciting the blessings.

1. בָּרוּךְ אַתָּה יְיָ אֱלֹהֵינוּ מֶלֶךְ הָעוֹלָם, שֶׁהַכֹּל בָּרָא לִכְבוֹדוֹ:

2. בָּרוּךְ אַתָּה יְיָ אֱלֹהֵינוּ מֶלֶךְ הָעוֹלָם, יוֹצֵר הָאָדָם:

3. בָּרוּךְ אַתָּה יְיָ אֱלֹהֵינוּ מֶלֶךְ הָעוֹלָם, אֲשֶׁר יָצַר אֶת הָאָדָם בְּצַלְמוֹ, בְּצֶלֶם דְּמוּת תַּבְנִיתוֹ, וְהִתְקִין לוֹ מִמֶּנּוּ בִּנְיַן עֲדֵי עַד. בָּרוּךְ אַתָּה יְיָ, יוֹצֵר הָאָדָם:

4. שׂוֹשׂ תָּשִׂישׂ וְתָגֵל הָעֲקָרָה בְּקִבּוּץ בָּנֶיהָ לְתוֹכָהּ (בִּמְהֵרָה) בְּשִׂמְחָה. בָּרוּךְ אַתָּה יְיָ, מְשַׂמֵּחַ צִיּוֹן בְּבָנֶיהָ:

5. שַׂמֵּחַ תְּשַׂמַּח רֵעִים הָאֲהוּבִים כְּשַׂמֵּחֲךָ יְצִירְךָ בְּגַן עֵדֶן מִקֶּדֶם. בָּרוּךְ אַתָּה יְיָ, מְשַׂמֵּחַ חָתָן וְכַלָּה:

THE SEVEN NUPTIAL BLESSINGS
These seven blessings, whose origin is to be found in the Talmud (B.T. Ketubot 7b, 8a) emphasize the fact that the joy of the couple is not only in each other but also involves the historic community of Israel: the young couple must see themselves as another glorious link in the golden chain of the Jewish eternity. The first blessing teaches that even in the midst of our

ere

 172

The bridegroom and the bride sip from the wine. The groom then recites the following and places the wedding ring on the forefinger of the right hand of the bride, in the presence of two witnesses:

You are hereby married to me with this ring according to the law of Moses and Israel.

The *ketubah* is read and the bridegroom presents it to the bride. The seven nuptial blessings are then recited.

The Seven Nuptial Blessings

Under the *huppah*, a second cup is filled with wine and the Seven Blessings are recited, the first one being בורא פרי הגפן.

After *Birkat Ha-Mazon*, the second cup is now held aloft during the recitation of the Seven Blessings, of which בורא פרי הגפן is recited last. It is customary to honor various participants with one of these blessings, passing the goblet of wine in turn to each of those reciting the blessings.

1. You are blessed, Lord our God, Sovereign of the world, Who created everything for His glory.

2. You are blessed, Lord our God, Sovereign of the world, Creator of man.

3. You are blessed, Lord our God, Sovereign of the world, Who created man in His image, in the pattern of His own likeness, and provided for the perpetuation of His kind. You are blessed, Lord, Creator of man.

4. Let the barren city be jubilantly happy and joyful at her joyous reunion with her children. You are blessed, Lord, Who makes Zion rejoice with her children.

5. Let the loving couple be very happy, just as You made Your creation happy in the Garden of Eden, so long ago. You are blessed, Lord, Who makes the bridegroom and the bride rejoice together.

most passionate moments we must give the God Who created love and humanity His just due. In the next two blessings which, strangely enough, share the same ending, we thank God for having fashioned the human being. Why two blessings with the same ending or seal? Each of

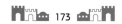

6. בָּרוּךְ אַתָּה יְיָ אֱלֹהֵינוּ מֶלֶךְ הָעוֹלָם, אֲשֶׁר בָּרָא שָׂשׂוֹן וְשִׂמְחָה, חָתָן וְכַלָּה, גִּילָה, רִנָּה, דִּיצָה וְחֶדְוָה, אַהֲבָה וְאַחֲוָה, שָׁלוֹם וְרֵעוּת. מְהֵרָה יְיָ אֱלֹהֵינוּ, יִשָּׁמַע בְּעָרֵי יְהוּדָה וּבְחוּצוֹת יְרוּשָׁלַיִם, קוֹל שָׂשׂוֹן וְקוֹל שִׂמְחָה, קוֹל חָתָן וְקוֹל כַּלָּה, קוֹל מִצְהֲלוֹת חֲתָנִים מֵחֻפָּתָם וּנְעָרִים מִמִּשְׁתֵּה נְגִינָתָם. בָּרוּךְ אַתָּה יְיָ, מְשַׂמֵּחַ הֶחָתָן עִם הַכַּלָּה:

After the six blessings have been recited, the one who led the Grace takes the cup with which he began the Grace and pours from it into an empty cup. He likewise takes the cup over which the six blessings were recited and pours from it into the empty cup. He then pours from the cup of the mixture into the cup with which he began the Grace as well as into the cup of the six blessings. He then recites the blessing over wine over the cup of the Grace and gives the other two cups to the bride and groom respectively. Hence each of the three, the leader, the bride and the groom, drink wine from the Grace after meals as well as from the nuptial blessings.

7. בָּרוּךְ אַתָּה יְיָ אֱלֹהֵינוּ מֶלֶךְ הָעוֹלָם, בּוֹרֵא פְּרִי הַגָּפֶן:

זימון לשבע ברכות

Leader: רַבּוֹתַי, נְבָרֵךְ: The others respond :יְהִי שֵׁם יְיָ מְבֹרָךְ מֵעַתָּה וְעַד עוֹלָם

The leader continues :יְהִי שֵׁם יְיָ מְבֹרָךְ מֵעַתָּה וְעַד עוֹלָם: דְּוַי הָסֵר וְגַם חָרוֹן, וְאָז אִלֵּם בְּשִׁיר יָרוֹן. נְחֵנוּ בְּמַעְגְּלֵי צֶדֶק וְכִשְׁרוֹן. שְׂעֵה בִרְכַּת בְּנֵי יְשֻׁרוּן, כְּבִרְכַּת בְּנֵי אַהֲרֹן:

בִּרְשׁוּת מָרָנָן וְרַבָּנָן וְרַבּוֹתַי, נְבָרֵךְ אֱלֹהֵינוּ שֶׁהַשִּׂמְחָה בִּמְעוֹנוֹ וְשֶׁאָכַלְנוּ מִשֶּׁלּוֹ:

The others respond בָּרוּךְ אֱלֹהֵינוּ שֶׁהַשִּׂמְחָה בִּמְעוֹנוֹ וְשֶׁאָכַלְנוּ מִשֶּׁלּוֹ וּבְטוּבוֹ חָיִינוּ:

The leader continues בָּרוּךְ אֱלֹהֵינוּ שֶׁהַשִּׂמְחָה בִּמְעוֹנוֹ וְשֶׁאָכַלְנוּ מִשֶּׁלּוֹ וּבְטוּבוֹ חָיִינוּ:

All say בָּרוּךְ הוּא וּבָרוּךְ שְׁמוֹ:

these two blessings is speaking of a different aspect of the couple — and indeed of every human being. In the first of these two blessings, we thank God for having destined these two particular individuals — each with his/her physical form, unique personality and specific family background — who have discovered in each other the miracle of love. The second of the two reminds us that we are not merely temporal creatures, children of a specific age and environment; we were formed "in God's image" with gifts of past memory and future anticipation which bind us to an eternal people. Such a realization carries with it ancestral pride as well as future responsibility.

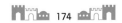

6. You are blessed, Lord our God, Sovereign of the world, Who created joy and celebration, bridegroom and bride, rejoicing, jubilation, pleasure and delight, love and companionship, peace and friendship. May there soon be heard, Lord our God, in the cities of Judea and in the streets of Jerusalem, the sound of joy and the sound of celebration, the voice of the bridegroom and the voice of the bride; the happy shouting of bridegrooms from their weddings and of young men from their feasts of song. You are blessed, Lord, Who makes the bridegroom and the bride rejoice together.

After the six blessings have been recited, the one who led the Grace takes the cup with which he began the Grace and pours from it into an empty cup. He likewise takes the cup over which the six blessings were recited and pours from it into the empty cup. He then pours from the cup of the mixture into the cup with which he began the Grace as well as into the cup of the six blessings. He then recites the blessing over wine over the cup of the Grace and gives the other two cups to the bride and groom respectively. Hence each of the three, the leader, the bride and the groom, drink wine from the Grace after meals as well as from the nuptial blessings.

7. You are blessed, Lord our God, Sovereign of the world, Creator of the fruit of the vine.

ZIMUN FOR THE WEDDING FEAST AND THE FOLLOWING SEVEN DAYS

Leader: My masters (or friends), let us say the blessing.

The others respond: Blessed be the name of the Lord now and forever.

The leader continues: Blessed be the name of the Lord now and forever. Banish grief and anger. Let those that cannot speak exult in song. Lead us in the path of righteousness. Listen to blessings of the priests. With the permission of all those present, let us now bless our God in whose abode is joy and of whose food we have eaten.

The others respond: Blessed our God in whose abode is joy, of whose food we have eaten and through whose goodness we live.

The leader repeats the previous sentence, followed by all saying in unison: May He be blessed and may His name be blessed.

The fourth of the nuptial blessings expresses the joy of the land of Israel, whose children are engaged in fostering a Jewish future. The fifth blessing reminds us of our links to universal humanity and the necessity of our helping to recapture the perfection of Eden. We conclude this historic vision with the prayer for redemption in Jerusalem reborn, when sounds of happiness and joy, sounds of bride and groom, will be heard in the cities of Judea and the highways of Jerusalem.

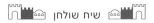
SHALOM ZAKHAR, SHALOM BAT

On the first Friday evening after the birth, there is a beautiful custom to gather at the home of the parents of the new-born baby (or another suitable home) for a dessert repast, singing *zemirot*, sharing words of Torah, and wishing the family *'mazal tov'*. The precise source of and reason for this custom are not known. Some suggest that it is an opportunity to utilize the combined merits of Shabbat and Torah to protect the new-born boy until after the circumcision — a period which was considered fraught with danger. If this is indeed the reason, the celebration applies specifically to the birth of boys — hence the name, "Shalom Zakhar" — "peace for the male child."

The Ba'al Ha-Ittur, however, maintains that the celebration is in thanksgiving to God for the mother having emerged from the ordeal of childbirth alive and well.

Another opinion posits that the gathering is actually a kind of mourning over the lost Torah knowledge of the new-born infant, since according the Midrash, a special angel has taught the fetus in the womb the entire Torah, but just before birth he kisses the fetus above the lips and all the Torah is forgotten. Since the Torah has nevertheless left an impression (and will therefore be relearned rather than having to be acquired *de novo* after birth), and since the newborn will merit the fulfillment of the commandment to study Torah as a result of the forgetfulness, the loss is offset by a positive gain. According to these two explanations, the celebration ought apply to baby girls as well as baby boys.

It is customary to serve chickpeas (*arbes* in Yiddish) at a Shalom Zakhar (or Shalom Bat). The reason for this is either because chickpeas are round and therefore reminiscent of the cycle of life, (paralleling bagels and hard-

boiled eggs at the *se'udat havraah* of mourners returning home from the funeral), or because of the verse of God's promise to Abraham, "I shall surely increase your seed" — *harbeh arbeh* ("increase" in Hebrew) being reminiscent of *arbes* (Gen. 22:17), and likewise linked to the joy of a birth in general.

A TALE OF TWO CIRCUMCISIONS

1. Riga, Soviet Union

In 1970 I was asked by the Lubavitcher Rebbe to visit the then Communist Soviet Union in order to open four underground Yeshivot and Hebrew Ulpanim in Moscow, Leningrad, Riga and Vilna. By the time I reached Riga, the capital of Latvia and the once-proud center of Judaism which had at that time barely 25 Jews in a synagogue that had once attracted close to 1,000 worshippers, the Soviet secret Police (K.G.B.) was on to me; indeed, there were four goons following my every movement from dawn to dusk. 4 a.m. Saturday night there was a loud banging on my hotel door. Understandably frightened, I reluctantly let my nocturnal visitors enter. Standing before me was a father holding a baby, with his two other sons, one aged ten and the other not quite thirteen. He had seen me enter the synagogue, had somehow ascertained that I was a rabbi, and now asked that I travel with him, his sons and a doctor to the outskirts of Rombula cemetery just beyond the Riga city limits. There, under the cover of darkness, the doctor had agreed to perform a circumcision on the newborn baby and his two brothers, the older one about to celebrate his Bar Mitzvah the next Shabbat. The father explained that a rabbi was needed to recite the blessings and to ascertain that the ritual was performed properly.

Although I'm generally squeamish even at ordinary circumcisions

performed on eight-day-old baby boys in homes or celebration halls by certified *Mohalim*, I felt I had no choice but to agree to try to be worthy of the challenge. At that time and place religious ritual circumcision was considered a serious criminal act against the State; all the participants hoped that a deserted cemetery and the cover of darkness would prevent any kind of discovery.

The children were given only local anesthetics. I instructed the doctor as best as I could, intoned the blessings, acted as *Sandak* (godfather, who holds the baby during the circumcision) and braced myself with every fiber of my being. At the conclusion of the rituals I intoned the usual formula: "Just as (*ke-shem*) the child has entered the covenant, so may he enter a life of Torah (at his Bar Mitzvah), stand under the nuptial canopy, and live a life of good deeds." Suddenly the father of the boys, who had been pensively and even ominously silent during the ride as well as the ceremony, screamed out: "Not *'ke-shem'*! Not 'just as'! Take the words back! I don't want his Bar Mitzvah or his wedding in the middle of the night in the cemetery. I want it in the open air in Jerusalem, before the place of the Holy Temple! Not *'ke-shem'*!"

The father then turned to me with tears streaming down his cheeks. "Please forgive my outburst. I don't really understand why I'm here and why I did this. I only know that I want my children to be Jews and that I couldn't live with myself if they were not circumcised."

Lonya Goldfarb, the father from Riga, came to Israel with his family in 1984. His son eventually studied at our Strauss Rabbinical Seminary, and it was in the Yeshiva Beit Midrash in Efrat that his grandson was circumcised, fulfilling his prayer at the outskirts of the Rombula cemetery....

2. Manipur, India

In the fall of 2002 I made a trip to the southeast of India in order to establish contact with a group of Jews — 5,000 strong — who call themselves Bnei Menashe, claiming to be descendants of the lost tribe of Menashe. They look Indian-Chinese and, mostly as a result of the indefatigable efforts of Rabbi Eliyahu Avihayil, are in large measure observant Jews. They do not have a Torah scroll, but they do have a lengthy narrative, in the dialect of Miso, which relates the history of Israel from the Garden of Eden to the Monarchs in Jerusalem. Their elders know the history-song by heart, and despite their isolation from the rest of Israel, they have staunchly remained committed to those rituals they preserved, like slaughtering a lamb on the 14th day of Nissan and painting its blood on their door posts. They stubbornly remained Jews despite their wanderings and in the face of much persecution. They also have a tradition of circumcision — which they performed with sharp flints, as did Tzipporah in the Torah, when she circumcised her son. In a synagogue in Manipur, India, overlooking the magnificent mountains, not far from Bangladesh, and to the tune of an Indian chant which seemd to contain ancient rhythms and secrets of eternity, I witnessed a Shabbat circumcision, which took literally twenty-two minutes to perform. Once again I was asked to intone the blessings. As I write these words, father and son — together with the rest of their Bnei Menashe family — are on their way to Israel, the land of the miracle of the ingathering of the exiles.

סדר ברית מילה

The ceremony is performed on the eighth day of the life of a baby boy.

As the baby is brought in, all rise and say:

בָּרוּךְ הַבָּא.

The Mohel says:

וַיְדַבֵּר יְיָ אֶל מֹשֶׁה לֵּאמֹר. פִּינְחָס בֶּן אֶלְעָזָר בֶּן אַהֲרֹן הַכֹּהֵן הֵשִׁיב אֶת חֲמָתִי מֵעַל בְּנֵי יִשְׂרָאֵל בְּקַנְאוֹ אֶת קִנְאָתִי בְּתוֹכָם, וְלֹא כִלִּיתִי אֶת בְּנֵי יִשְׂרָאֵל בְּקִנְאָתִי, לָכֵן אֱמֹר הִנְנִי נֹתֵן לוֹ אֶת בְּרִיתִי שָׁלוֹם.

The father of the baby, wrapped in a *tallit* (and in accordane with many customs, also *tefillin*) holds the baby and recites the following verses, repeated verse by verse by the assembled:

שְׁמַע יִשְׂרָאֵל יְיָ אֱלֹהֵינוּ יְיָ אֶחָד.

יְיָ מֶלֶךְ יְיָ מָלָךְ יְיָ יִמְלֹךְ לְעוֹלָם וָעֶד.

אָנָּא יְיָ הוֹשִׁיעָה נָּא. אָנָּא יְיָ הוֹשִׁיעָה נָּא.

אָנָּא יְיָ הַצְלִיחָה נָּא. אָנָּא יְיָ הַצְלִיחָה נָּא.

Two seats are prepared, one upon which the *"Sandak"* (godparent) will sit as he holds the baby during the circumcision. The second is prepared for Elijah the prophet. The baby is first placed upon the Throne of Elijah by one of the prominent guests, whereupon the Mohel says:

זֶה הַכִּסֵּא שֶׁל אֵלִיָּהוּ הַנָּבִיא זָכוּר לַטּוֹב. לִישׁוּעָתְךָ קִוִּיתִי יְיָ. שִׁבַּרְתִּי לִישׁוּעָתְךָ יְיָ וּמִצְוֹתֶיךָ עָשִׂיתִי. אֵלִיָּהוּ מַלְאַךְ הַבְּרִית. הִנֵּה שֶׁלְּךָ לְפָנֶיךָ. עֲמוֹד עַל יְמִינִי וְסָמְכֵנִי. שִׁבַּרְתִּי לִישׁוּעָתְךָ יְיָ. שָׂשׂ אָנֹכִי עַל אִמְרָתֶךָ כְּמוֹצֵא שָׁלָל רָב. שָׁלוֹם רָב לְאֹהֲבֵי תוֹרָתֶךָ וְאֵין לָמוֹ מִכְשׁוֹל. אַשְׁרֵי תִּבְחַר וּתְקָרֵב יִשְׁכֹּן חֲצֵרֶיךָ.

BERIT MILAH (Circumcision Ceremony)

The ceremony is performed on the eighth day of the life of a baby boy.

As the baby is brought in, all rise and say:

Blessed is he who arrives!

The Mohel says:

The Lord told Moses: Pinhas, the son of El'azar, the son of Aharon the Priest, calmed My anger against the children of Israel by expressing My rage at them, so I did not destroy the children of Israel in My rage. Therefore, say: I hereby confer on him My covenant of peace.

The father of the baby, wrapped in a *tallit* (and in accordance with many customs, also *tefillin*) holds the baby and recites the following verses, repeated verse by verse by the assembled:

Hear, O Israel, the Lord our God the Lord is One.
The Lord is King, the Lord was King, the Lord will be King forever and ever.
Please, Lord, save us Please, Lord, save us.
Please, Lord, prosper us Please, Lord, prosper us.

Two seats are prepared, one upon which the *"Sandak"* (godparent) will sit as he holds the baby during the circumcision. The second is prepared for Elijah the prophet. The baby is first placed upon the Throne of Elijah by one of the prominent guests, whereupon the Mohel says:

This chair is for Elijah, may he be remembered for good. I yearn for Your salvation, Lord. I await Your salvation, Lord, while I observe Your commandments. Elijah, emissary of the covenant, this is yours; stand by my right hand and assist me. I await Your salvation, Lord; I rejoice in Your word, like someone who discovers a great treasure. May those who love Your Torah enjoy profound peace and let there be no pitfalls for them. Happy is the man You choose and draw near, so that he may dwell in Your courts.

All present respond:

נִשְׂבְּעָה בְּטוּב בֵּיתֶךָ קְדֹשׁ הֵיכָלֶךָ.

When the Mohel is ready to perform the circumcision, the baby's father says:

הִנְנִי מוּכָן וּמְזֻמָּן לְקַיֵּם מִצְוַת עֲשֵׂה שֶׁצִּוָּנוּ הַבּוֹרֵא יִתְבָּרַךְ לָמוּל אֶת בְּנִי.

At this point, the father verbally appoints the Mohel as his agent to perform circumcision on his son. The Mohel then takes the infant and proclaims:

אָמַר הַקָּדוֹשׁ בָּרוּךְ הוּא לְאַבְרָהָם אָבִינוּ, הִתְהַלֵּךְ לְפָנַי וֶהְיֵה תָמִים. הִנְנִי מוּכָן וּמְזֻמָּן לְקַיֵּם מִצְוַת עֲשֵׂה שֶׁצִּוָּנוּ הַבּוֹרֵא יִתְבָּרַךְ לָמוּל.

The baby is placed on the Sandak's knees. Just before operating the Mohel says:

בָּרוּךְ אַתָּה יְיָ אֱלֹהֵינוּ מֶלֶךְ הָעוֹלָם, אֲשֶׁר קִדְּשָׁנוּ בְּמִצְוֹתָיו וְצִוָּנוּ עַל הַמִּילָה.

As the Mohel performs the circumcision, the father (or, if the father is not present, the *Sandak*) recites:

בָּרוּךְ אַתָּה יְיָ אֱלֹהֵינוּ מֶלֶךְ הָעוֹלָם, אֲשֶׁר קִדְּשָׁנוּ בְּמִצְוֹתָיו וְצִוָּנוּ לְהַכְנִיסוֹ בִּבְרִיתוֹ שֶׁל אַבְרָהָם אָבִינוּ.
בָּרוּךְ אַתָּה יְיָ אֱלֹהֵינוּ מֶלֶךְ הָעוֹלָם, שֶׁהֶחֱיָנוּ וְקִיְּמָנוּ וְהִגִּיעָנוּ לַזְּמַן הַזֶּה.

All respond joyfully and loudly:

אָמֵן. כְּשֵׁם שֶׁנִּכְנַס לַבְּרִית, כֵּן יִכָּנֵס לַתּוֹרָה, לַחֻפָּה וּלְמַעֲשִׂים טוֹבִים.

When the circumcision is complete, the baby is handed to one of the prominent guests to hold, while the following prayers (including the giving of the name) are recited. The honor of reciting them may be given to one person, or they may be divided between two people. If so, the first person recites the two blessings and the second person recites the prayer during which the baby is given his name.

All present respond:

May we be sated with the goodness of Your house; Your holy sanctuary.

When the Mohel is ready to perform the circumcision, the baby's father says:

I am ready and prepared to fulfill the positive commandment which the Creator, blessed be He, commanded us; to circumcise my son.

At this point the father verbally appoints the Mohel as his agent to perform circumcision on his son. The Mohel then takes the infant and proclaims:

God told Abraham, our father: Walk before Me and attain perfection. I am ready and prepared to fulfill the positive commandment which the Creator, blessed be He, commanded us — to perform circumcision.

The baby is placed on the Sandak's knees. Just before operating, the Mohel says:

You are blessed, Lord our God, Sovereign of the world, Who made us holy with His commandments and commanded us concerning circumcision.

As the mohel performs the circumcision, the father (or, if the father is not present, the Sandak) recites:

You are blessed, Lord our God, Sovereign of the world, Who made us holy with His commandments and commanded us to initiate him into the covenant of Abraham.
You are blessed, Lord our God, Sovereign of the world, Who has kept us alive and sustained us and enabled us to reach this occasion.

All respond, loudly and joyfully:

Amen. Just as he has been initiated into the covenant, so may he be initiated into learning Torah, marriage, and a life of good deeds.

When the circumcision is complete, the baby is handed to one of the prominent guests to hold, while the following prayers (including the giving of the name) are recited. The honor of reciting them may be given to one person, or they may be divided between two people. If so, the first person recites the two blessings and the second person recites the prayer during which the baby is given his name.

בָּרוּךְ אַתָּה יְיָ אֱלֹהֵינוּ מֶלֶךְ הָעוֹלָם, בּוֹרֵא פְּרִי הַגָּפֶן.

בָּרוּךְ אַתָּה יְיָ אֱלֹהֵינוּ מֶלֶךְ הָעוֹלָם, אֲשֶׁר קִדֵּשׁ יְדִיד מִבֶּטֶן וְחֹק
בִּשְׁאֵרוֹ שָׂם וְצֶאֱצָאָיו חָתַם בְּאוֹת בְּרִית קֹדֶשׁ. עַל כֵּן בִּשְׂכַר זֹאת אֵל
חַי חֶלְקֵנוּ צוּרֵנוּ. צַוֵּה לְהַצִּיל יְדִידוּת שְׁאֵרֵנוּ מִשַּׁחַת לְמַעַן בְּרִיתוֹ
אֲשֶׁר שָׂם בִּבְשָׂרֵנוּ. בָּרוּךְ אַתָּה יְיָ כּוֹרֵת הַבְּרִית.

A sip of wine is now taken by the reader of these two blessings.

אֱלֹהֵינוּ וֵאלֹהֵי אֲבוֹתֵינוּ, קַיֵּם אֶת הַיֶּלֶד הַזֶּה לְאָבִיו וּלְאִמּוֹ, וְיִקָּרֵא שְׁמוֹ
בְּיִשְׂרָאֵל .... בֶּן .... יִשְׂמַח הָאָב בְּיוֹצֵא חֲלָצָיו. וְתָגֵל אִמּוֹ בִּפְרִי בִטְנָהּ. כַּכָּתוּב:
יִשְׂמַח אָבִיךָ וְאִמֶּךָ וְתָגֵל יוֹלַדְתֶּךָ. וְנֶאֱמַר: וָאֶעֱבֹר עָלַיִךְ וָאֶרְאֵךְ מִתְבּוֹסֶסֶת
בְּדָמָיִךְ וָאֹמַר לָךְ בְּדָמַיִךְ חֲיִי וָאֹמַר לָךְ בְּדָמַיִךְ חֲיִי. וְנֶאֱמַר: זָכַר לְעוֹלָם בְּרִיתוֹ
דָּבָר צִוָּה לְאֶלֶף דּוֹר. אֲשֶׁר כָּרַת אֶת אַבְרָהָם וּשְׁבוּעָתוֹ לְיִשְׂחָק. וַיַּעֲמִידֶהָ
לְיַעֲקֹב לְחֹק. לְיִשְׂרָאֵל בְּרִית עוֹלָם. וְנֶאֱמַר: וַיָּמָל אַבְרָהָם אֶת יִצְחָק בְּנוֹ בֶּן
שְׁמוֹנַת יָמִים כַּאֲשֶׁר צִוָּה אֹתוֹ אֱלֹהִים.

All present recite the following, then the reader repeats:

הוֹדוּ לַיְיָ כִּי טוֹב כִּי לְעוֹלָם חַסְדּוֹ:
הוֹדוּ לַיְיָ כִּי טוֹב כִּי לְעוֹלָם חַסְדּוֹ:

The reader then continues:

.... בֶּן .... זֶה הַקָּטֹן גָּדוֹל יִהְיֶה. כְּשֵׁם שֶׁנִּכְנַס לַבְּרִית כֵּן יִכָּנֵס לְתוֹרָה, לְחֻפָּה
וּלְמַעֲשִׂים טוֹבִים וְנֹאמַר אָמֵן.

It is now customary in many communities for the mother to recite Birkat Ha-Gomel, *her prayer of thanksgiving, in the presence of the assembled:*

בָּרוּךְ אַתָּה יְיָ אֱלֹהֵינוּ מֶלֶךְ הָעוֹלָם, הַגּוֹמֵל לְחַיָּבִים טוֹבוֹת שֶׁגְּמָלַנִי כָּל טוֹב.

All present respond:

אָמֵן. מִי שֶׁגְּמָלֵךְ טוֹב. הוּא יִגְמָלֵךְ כָּל טוֹב, סֶלָה.

You are blessed, Lord our God, Sovereign of the world, Creator of the fruit of the vine. You are blessed, Lord our God, Sovereign of the world, Who singled out His beloved one in the womb and set an ordinance in his flesh, sealing a holy covenant with his descendants. Therefore, in the merit of this — living God, our Destiny, our Stronghold — deliver from destruction the dearly beloved of our flesh, for the sake of the covenant set in our flesh. You are blessed, Lord, Maker of the covenant.

A sip of wine is now taken by the reader of these two blessings.

Our God and God of our fathers: keep this boy safe for his father and mother. Let his name be known in Israel as ... the son of .... May his father be happy with his offspring and his mother rejoice in the fruit of her womb. As it is written: May your father and mother be happy and the one who gave birth to you rejoice. And it is also said: "And I passed by you and I saw you rooted in your blood. I said to you: By your blood shall you live. And I said to you: By your blood shall you live." And it is said: "He is mindful of His covenant forever — the word He decreed for a thousand generations, which He forged with Abraham — and also of His oath of Isaac. He established it as an ordinance for Jacob, and everlasting covenant for Israel." And it is said: "So Abraham circumcised his son Isaac when he was eight days old, as God commanded him."

All present recite the following, then the reader repeats:

Give thanks to the Lord for He is good, for His kindness is everlasting.
Give thanks to the Lord for He is good, for His kindness is everlasting.

The reader then continues:

May this little boy, ... the son of ..., become great. Just as he has been initiated into the covenant, so may he be initiated into learning Torah, marriage, and a life of good deeds, and let us say, Amen.

It is now customary in many communities for the mother to recite Birkat Ha-Gomel, *her prayer of thanksgiving, in the presence of the assembled:*

You are blessed, Lord our God, Sovereign of the world, Who provides good things to those who are obligated to Him, and Who has provided me with such good.

All present respond:

Amen. May He Who has provided you with such good, always provide you with good, Selah.

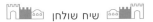

זימון לברית מילה

Begin with *Shir Ha-Ma'alot* (page 12). Then the leader continues here:

רַבּוֹתַי, נְבָרֵךְ.

The others answer:

יְהִי שֵׁם יְיָ מְבֹרָךְ מֵעַתָּה וְעַד עוֹלָם.

The leader continues:

יְהִי שֵׁם יְיָ מְבֹרָךְ מֵעַתָּה וְעַד עוֹלָם.
נוֹדֶה לְשִׁמְךָ בְּתוֹךְ אֱמוּנַי, בְּרוּכִים אַתֶּם לַיְיָ.

The others repeat:

נוֹדֶה לְשִׁמְךָ בְּתוֹךְ אֱמוּנַי, בְּרוּכִים אַתֶּם לַיְיָ.

Leader:

בִּרְשׁוּת הַתּוֹרָה הַקְּדוֹשָׁה, טְהוֹרָה הִיא וְגַם פְּרוּשָׁה, צִוָּה לָנוּ מוֹרָשָׁה, מֹשֶׁה עֶבֶד יְיָ.

GRACE AFTER THE MEAL CELEBRATING A BERIT MILAH

Just as in the case of the *Sheva Berakhot* meals after the wedding feast and during the week, there is a special *zimun* for the meal following the circumcision, giving praise to God, our Fortress and Refuge. The refrain, repeated after each stanza, declares: "We give thanks to Your Name among my faithful; blessed are you to the Lord." The ritual circumcision is certainly an act of faith which has demonstrated amazing staying power throughout the generations. Towards the end of the Grace After Meals, after reciting "in the eyes of God and man", the following prayers are recited. It is customary to hand the goblet of wine to each participant who is honored with one of these prayers. God is called "the Compassionate One" at the opening for each of these prayers, attesting to the fact that at the circumcision there is only a

ZIMUN FOR A CIRCUMCISION

Begin with *Shir Ha-Ma'alot* (page 12). Then the leader continues here:

My friends, let us say the blessing.

The others answer:

May the Name of the Lord be blessed from now on and forever more.

The leader continues:

May the Name of the Lord be blessed from now on and forever more.
We give thanks to Your Name among the faithful; you are blessed by the Lord.

The others repeat:

We give thanks to Your Name among the faithful; you are blessed by the Lord.

Leader:

With the consent of the holy, pure and clear Torah, which Moses, the Lord's servant gave us as a heritage.

---

little bit of blood and pain, but hopefully a long life of health and happiness. The first prayer grants a special blessing to the parents of the child, and the second to the *Sandak* who held the infant during the circumcision and is considered to be the godparent of the baby. The status of the place of the circumcision is like that of an altar, and the circumcision blood like a sacrifice accepted by the Almighty. The third prayer blesses the baby himself, praying that he merit visiting the Temple in Jerusalem during the three pilgrim festivals. The fourth blesses the Mohel, and the fifth blesses the Messiah.

The birth of every Jewish child raises optimistic hope of new beginnings and the constant possibility that this newborn infant may indeed become the Messiah of redemption. Our tradition teaches that there can be no salvation without commitment — even commitment unto shedding of blood. It is for this reason that the Pesach sacrifice on the fourteenth day of Nissan (as well as the circumcision of every male baby, which the Midrash records took place on the 11th of Nissan) preceded the salvation and exodus from Egypt on the fifteenth day of Nissan.

(continued on page 190)

All say:

נוֹדֶה לְשִׁמְךָ בְּתוֹךְ אֱמוּנֵי, בְּרוּכִים אַתֶּם לַיְיָ.

Leader:

בִּרְשׁוּת הַכֹּהֲנִים וְהַלְוִיִּם, אֶקְרָא לֵאלֹהֵי הָעִבְרִיִּים, אֲהוֹדֶנּוּ בְּכָל אִיִּים, אֲבָרְכָה אֶת יְיָ.

All say:

נוֹדֶה לְשִׁמְךָ בְּתוֹךְ אֱמוּנֵי, בְּרוּכִים אַתֶּם לַיְיָ.

Leader:

בִּרְשׁוּת מָרָנָן וְרַבָּנָן וְרַבּוֹתַי, אֶפְתְּחָה בְּשִׁיר פִּי וּשְׂפָתַי, וְתֹאמַרְנָה עַצְמוֹתַי, בָּרוּךְ הַבָּא בְּשֵׁם יְיָ.

All say:

נוֹדֶה לְשִׁמְךָ בְּתוֹךְ אֱמוּנֵי, בְּרוּכִים אַתֶּם לַיְיָ.

Leader:

בִּרְשׁוּת מָרָנָן וְרַבָּנָן וְרַבּוֹתַי, נְבָרֵךְ אֱלֹהֵינוּ שֶׁאָכַלְנוּ מִשֶּׁלּוֹ.

The others say:

בָּרוּךְ אֱלֹהֵינוּ שֶׁאָכַלְנוּ מִשֶּׁלּוֹ וּבְטוּבוֹ חָיִינוּ.

All say:

בָּרוּךְ הוּא וּבָרוּךְ שְׁמוֹ.

Continue with the Blessing After the Meal until "in the sight of God and man" (p. 16-28). Then the leader continues:

הָרַחֲמָן הוּא יְבָרֵךְ אֲבִי הַיֶּלֶד וְאִמּוֹ, וְיִזְכּוּ לְגַדְּלוֹ וּלְחַנְּכוֹ וּלְחַכְּמוֹ, מִיּוֹם הַשְּׁמִינִי וָהָלְאָה יֵרָצֶה דָמוֹ, וִיהִי יְיָ אֱלֹהָיו עִמּוֹ.

All say:

We give thanks to Your Name among the faithful; you are blessed by the Lord.

Leader:

With the consent of the priests, the levites, I will call to the God of the Hebrews. I will extol Him in all the far-flung lands; I will bless the Lord.

All say:

We give thanks to Your Name among the faithful; you are blessed by the Lord.

Leader:

With the consent of all present I will open my mouth, my lips in song, and let my whole being declare: Blessed is he who comes in the name of the Lord!

All say:

We give thanks to Your Name among the faithful; you are blessed by the Lord.

With the consent of all present, let us bless Him — (if there are ten or more men present, say "our God")
Whose food we have eaten.

The others say:

Blessed is He (our God) Whose food we have eaten and through Whose goodness we live.

All say:

May He be blessed and may His Name be blessed.

Continue with the Blessing After the Meal until "in the sight of God and man" (p.16-29). Then the leader continues:

May the Merciful One bless the child's father and mother and permit them to raise him, educate him and teach him wisdom. From this eighth day on may his blood be accepted, and may the Lord his God be with him.

הָרַחֲמָן הוּא יְבָרֵךְ בַּעַל בְּרִית הַמִּילָה, אֲשֶׁר שָׂשׂ לַעֲשׂוֹת צֶדֶק בְּגִילָה, וִישַׁלֵּם פָּעֳלוֹ וּמַשְׂכֻּרְתּוֹ כְּפוּלָה, וְיִתְּנֵהוּ לְמַעְלָה לְמָעְלָה.

הָרַחֲמָן הוּא יְבָרֵךְ רַךְ הַנִּמּוֹל לִשְׁמוֹנָה, וְיִהְיוּ יָדָיו וְלִבּוֹ לָאֵל אֱמוּנָה, וְיִזְכֶּה לִרְאוֹת פְּנֵי הַשְּׁכִינָה, שָׁלֹשׁ פְּעָמִים בַּשָּׁנָה.

הָרַחֲמָן הוּא יְבָרֵךְ הַמָּל בְּשַׂר הָעָרְלָה, וּפָרַע וּמָצַץ דְּמֵי הַמִּילָה, אִישׁ הַיָּרֵא וְרַךְ הַלֵּבָב עֲבוֹדָתוֹ פְּסוּלָה. אִם שָׁלֹשׁ אֵלֶּה לֹא יַעֲשֶׂה לָהּ.

הָרַחֲמָן הוּא יִשְׁלַח לָנוּ מְשִׁיחוֹ הוֹלֵךְ תָּמִים, בִּזְכוּת חֲתַן לַמּוּלוֹת דָּמִים, לְבַשֵּׂר בְּשׂוֹרוֹת טוֹבוֹת וְנִחוּמִים, לְעַם אֶחָד מְפֻזָּר וּמְפֹרָד בֵּין הָעַמִּים.

הָרַחֲמָן הוּא יִשְׁלַח לָנוּ כֹּהֵן צֶדֶק אֲשֶׁר לֻקַּח לְעֵילוֹם, עַד הוּכַן כִּסְאוֹ כַּשֶּׁמֶשׁ וְיַהֲלוֹם, וַיָּלֶט פָּנָיו בְּאַדַּרְתּוֹ וַיִּגְלוֹם, בְּרִיתִי הָיְתָה אִתּוֹ הַחַיִּים וְהַשָּׁלוֹם.

Continue with "May the Merciful One..." to the end of the Blessing After the Meal (on pages 29-30).

This is the reference in the circumcision ceremony, "By your blood shall you live; by your blood shall you live" — the blood of circumcision and the blood of the Pesach sacrifice.

We especially pray at each circumcision that the merit of the blood of this ritual commitment may bring about the ultimate redemption. Indeed, the infant is circumcised on the knees of the *Sandak* who sits on the special chair of Elijah, for Elijah the prophet is the forerunner of the

May the Merciful One bless the Sandek who was happy to perform this righteous act; may He reward his efforts in double measure and exalt him more and more.

May the Merciful One bless the tender eight-day-old infant who was circumcised; may his hands and his heart be faithful to God. May he be worthy to appear in the Divine Presence three times a year.

May the Merciful One bless the Mohel who performed the circumcision, split the membrane and drew off some blood. The efforts of a timid or faint-hearted man would be invalid if he did not include these three steps.

May the Merciful One send us His faultless Messiah, in the merit of those related by circumcision, to bring good tidings and comfort to the unique people, scattered and dispersed among the nations.

May the Merciful One send us the righteous priest who remains unseen until his shining and sparkling throne is ready; he who enveloped himself in his mantle; he who has God's covenant of life and peace.

Continue with "May the Merciful One..." to the end of the Blessing After the Meal (on pages 29-30).

Messiah and herald of the good tidings of salvation and comfort. The sixth prayer specifically relates to Elijah, who is called "the righteous Kohen-priest" and who will be revealed in all of his glory with the establishment of the Third Temple. ✦

סדר פדיון הבן

Once the meal has started, the baby boy is brought in. The parents present their son to the kohen and say, individually or together:

זֶה בְּנִי בְכוֹרִי הוּא פֶּטֶר רֶחֶם לְאִמּוֹ וְהַקָּדוֹשׁ בָּרוּךְ הוּא צִוָּה הוּא לִפְדּוֹתוֹ, שֶׁנֶּאֱמַר: וּפְדוּיָו מִבֶּן חֹדֶשׁ תִּפְדֶּה בְּעֶרְכְּךָ כֶּסֶף חֲמֵשֶׁת שְׁקָלִים בְּשֶׁקֶל הַקֹּדֶשׁ עֶשְׂרִים גֵּרָה הוּא, וְנֶאֱמַר: קַדֶּשׁ לִי כָל בְּכוֹר פֶּטֶר כָּל רֶחֶם בִּבְנֵי יִשְׂרָאֵל בָּאָדָם וּבַבְּהֵמָה לִי הוּא.

The kohen asks:

מַה בָּעֵית טְפֵי לִתֶּן לִי, בִּנְךָ בְּכוֹרְךָ שֶׁהוּא פֶּטֶר רֶחֶם לְאִמּוֹ, אוֹ בָּעֵית לִפְדּוֹתוֹ בְּעַד חָמֵשׁ סְלָעִים כִּדְמְחַיַּבְתָּא מִדְּאוֹרַיְתָא?

The father, holding five shekels or silver dollars, replies:

חָפֵץ אֲנִי לִפְדּוֹת אֶת בְּנִי, וְהֵילָךְ דְּמֵי פִדְיוֹנוֹ כִּדְמְחַיַּבְתִּי מִדְּאוֹרַיְתָא.

He continues:

בָּרוּךְ אַתָּה יְיָ אֱלֹהֵינוּ מֶלֶךְ הָעוֹלָם, אֲשֶׁר קִדְּשָׁנוּ בְּמִצְוֹתָיו וְצִוָּנוּ עַל פִּדְיוֹן הַבֵּן.

PIDYON HA-BEN: REDEMPTION OF THE FIRSTBORN MALE

The redemption ceremony is performed by a kohen at a festive meal on the 31st day of the life of a firstborn son to a mother. If the family of the mother or of the father are kohanim or levites, or if the birth was by caesarean section, no redemption ceremony is necessary. The ceremony is usually held in the daytime, but should the 31st day be a Shabbat, a festival or a fast day, it is postponed until that evening.

The Redemption of the Firstborn ceremony harks back to the ancient biblical period even before there was a class of kohanim-priests or a formalized Temple Sanctuary. The initial biblical plan was a much more democratic one, with every household having its own sacrificial altar and prayer rooms which would be ministered by the firstborn son. It was, after all, the firstborn who was expected to take ultimate responsibility for his younger siblings if anything happened to compromise the effectiveness of the parents. And therefore it was the firstborn who was likewise responsible for the religious and ritual devotions of the family. The Torah

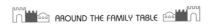
PIDYON HA-BEN (Redemption of the Firstborn Male)

Once the meal has started, the baby boy is brought in. The parents present their son to the kohen and say, individually or together:

This is our firstborn son, his mother's first delivery, and the Holy One, blessed be He, has commanded me to redeem him, as it is said: "The price of his redemption, when you redeem him at one month old, shall be five silver shekels, according to your valuation, of the Temple shekels, each of twenty *gerahs*." And it is said: "Sanctify for Me every firstborn son that is first out of the womb among the children of Israel, of both men and animals; it is Mine."

The kohen asks:

Which do you prefer, to give me your firstborn son, his mother's first delivery, or would you redeem him for five shekels, as required by the Torah?

The father, holding five shekels or silver dollars, replies:

I wish to redeem my son, and here is the money for the redemption, as required by the Torah.

He continues:

You are blessed, Lord our God, Sovereign of the world, Who made us holy with His commandments and commanded us to redeem the firstborn.

initially seemed to favor a religious system centered around the family and devoid of an institutionalized and professional religious structure, with a centralized Temple and priestly class. However, when the Israelites in the desert worshipped the Golden Calf — a sin in which the firstborn sons participated but the children of Aaron did not — the Almighty recognized, as it were, the necessity of a centralized Sanctuary and of a specifically appointed kohen-priest class comprising the religious establishment. Many commentaries believe that eventually this professionalized and institutionalized religious center, as well as the priestly tribal class, will give way to the more personalized and family-oriented home altar and firstborn minister. This ceremony therefore reminds us of the situation in Israel's ancient past as well as what may lie in store for us in Israel's future.

The question which the kohen asks the parents: "Which do you prefer, to give me your firstborn son or to redeem him for five shekels?" sounds rather strange to the modern ear. What parent would prefer five shekels to his own child?

בָּרוּךְ אַתָּה יְיָ אֱלֹהֵינוּ מֶלֶךְ הָעוֹלָם, שֶׁהֶחֱיָנוּ וְקִיְּמָנוּ וְהִגִּיעָנוּ לַזְּמַן הַזֶּה.

The father gives the coins to the kohen, who holds them over the baby's head and says:

זֶה תַּחַת זֶה, זֶה חִלּוּף זֶה, זֶה מָחוּל עַל זֶה, וְיִכָּנֵס זֶה הַבֵּן לְחַיִּים, לַתּוֹרָה וּלְיִרְאַת שָׁמַיִם. יְהִי רָצוֹן שֶׁכְּשֵׁם שֶׁנִּכְנַס לַפִּדְיוֹן כֵּן יִכָּנֵס לַתּוֹרָה וּלְחֻפָּה וּלְמַעֲשִׂים טוֹבִים.

The kohen then gives the baby boy his blessing:

יְשִׂימְךָ אֱלֹהִים כְּאֶפְרַיִם וְכִמְנַשֶּׁה. יְבָרֶכְךָ יְיָ וְיִשְׁמְרֶךָ. יָאֵר יְיָ פָּנָיו אֵלֶיךָ וִיחֻנֶּךָּ. יִשָּׂא יְיָ פָּנָיו אֵלֶיךָ וְיָשֵׂם לְךָ שָׁלוֹם. יְיָ שֹׁמְרֶךָ, יְיָ צִלְּךָ עַל יַד יְמִינֶךָ. כִּי אֹרֶךְ יָמִים וּשְׁנוֹת חַיִּים וְשָׁלוֹם יוֹסִיפוּ לָךְ. יְיָ יִשְׁמָרְךָ מִכָּל רָע יִשְׁמֹר אֶת נַפְשֶׁךָ.

The kohen recites the blessing for wine to conclude the ceremony:

בָּרוּךְ אַתָּה יְיָ אֱלֹהֵינוּ מֶלֶךְ הָעוֹלָם, בּוֹרֵא פְּרִי הַגָּפֶן.

However, we do find many families, professional and upwardly mobile, in which parents have relatively little time — and even little emotional energy — to give to their children. It would seem that the parents do prefer the shekels to their children — who, although they certainly might benefit from the material luxuries provided by the extra hours spent by the parents at work, would probably do better by having their parents themselves rather than their parents' largesse. As my wife never tires of pointing out, when it comes to our children, "quality time" is quantity time.

Rav Yisrael Meir Kagan, known as the Hafetz Hayim, teaches a charming allegory to express the topsy-turvy priorities of concern for a child's extra physical comfort before the necessity of

You are blessed, Lord our God, Sovereign of the world, Who has kept us alive and sustained us and enabled us to reach this occasion.

The father gives the coins to the kohen, who holds them over the baby's head and says:

This instead of that, this in substitution for that, this in remission for that. May this boy be granted life, Torah and respect for God. May it be God's will that, just as he has experienced his redemption, so may he experience Torah, marriage and a life of good deeds. Amen.

The kohen then gives the baby boy his blessing:

May God make you like Efraim and Menashe. May the Lord bless you and watch over you. May the Lord shine His face towards you and show you favor. May the Lord lift His face towards you and grant you peace. The Lord watches over you; the Lord is your haven at your right hand. For a long life — years of life and of peace — will be extended to you. The Lord will guard you from all evil; He will watch over your soul. Amen.

The kohen recites the blessing for wine to conclude the ceremony:

You are blessed, Lord our God, Sovereign of the world, Creator of the fruit of the vine.

providing ample human contact and time for protracted dialogue with our children. He writes that a house was once ravaged by a fire which broke out in the middle of the night. The firemen saved the husband and wife. Suddenly the wife rushed back into the flames, crying, "I forgot, I forgot!" and soon emerged safely from the conflagration — albeit a bit charred and coughing — holding aloft a rescued jacket and cap. "It's for my baby — it's cold in the night air," she explained. "But where is your baby?" asked the firemen. "I forgot him in the house," groaned the hapless woman. The dialogue with the kohen teaches young parents that they must never favor material provisions for children over their fundamental emotional needs! ◈

שמחת בת / זבד הבת

As the baby girl is brought in by her parents, all rise and say:

בְּרוּכָה הַבָּאָה!

The baby is presented to the grandmothers (or aunts) who declare:

יוֹנָתִי בְּחַגְוֵי הַסֶּלַע בְּסֵתֶר הַמַּדְרֵגָה הַרְאִינִי אֶת-מַרְאַיִךְ הַשְׁמִיעִינִי
אֶת-קוֹלֵךְ כִּי-קוֹלֵךְ עָרֵב וּמַרְאֵיךְ נָאוֶה:

For a firstborn daughter, add:

אַחַת הִיא יוֹנָתִי תַמָּתִי אַחַת הִיא לְאִמָּהּ בָּרָה הִיא לְיוֹלַדְתָּהּ רָאוּהָ
בָנוֹת וַיְאַשְׁרוּהָ מְלָכוֹת וּפִילַגְשִׁים וַיְהַלְלוּהָ:

The Rabbi or honored guest recites:

מִי שֶׁבֵּרַךְ שָׂרָה וְרִבְקָה רָחֵל וְלֵאָה וּמִרְיָם הַנְּבִיאָה וַאֲבִיגַיִל, וְאֶסְתֵּר
הַמַּלְכָּה בַּת אֲבִיחַיִל, הוּא יְבָרֵךְ אֶת הַיַּלְדָּה הַנְּעִימָה הַזֹּאת (פלונית בת
פלונית) בְּמַזָּל טוֹב וּבְשָׁעַת בְּרָכָה, וִיגַדְּלֶהָ לְתוֹרָה בִּבְרִיאוּת שָׁלוֹם
וּמְנוּחָה. וִיזַכֶּה אֶת אָבִיהָ וְאֶת אִמָּהּ לִרְאוֹת בְּשִׂמְחָתָהּ וּבְחֻפָּתָהּ,
בְּבָנִים וּבְבָנוֹת, עֹשֶׁר וְכָבוֹד, דְּשֵׁנִים וְרַעֲנַנִּים יְנוּבוּן בְּשֵׂיבָה, וְכֵן יְהִי
רָצוֹן, וְנֹאמַר אָמֵן:

SIMHAT BAT/ZEVED HA-BAT

The special ceremony for the birth of a baby girl is based upon the ancient Zeved Ha-Bat (literally, "the gift of a daughter") ceremony of the Spanish and Portuguese tradition. It ought take place within 30 days of the birth of the baby girl, after she has been officially named at a public Torah reading on the closest possible Shabbat (or Monday/Thursday) service following the birth.

The Torah relates, "And Abraham was old, and God blessed Abraham with everything (Hebrew: *ba-kol*)" (Gen. 24:1). The Midrash explains that "everything" in this context means a

SIMHAT BAT / ZEVED HA-BAT

As the baby girl is brought in by her parents, all rise and say:

Blessed is she who arrives!

The baby is presented to the grandmothers (or aunts) who declare:

My dove, in the clefts of the rock, in the hidden places of the mountainside, show me your form, let me hear your voice, for your voice is sweet and your form is beautiful.

For a firstborn daughter, add:

One alone is my dove, my innocent one, the only one of her mother, the darling of the one who gave birth to her. The girls who have seen her have acclaimed her; queens and consorts have praised her.

The Rabbi or honored guest recites:

May He Who blessed Sarah and Rebecca, Rachel and Leah, Miriam the prophetess and Avigayil, and Queen Esther, daughter of Avihayil, bless this lovely little girl (name)... the daughter of (mother's name)... with good fortune and a timely blessing, and raise her to a life of Torah, health, peacefulness and tranquility. May He permit her father and mother to see her happily married, with sons and daughters, prosperous and well respected, vigorous and flourishing into a productive old age. May this be Your will, and let us say, Amen.

daughter, whom he named Bakol. Clearly, the assumption of this midrash is that happiness can never be complete without the birth of a daughter.

Our Sages of the Talmud also teach, "If one has a daughter first, it is a good sign for the (following) children (*banim*, sometimes — I believe incorrectly — translated as "sons")." Apparently an eldest daughter is presumed to be a virtual "Godsend" in helping with the younger children. ♦

The parents bless their daughter:

יְשִׂמֵךְ אֱלֹהִים כְּשָׂרָה רִבְקָה רָחֵל וְלֵאָה.
יְבָרֶכְךָ יְיָ וְיִשְׁמְרֶךָ.
יָאֵר יְיָ פָּנָיו אֵלֶיךָ וִיחֻנֶּךָּ.
יִשָּׂא יְיָ פָּנָיו אֵלֶיךָ וְיָשֵׂם לְךָ שָׁלוֹם.

The father says:

בָּרוּךְ אַתָּה יְיָ אֱלֹהֵינוּ מֶלֶךְ הָעוֹלָם, הַטּוֹב וְהַמֵּטִיב.

The mother says:

בָּרוּךְ אַתָּה יְיָ אֱלֹהֵינוּ מֶלֶךְ הָעוֹלָם, הַגּוֹמֵל לְחַיָּבִים טוֹבוֹת שֶׁגְּמָלַנִי כָּל
טוֹב.

All present respond:

אָמֵן. מִי שֶׁגְּמָלֵךְ טוֹב. הוּא יִגְמָלֵךְ כָּל טוֹב, סֶלָה.

The baby is now presented to the eldest maternal relative in the family, who holds the baby on her lap; all the other women relatives join hands in a circle around the matriarch and infant, chanting "Eshet Hayil."

אֵשֶׁת חַיִל מִי יִמְצָא וְרָחֹק מִפְּנִינִים מִכְרָהּ. בָּטַח בָּהּ לֵב בַּעְלָהּ וְשָׁלָל
לֹא יֶחְסָר. גְּמָלַתְהוּ טוֹב וְלֹא רָע כֹּל יְמֵי חַיֶּיהָ. דָּרְשָׁה צֶמֶר וּפִשְׁתִּים
וַתַּעַשׂ בְּחֵפֶץ כַּפֶּיהָ. הָיְתָה כָּאֳנִיּוֹת סוֹחֵר מִמֶּרְחָק תָּבִיא לַחְמָהּ. וַתָּקָם
בְּעוֹד לַיְלָה וַתִּתֵּן טֶרֶף לְבֵיתָהּ וְחֹק לְנַעֲרֹתֶיהָ. זָמְמָה שָׂדֶה וַתִּקָּחֵהוּ
מִפְּרִי כַפֶּיהָ נָטְעָה כָּרֶם. חָגְרָה בְעוֹז מָתְנֶיהָ וַתְּאַמֵּץ זְרוֹעֹתֶיהָ. טָעֲמָה
כִּי טוֹב סַחְרָהּ לֹא יִכְבֶּה בַלַּיְלָה נֵרָהּ. יָדֶיהָ שִׁלְּחָה בַכִּישׁוֹר וְכַפֶּיהָ
תָּמְכוּ פָלֶךְ. כַּפָּהּ פָּרְשָׂה לֶעָנִי וְיָדֶיהָ שִׁלְּחָה לָאֶבְיוֹן. לֹא תִירָא לְבֵיתָהּ
מִשָּׁלֶג כִּי כָל־בֵּיתָהּ לָבֻשׁ שָׁנִים. מַרְבַדִּים עָשְׂתָה־לָּהּ שֵׁשׁ וְאַרְגָּמָן
לְבוּשָׁהּ. נוֹדָע בַּשְּׁעָרִים בַּעְלָהּ בְּשִׁבְתּוֹ עִם־זִקְנֵי־אָרֶץ. סָדִין עָשְׂתָה

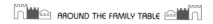

The parents bless their daughter:

May God make you like Sarah, Rebecca, Rachel and Leah.
May the Lord bless you and watch over you;
May the Lord shine His face towards you and show you favor;
May the Lord turn His face towards you and grant you peace.

The father says:

You are blessed, Lord our God, Sovereign of the world, Who is good and Who does good.

The mother says:

You are blessed, Lord our God, Sovereign of the world, Who provides good things to those who are obligated to Him, and Who has provided me with such good.

All present respond:

Amen. May He Who has provided you with such good, always provide you with good, Selah.

The baby is now presented to the eldest maternal relative in the family, who holds the baby on her lap; all the other women relatives join hands in a circle around the matriarch and infant, chanting "Eshet Hayil."

A woman of valor who can find? She is more precious than pearls. Her husband places his trust in her, and only profits thereby. She brings him good, and no evil, all the days of her life. She seeks out wool and flax and cheerfully performs her handiwork. She is like the trading ships, bringing food from afar. She arises while it is still night to provide food for her household and a fair share for her staff. She considers a field and purchases it, and plants a vineyard with the fruit of her labors. She girds herself with strength and her arms with energy. She senses that her trade is profitable, her light is not extinguished at night. She stretches out her hand to the distaff, while her palms hold the spindle. She opens her palm to the poor and stretches her hand to the needy. She has no fear of the snow for her household, for all her household is dressed in fine clothing. She makes her own coverlets; she is dressed in fine linen and luxurious cloth. Her husband is known at the gates,

וַתִּמְכֹּר וַחֲגוֹר נָתְנָה לַכְּנַעֲנִי. עֹז־וְהָדָר לְבוּשָׁהּ וַתִּשְׂחַק לְיוֹם אַחֲרוֹן. פִּיהָ פָּתְחָה בְחָכְמָה וְתוֹרַת־חֶסֶד עַל־לְשׁוֹנָהּ. צוֹפִיָּה הֲלִיכוֹת בֵּיתָהּ וְלֶחֶם עַצְלוּת לֹא תֹאכֵל. קָמוּ בָנֶיהָ וַיְאַשְּׁרוּהָ בַּעְלָהּ וַיְהַלְלָהּ. רַבּוֹת בָּנוֹת עָשׂוּ חָיִל וְאַתְּ עָלִית עַל־כֻּלָּנָה. שֶׁקֶר הַחֵן וְהֶבֶל הַיֹּפִי אִשָּׁה יִרְאַת־יְיָ הִיא תִתְהַלָּל. תְּנוּ־לָהּ מִפְּרִי יָדֶיהָ וִיהַלְלוּהָ בַשְּׁעָרִים מַעֲשֶׂיהָ:

Psalm 128

שִׁיר הַמַּעֲלוֹת אַשְׁרֵי כָּל יְרֵא יְיָ הַהֹלֵךְ בִּדְרָכָיו: יְגִיעַ כַּפֶּיךָ כִּי תֹאכֵל אַשְׁרֶיךָ וְטוֹב לָךְ: אֶשְׁתְּךָ כְּגֶפֶן פֹּרִיָּה בְּיַרְכְּתֵי בֵיתֶךָ בָּנֶיךָ כִּשְׁתִלֵי זֵיתִים סָבִיב לְשֻׁלְחָנֶךָ: הִנֵּה כִי כֵן יְבֹרַךְ גָּבֶר יְרֵא יְיָ: יְבָרֶכְךָ יְיָ מִצִּיּוֹן וּרְאֵה בְּטוּב יְרוּשָׁלָיִם כֹּל יְמֵי חַיֶּיךָ: וּרְאֵה בָנִים לְבָנֶיךָ שָׁלוֹם עַל יִשְׂרָאֵל:

The ceremony is concluded with the blessing for wine:

בָּרוּךְ אַתָּה יְיָ אֱלֹהֵינוּ מֶלֶךְ הָעוֹלָם, בּוֹרֵא פְּרִי הַגָּפֶן:

where he sits with the elders of the land. She makes and sells linens; she supplies the merchants with sashes. She is robed in strength and dignity, and faces the future with optimism. She opens her mouth with wisdom, and the teaching of kindness is upon her tongue. She looks after the conduct of her household, never tasting the bread of sloth. Her children rise up and make her happy; her husband praises her: Many women have been valiant, but you have outshone them all. Grace is deceptive and beauty is empty; a woman who fears the Lord — she shall be praised. Give her credit for the fruit of her labors, and let her achievements praise her at the gates.

Psalm 128

A song of Ascents. Happy is everyone who stands in awe of the Lord, who follows His ways. When you eat of the toil of your own hands, you will be happy and fortunate. Your wife shall be as a fruitful vine inside your house; your children will be like olive plants around your table. This indeed is how the individual who respects the Lord is blessed. May the Lord bless you from Zion and may you see the prosperity of Jerusalem all the days of your life. And may you see you children's children; peace be upon Israel!

The ceremony is concluded with the blessing for wine:

You are blessed, Lord our God, Sovereign of the world, Creator of the fruit of the vine.

חנוכת הבית

The ceremony for the dedication of a home has many variations. The procedure set out below follows the Spanish and Portuguese tradition.

The Mezuzah, commanded in Deuteronomy 6:9 and 11:20, must be attached to the doorpost of each room on the right as one enters. It is affixed according to the Ashkenazi tradition, slanting from top left to right at about two-thirds of the height of the doorpost, as the following blessing is recited:

בָּרוּךְ אַתָּה יְיָ אֱלֹהֵינוּ מֶלֶךְ הָעוֹלָם, אֲשֶׁר קִדְּשָׁנוּ בְּמִצְוֹתָיו וְצִוָּנוּ לִקְבֹּעַ מְזוּזָה:

If you are building a home for the first time in an area in Israel which had not been settled by Jews in the previous generation, recite:

בָּרוּךְ אַתָּה יְיָ אֱלֹהֵינוּ מֶלֶךְ הָעוֹלָם, הַמַּצִּיב גְּבוּל אַלְמָנָה:

The home owner then recites aloud Psalm 30:

מִזְמוֹר שִׁיר חֲנֻכַּת הַבַּיִת לְדָוִד. אֲרוֹמִמְךָ יְיָ כִּי דִלִּיתָנִי. וְלֹא שִׂמַּחְתָּ אֹיְבַי לִי. יְיָ אֱלֹהָי. שִׁוַּעְתִּי אֵלֶיךָ וַתִּרְפָּאֵנִי. יְיָ הֶעֱלִיתָ מִן שְׁאוֹל נַפְשִׁי. חִיִּיתַנִי מִיָּרְדִי בוֹר. זַמְּרוּ לַיהֹוָה חֲסִידָיו. וְהוֹדוּ לְזֵכֶר קָדְשׁוֹ. כִּי רֶגַע בְּאַפּוֹ חַיִּים בִּרְצוֹנוֹ. בָּעֶרֶב יָלִין בֶּכִי וְלַבֹּקֶר רִנָּה. וַאֲנִי אָמַרְתִּי בְשַׁלְוִי. בַּל אֶמּוֹט לְעוֹלָם. יְיָ בִּרְצוֹנְךָ הֶעֱמַדְתָּה לְהַרְרִי עֹז. הִסְתַּרְתָּ פָנֶיךָ הָיִיתִי נִבְהָל. אֵלֶיךָ יְיָ אֶקְרָא וְאֶל אֲדֹנָי אֶתְחַנָּן. מַה בֶּצַע בְּדָמִי בְּרִדְתִּי אֶל שָׁחַת. הֲיוֹדְךָ עָפָר הֲיַגִּיד אֲמִתֶּךָ. שְׁמַע יְיָ וְחָנֵּנִי יְיָ הֱיֵה עֹזֵר לִי. הָפַכְתָּ מִסְפְּדִי לְמָחוֹל לִי פִּתַּחְתָּ שַׂקִּי וַתְּאַזְּרֵנִי שִׂמְחָה. לְמַעַן יְזַמֶּרְךָ כָבוֹד וְלֹא יִדֹּם. יְיָ אֱלֹהַי לְעוֹלָם אוֹדֶךָּ:

DEDICATION OF A HOUSE

The ceremony for the dedication of a home has many variations. The procedure set out below follows the Spanish and Portuguese tradition.

The mezuzah, commanded in Deuteronomy 6:9 and 11:20, must be attached to the doorpost of each room on the right as one enters. It is affixed according to the Ashkenazi tradition, slanting from top left to right at about two-thirds of the height of the doorpost, as the following blessing is recited:

You are blessed, Lord our God, Sovereign of the world, Who has commanded us to affix the mezuzah.

If you are building a home for the first time in an area in Israel which had not been settled by Jews in the previous generation, recite:

You are blessed, Lord our God, Sovereign of the world, Who re-establishes the widow's boundaries.

The home owner then recites aloud Psalm 30:

A psalm: A song at the dedication of the house of David. I will extol you, Lord, for You have lifted me up, and have not caused my enemies to rejoice over me. O Lord my God, I cried to You and You have healed me. O Lord, You have brought up my soul from Sheol; You have kept me alive, that I should not descend to the pit. Sing to the Lord, His pious ones, and give thanks to His holy Name. For His anger lasts but a moment; in His favor is life. Weeping may endure for a night, but joy comes in the morning. In my prosperity I said, I shall never be moved. Lord, by Your favor You have made my mountain stand strong; You hid Your face and I was afraid. I cried to You, Lord, and to the Lord I made my supplication. What profit is there in my blood, when I go down to the pit? Will dust then praise You; will it declare Your truth? Hear, O Lord, and be gracious to me; Lord, be my helper. You have turned my mourning into dancing; You have removed my sackcloth and girded me with joy, in order that glory may sing praise to You and not be silent. O Lord my God, I will give thanks to You forever.

The custom is then to pray either the afternoon or the evening service, whichever is appropriate.

At this point a repast may be served, during which (or prior to which) the following sections from the Torah and the Mishnah are recited:

כִּי תִבְנֶה בַּיִת חָדָשׁ וְעָשִׂיתָ מַעֲקֶה לְגַגֶּךָ וְלֹא תָשִׂים דָּמִים בְּבֵיתֶךָ כִּי יִפֹּל הַנֹּפֵל מִמֶּנּוּ: (דברים כב:ח)

וְהָיָה כִּי יְבִיאֲךָ יְיָ אֱלֹהֶיךָ אֶל הָאָרֶץ אֲשֶׁר נִשְׁבַּע לַאֲבֹתֶיךָ לְאַבְרָהָם לְיִצְחָק וּלְיַעֲקֹב לָתֶת לָךְ עָרִים גְּדֹלֹת וְטֹבֹת אֲשֶׁר לֹא בָנִיתָ. וּבָתִּים מְלֵאִים כָּל טוּב אֲשֶׁר לֹא מִלֵּאתָ וּבֹרֹת חֲצוּבִים אֲשֶׁר לֹא חָצַבְתָּ כְּרָמִים וְזֵיתִים אֲשֶׁר לֹא נָטָעְתָּ וְאָכַלְתָּ וְשָׂבָעְתָּ. הִשָּׁמֶר לְךָ פֶּן תִּשְׁכַּח אֶת יְיָ אֲשֶׁר הוֹצִיאֲךָ מֵאֶרֶץ מִצְרַיִם מִבֵּית עֲבָדִים: (דברים ו:י-יב)

מֵאֵל אָבִיךָ וְיַעְזְרֶךָּ וְאֵת שַׁדַּי וִיבָרְכֶךָּ בִּרְכֹת שָׁמַיִם מֵעָל בִּרְכֹת תְּהוֹם רֹבֶצֶת תָּחַת בִּרְכֹת שָׁדַיִם וָרָחַם: (בראשית מט:כה)

לְבִנְיָמִן אָמַר יְדִיד יְיָ יִשְׁכֹּן לָבֶטַח עָלָיו חֹפֵף עָלָיו כָּל הַיּוֹם וּבֵין כְּתֵפָיו שָׁכֵן: דברים (לג:יב)

וְהָיָה אִם שָׁמוֹעַ תִּשְׁמַע בְּקוֹל יְיָ אֱלֹהֶיךָ לִשְׁמֹר לַעֲשׂוֹת אֶת כָּל מִצְוֹתָיו אֲשֶׁר אָנֹכִי מְצַוְּךָ הַיּוֹם וּנְתָנְךָ יְיָ אֱלֹהֶיךָ עֶלְיוֹן עַל כָּל גּוֹיֵי הָאָרֶץ. וּבָאוּ עָלֶיךָ כָּל הַבְּרָכוֹת הָאֵלֶּה וְהִשִּׂיגֻךָ כִּי תִשְׁמַע בְּקוֹל יְיָ אֱלֹהֶיךָ. בָּרוּךְ אַתָּה בָּעִיר וּבָרוּךְ אַתָּה בַּשָּׂדֶה. בָּרוּךְ פְּרִי בִטְנְךָ וּפְרִי אַדְמָתְךָ וּפְרִי בְהֶמְתֶּךָ שְׁגַר אֲלָפֶיךָ וְעַשְׁתְּרֹת צֹאנֶךָ: בָּרוּךְ טַנְאֲךָ וּמִשְׁאַרְתֶּךָ. בָּרוּךְ אַתָּה בְּבֹאֶךָ וּבָרוּךְ אַתָּה בְּצֵאתֶךָ. יִתֵּן יְיָ אֶת אֹיְבֶיךָ הַקָּמִים עָלֶיךָ נִגָּפִים לְפָנֶיךָ בְּדֶרֶךְ אֶחָד יֵצְאוּ אֵלֶיךָ וּבְשִׁבְעָה דְרָכִים

The custom is then to pray either the afternoon or the evening service, whichever is appropriate.

At this point a repast may be served, during which (or prior to which) the following sections from the Torah and the Mishnah are recited:

When you build a new house, you shall make a parapet for your roof, that you shall not bring blood-guilt upon your house if a person should fall from it. (Deut. 22:8)

And it shall be when the Lord your God brings you to the land which He promised to your forefathers, to Abraham, to Isaac and to Jacob to give to you — great and strong cities which you did not build; and houses full of all kinds of goods with which you did not fill them; hewn-out cisterns which you did not hew; vineyards and olive groves which you did not plant, and you shall eat and be satisfied — then guard yourself lest you forget the Lord Who brought you out of the land of Egypt, from the house of slavery. (Deut. 6:10-12)

From the God of your father — may He help you — and the Almighty — may He bless you — the blessings of heaven above and the blessings of the deep couched beneath; the blessings of the breasts and of the womb. (Gen. 49:25)

To Benjamin he said: The beloved of the Lord shall dwell in safety by Him, He protects him all day long and He shall dwell between his ridges. (Deut. 33:12)

And it shall be, if you will diligently listen to the voice of the Lord your God, to observe to do all His commandments which I command you this day, then the Lord your God will place you on high over all the nations of the earth. And all of these blessings shall come upon you and overtake you, for you listen to the voice of the Lord your God. Blessed shall you be in the city, and blessed shall you be in the field. Blessed shall be the fruit of your body, the fruit of your ground and the fruit of your cattle, the increase of your kine and the lambs of your flock. Blessed shall be your basket and your kneading trough. Blessed shall you be when you come in, and blessed shall you be when you go out. The Lord will cause your enemies who rise upon against you to be

יָנוּסוּ לְפָנֶיךָ. יְצַו יְיָ אִתְּךָ אֶת הַבְּרָכָה בַּאֲסָמֶיךָ וּבְכֹל מִשְׁלַח יָדֶךָ וּבֵרַכְךָ
בָּאָרֶץ אֲשֶׁר יְיָ אֱלֹהֶיךָ נֹתֵן לָךְ: (דברים כח:א-ח)

וַיְהִי דְבַר יְיָ אֶל שְׁלֹמֹה לֵאמֹר. הַבַּיִת הַזֶּה אֲשֶׁר אַתָּה בֹנֶה אִם תֵּלֵךְ
בְּחֻקֹּתַי וְאֶת מִשְׁפָּטַי תַּעֲשֶׂה וְשָׁמַרְתָּ אֶת כָּל מִצְוֹתַי לָלֶכֶת בָּהֶם
וַהֲקִמֹתִי אֶת דְּבָרַי אִתָּךְ אֲשֶׁר דִּבַּרְתִּי אֶל דָּוִד אָבִיךָ. וְשָׁכַנְתִּי בְּתוֹךְ בְּנֵי
יִשְׂרָאֵל וְלֹא אֶעֱזֹב אֶת עַמִּי יִשְׂרָאֵל. (מלכים א' ו:יא-יג)

הַרְחִיבִי מְקוֹם אָהֳלֵךְ וִירִיעוֹת מִשְׁכְּנוֹתַיִךְ יַטּוּ אַל תַּחְשֹׂכִי הַאֲרִיכִי
מֵיתָרַיִךְ וִיתֵדֹתַיִךְ חַזֵּקִי: (ישעיהו נד:ב)

וּבָנוּ בָתִּים וְיָשָׁבוּ וְנָטְעוּ כְרָמִים וְאָכְלוּ פִרְיָם. לֹא יִבְנוּ וְאַחֵר יֵשֵׁב לֹא
יִטְּעוּ וְאַחֵר יֹאכֵל כִּי כִימֵי הָעֵץ יְמֵי עַמִּי וּמַעֲשֵׂה יְדֵיהֶם יְבַלּוּ בְחִירָי.
לֹא יִיגְעוּ לָרִיק וְלֹא יֵלְדוּ לַבֶּהָלָה כִּי זֶרַע בְּרוּכֵי יְיָ הֵמָּה וְצֶאֱצָאֵיהֶם
אִתָּם. וְהָיָה טֶרֶם יִקְרָאוּ וַאֲנִי אֶעֱנֶה עוֹד הֵם מְדַבְּרִים וַאֲנִי אֶשְׁמָע:
(ישעיהו סה:כא-כד)

(The following excerpt is recited only in the Diaspora:)

כֹּה אָמַר יְיָ צְבָאוֹת אֱלֹהֵי יִשְׂרָאֵל לְכָל הַגּוֹלָה אֲשֶׁר הִגְלֵיתִי מִירוּשָׁלַם
בָּבֶלָה. בְּנוּ בָתִּים וְשֵׁבוּ וְנִטְעוּ גַנּוֹת וְאִכְלוּ אֶת פִּרְיָן. קְחוּ נָשִׁים
וְהוֹלִידוּ בָּנִים וּבָנוֹת וּקְחוּ לִבְנֵיכֶם נָשִׁים וְאֶת בְּנוֹתֵיכֶם תְּנוּ לַאֲנָשִׁים
וְתֵלַדְנָה בָּנִים וּבָנוֹת וּרְבוּ שָׁם וְאַל תִּמְעָטוּ. וְדִרְשׁוּ אֶת שְׁלוֹם הָעִיר
אֲשֶׁר הִגְלֵיתִי אֶתְכֶם שָׁמָּה וְהִתְפַּלְלוּ בַעֲדָהּ אֶל יְיָ כִּי בִשְׁלוֹמָהּ יִהְיֶה
לָכֶם שָׁלוֹם: (ירמיהו כט:ד-ז)

smitten before you; they will come out against you on one path but shall flee before you on seven paths. The Lord will command this blessing upon you in your store-houses and in all that you put your hand to, and bless you in the land which the Lord your God gives you. (Deut. 28:1-8)

And the word of the Lord came to Solomon saying: This house that you build — if you walk in My statutes and fulfill My judgments and observe all My commandments, to walk in them, then I shall establish My word with you, concerning which I spoke to David your father. And I shall dwell among the children of Israel, and I shall not forsake My people Israel. (I Kings 6:11-13)

Extend the place of your tent; stretch out the curtains of your dwelling, spare not; lengthen your tent ropes and make your stakes firm. (Is. 54:2)

And they shall build houses and inhabit them, and plant vineyards and eat their fruit. They shall not build and another inhabit, they shall not plant and another eat, for as the days of a tree shall be the days of My people, and My chosen ones shall long enjoy the work of their hands. They shall not labor in vain, nor bring forth disaster, for these are the seed of the blessed of the Lord, and their descendants with them. And it shall be that even before they call, I shall answer; while they yet speak, I shall hear. (Is. 65:21-24)

(The following excerpt is recited only in the Diaspora:)

Thus says the Lord of hosts, the God of Israel: To all the exiles whom I have carried away from Jerusalem to Babylon: Build houses and dwell in them; plant gardens and eat their fruit. Take wives and bear sons and daughters, and take wives for your sons and give your daughters to husbands, that they may bear sons and daughters and increase there and not be diminished. And seek the welfare of the city to which I have exiled you, and pray to the Lord on its behalf, for in its welfare shall be your welfare. (Jer. 29:4-7)

כִּי אַתָּה יְיָ צְבָאוֹת אֱלֹהֵי יִשְׂרָאֵל גָּלִיתָה אֶת אֹזֶן עַבְדְּךָ לֵאמֹר בַּיִת אֶבְנֶה לָּךְ עַל כֵּן מָצָא עַבְדְּךָ אֶת לִבּוֹ לְהִתְפַּלֵּל אֵלֶיךָ אֶת הַתְּפִלָּה הַזֹּאת. וְעַתָּה אֲדֹנָי יְהוִֹה אַתָּה הוּא הָאֱלֹהִים וּדְבָרֶיךָ יִהְיוּ אֱמֶת וַתְּדַבֵּר אֶל עַבְדְּךָ אֶת הַטּוֹבָה הַזֹּאת. וְעַתָּה הוֹאֵל וּבָרֵךְ אֶת בֵּית עַבְדְּךָ לִהְיוֹת לְעוֹלָם לְפָנֶיךָ כִּי אַתָּה אֲדֹנָי יְהוִֹה דִּבַּרְתָּ וּמִבִּרְכָתְךָ יְבֹרַךְ בֵּית עַבְדְּךָ לְעוֹלָם: (שמואל ב ז:כז-ל)

שִׁיר הַמַּעֲלוֹת לִשְׁלֹמֹה אִם יְיָ לֹא יִבְנֶה בַיִת שָׁוְא עָמְלוּ בוֹנָיו בּוֹ אִם יְיָ לֹא יִשְׁמָר עִיר שָׁוְא שָׁקַד שׁוֹמֵר. שָׁוְא לָכֶם מַשְׁכִּימֵי קוּם מְאַחֲרֵי שֶׁבֶת אֹכְלֵי לֶחֶם הָעֲצָבִים כֵּן יִתֵּן לִידִידוֹ שֵׁנָא. הִנֵּה נַחֲלַת יְיָ בָּנִים שָׂכָר פְּרִי הַבָּטֶן. כְּחִצִּים בְּיַד גִּבּוֹר כֵּן בְּנֵי הַנְּעוּרִים. אַשְׁרֵי הַגֶּבֶר אֲשֶׁר מִלֵּא אֶת אַשְׁפָּתוֹ מֵהֶם לֹא יֵבֹשׁוּ כִּי יְדַבְּרוּ אֶת אוֹיְבִים בַּשָּׁעַר: (תהלים פרק קכז)

כָּל יִשְׂרָאֵל יֵשׁ לָהֶם חֵלֶק לָעוֹלָם הַבָּא, שֶׁנֶּאֱמַר (ישעיה ס) וְעַמֵּךְ כֻּלָּם צַדִּיקִים לְעוֹלָם יִירְשׁוּ אָרֶץ נֵצֶר מַטָּעַי מַעֲשֵׂה יָדַי לְהִתְפָּאֵר: (משנה סנהדרין י:א)

אָמַר רַבִּי יְהוֹשֻׁעַ בֶּן לֵוִי, עָתִיד הַקָּדוֹשׁ בָּרוּךְ הוּא לְהַנְחִיל לְכָל צַדִּיק וְצַדִּיק שְׁלֹשׁ מֵאוֹת וַעֲשָׂרָה עוֹלָמוֹת, שֶׁנֶּאֱמַר (משלי ח), לְהַנְחִיל אֹהֲבַי יֵשׁ וְאֹצְרֹתֵיהֶם אֲמַלֵּא. אָמַר רַבִּי שִׁמְעוֹן בֶּן חֲלַפְתָּא, לֹא מָצָא הַקָּדוֹשׁ בָּרוּךְ הוּא כְּלִי מַחֲזִיק בְּרָכָה לְיִשְׂרָאֵל אֶלָּא הַשָּׁלוֹם, שֶׁנֶּאֱמַר (תהלים כט), יְיָ עֹז לְעַמּוֹ יִתֵּן יְיָ יְבָרֵךְ אֶת עַמּוֹ בַשָּׁלוֹם: (משנה עוקצים ג:יב)

For you, the Lord of hosts, God of Israel, have revealed to the ear of Your servant, saying: A house I shall build for you. Therefore your servant has taken heart to pray to you this prayer. Now, Lord God — You are God and Your words will be fulfilled; You have promised this good to Your servant. Now therefore be pleased to bless the house of Your servant, that it may exist forever before You. For You, Lord God, have spoken, and may the house of Your servant be blessed with Your blessing forever. (II Samuel 7:27-30)

A Song of Maalot for Solomon. Unless the Lord builds the house, those who build it labor in vain; unless the Lord watches over the city, the watchman stays awake in vain. It is vain for you to rise up early, to sit up late, to eat the bread of toil; for truly to his beloved he gives sleep. Behold, children are a heritage of the Lord; and the fruit of the womb is a reward. As arrows are in the hand of a mighty man; so are the children of one's youth. Happy is the man who has his quiver full of them; they shall not be put to shame, but they shall speak with the enemies in the gate. (Psalm 127)

All Israel have a share in the world to come. As it is written, "Your people shall all be righteous and shall inherit the land forever. They are the shoot of My planting, the work of My hands, for My glory. (Mishnah Sanhedrin 10:1)

Rabbi Joshua the son of Levi said: The Holy One, blessed be He, is destined to bequeath to every righteous person three hundred and ten worlds, as it is written, "that I may bequeath substance to those who love Me, and that I may fill their treasuries."
Rabbi Simon the son of Halafta said: The Holy One, blessed be He, found no better vessel to contain blessing for Israel than peace, as it is written: "The Lord will give strength to His people; the Lord will bless His people with peace." (Mishnah Uktzin 3:12)

The ceremony concludes with Kaddish De-Rabbanan (if a *minyan* is present), and a blessing for the home owners:

יִתְגַּדַּל וְיִתְקַדַּשׁ שְׁמֵהּ רַבָּא. (אָמֵן)

בְּעָלְמָא דִּי בְרָא כִרְעוּתֵהּ וְיַמְלִיךְ מַלְכוּתֵהּ בְּחַיֵּיכוֹן וּבְיוֹמֵיכוֹן וּבְחַיֵּי דְכָל בֵּית יִשְׂרָאֵל בַּעֲגָלָא וּבִזְמַן קָרִיב. וְאִמְרוּ אָמֵן:

יְהֵא שְׁמֵהּ רַבָּא מְבָרַךְ לְעָלַם וּלְעָלְמֵי עָלְמַיָּא:

יִתְבָּרַךְ. וְיִשְׁתַּבַּח וְיִתְפָּאַר וְיִתְרוֹמַם וְיִתְנַשֵּׂא וְיִתְהַדָּר וְיִתְעַלֶּה וְיִתְהַלָּל שְׁמֵהּ דְּקֻדְשָׁא בְּרִיךְ הוּא.

לְעֵלָּא מִן כָּל (בעשי״ת לְעֵלָּא לְעֵלָּא מִכָּל) בִּרְכָתָא וְשִׁירָתָא תֻּשְׁבְּחָתָא וְנֶחֱמָתָא דַּאֲמִירָן בְּעָלְמָא. וְאִמְרוּ אָמֵן:

עַל יִשְׂרָאֵל וְעַל רַבָּנָן. וְעַל תַּלְמִידֵיהוֹן וְעַל כָּל תַּלְמִידֵי תַלְמִידֵיהוֹן. וְעַל כָּל מַאן דְּעָסְקִין בְּאוֹרַיְתָא. דִּי בְאַתְרָא קַדִּישָׁא הָדֵין וְדִי בְכָל אֲתַר וַאֲתַר.
יְהֵא לְהוֹן וּלְכוֹן שְׁלָמָא רַבָּא חִנָּא וְחִסְדָּא וְרַחֲמִין וְחַיִּין אֲרִיכִין וּמְזוֹנֵי רְוִיחֵי וּפֻרְקָנָא מִן קֳדָם אֲבוּהוֹן דְּבִשְׁמַיָּא וְאַרְעָא וְאִמְרוּ אָמֵן:

יְהֵא שְׁלָמָא רַבָּא מִן שְׁמַיָּא וְחַיִּים עָלֵינוּ וְעַל כָּל יִשְׂרָאֵל. וְאִמְרוּ אָמֵן:

עוֹשֶׂה שָׁלוֹם (בעשי״ת הַשָּׁלוֹם) בִּמְרוֹמָיו הוּא יַעֲשֶׂה בְרַחֲמָיו שָׁלוֹם עָלֵינוּ וְעַל כָּל יִשְׂרָאֵל וְאִמְרוּ אָמֵן:

The ceremony concludes with Kaddish De-Rabbanan (if a *minyan* is present), and a blessing for the home owners.

Magnified and sanctified be His great name. (Cong. Amen)
In the world which He has created according to His will.

In your lifetime and in your days, and in the lifetime of the whole house of Israel, speedily and soon, and say, Amen.

May His great name be blessed forever and ever.

Blessed, praised, glorified, exalted, elevated and honored, magnified and extolled be the name of the Holy One, blessed be He; (Cong. Amen)

Though He be high above all the blessings and hymns, praises and consolations, that are uttered in the world, and say, Amen. (Cong. Amen)

Unto Israel, unto the Rabbis, unto their disciples, and unto all the disciples of their disciples, that occupy themselves with the holy Torah, whether here or elsewhere.
May there be to us, to them, and to you, grace, lovingkindness and mercy, from before the Master of heaven and earth, and say, Amen.

May abundant peace from heaven, with life, be granted to us and to all Israel, and say, Amen.

May He who makes peace in His high heavens, through His mercy grant peace to us and to all Israel, and say, Amen. (Cong. Amen)

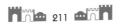

ירושלים של זהב

וְרֵיחַ אֳרָנִים   אֲוִיר הָרִים צָלוּל כַּיַּיִן
עִם קוֹל פַּעֲמוֹנִים   נִשָּׂא בְּרוּחַ הָעַרְבַּיִם

שְׁבוּיָה בַּחֲלוֹמָהּ   וּבְתַרְדֵּמַת אִילָן וָאֶבֶן
וּבְלִבָּהּ חוֹמָה.   הָעִיר אֲשֶׁר בָּדָד יוֹשֶׁבֶת

וְשֶׁל נְחֹשֶׁת וְשֶׁל אוֹר   יְרוּשָׁלַיִם שֶׁל זָהָב
הֲלֹא לְכָל שִׁירַיִךְ אֲנִי כִּנּוֹר.

לַשּׁוּק וְלַכִּכָּר   חָזַרְנוּ אֶל בּוֹרוֹת הַמַּיִם
בָּעִיר הָעַתִּיקָה.   שׁוֹפָר קוֹרֵא בְּהַר הַבַּיִת

אַלְפֵי שְׁמָשׁוֹת זוֹרְחוֹת   וּבַמְּעָרוֹת אֲשֶׁר בַּסֶּלַע
בְּדֶרֶךְ יְרִיחוֹ.   נָשׁוּב נֵרֵד אֶל יָם הַמֶּלַח

וְשֶׁל נְחֹשֶׁת וְשֶׁל אוֹר   יְרוּשָׁלַיִם שֶׁל זָהָב
הֲלֹא לְכָל שִׁירַיִךְ אֲנִי כִּנּוֹר.

וְלֵךְ לִקְשֹׁר כְּתָרִים   אַךְ בְּבוֹאִי הַיּוֹם לָשִׁיר לָךְ
וּמֵאַחֲרוֹן הַמְשׁוֹרְרִים   קָטֹנְתִּי מִצְּעִיר בָּנַיִךְ

כִּי שְׁמֵךְ צוֹרֵב אֶת הַשְּׂפָתַיִם כִּנְשִׁיקַת שָׂרָף
אִם אֶשְׁכָּחֵךְ יְרוּשָׁלַיִם   אֲשֶׁר כֻּלָּהּ זָהָב.

וְשֶׁל נְחֹשֶׁת וְשֶׁל אוֹר   יְרוּשָׁלַיִם שֶׁל זָהָב
הֲלֹא לְכָל שִׁירַיִךְ אֲנִי כִּנּוֹר.

Jerusalem of Gold

As clear as wine, the wind is flying
As evening light is slowly dying

Among the dreamy pines
A lonely bell still chimes.

So many songs, so many stories
Around her heart my city carries

The stony hills recall.
A lonely ancient wall.

Jerusalem all of gold
Within my heart I shall treasure

Jerusalem, bronze and light
Your song and sight.

Back to the wells and to the fountains Within the ancient walls
The sound of horn from Temple's mountain Again so loudly calls

From rocky caves, this very morning
As we shall go down to the Jordan

A thousand suns will glow
By way of Jericho.

Jerusalem all of gold
Within my heart I shall treasure

Jerusalem, bronze and light
Your song and sight.

But when I come to count your praises   And sing Hallel to you
With pretty rhymes I dare not crown you As other poets do

Upon my lips is always burning
If I forget Jerusalem

Your name, so dear, so old:
Of bronze and light and gold.

Jerusalem all of gold
Within my heart I shall treasure

Jerusalem, bronze and light
Your song and sight.

עַל הַדְּבַשׁ וְעַל הָעֹקֶץ

עַל הַדְּבַשׁ וְעַל הָעֹקֶץ, עַל הַמַּר וְהַמָּתוֹק,
עַל בִּתֵּנוּ הַתִּינוֹקֶת שְׁמֹר אֵלִי הַטּוֹב.
עַל הָאֵשׁ הַמְבֹעֶרֶת עַל הַמַּיִם הַזַּכִּים,
עַל הָאִישׁ הַשָּׁב הַבַּיְתָה מִן הַמֶּרְחַקִּים.

עַל כָּל אֵלֶּה, עַל כָּל אֵלֶּה שְׁמֹר נָא לִי אֵלִי הַטּוֹב.
עַל הַדְּבַשׁ וְעַל הָעֹקֶץ, עַל הַמַּר וְהַמָּתוֹק.
אַל נָא תַּעֲקֹר נָטוּעַ, אַל תִּשְׁכַּח אֶת הַתִּקְוָה.
הֲשִׁיבֵנִי וְאָשׁוּבָה אֶל הָאָרֶץ הַטּוֹבָה.

שְׁמֹר אֵלִי עַל זֶה הַבַּיִת עַל הַגַּן, עַל הַחוֹמָה,
מִיָּגוֹן, מִפַּחַד פֶּתַע וּמִמִּלְחָמָה.
שְׁמֹר עַל הַמְּעַט שֶׁיֵּשׁ לִי עַל הָאוֹר וְעַל הַטַּף,
עַל הַפְּרִי שֶׁלֹּא הִבְשִׁיל עוֹד וְשֶׁנֶּאֱסַף.

עַל כָּל אֵלֶּה, עַל כָּל אֵלֶּה...

מַרְשְׁרֵשׁ אִילָן בָּרוּחַ, מֵרָחוֹק נוֹשֵׁר כּוֹכָב,
מִשְׁאֲלוֹת לִבִּי בַּחֹשֶׁךְ נִרְשָׁמוֹת עַכְשָׁו.
אָנָּא, שְׁמֹר לִי עַל כָּל אֵלֶּה וְעַל אֲהוּבֵי נַפְשִׁי,
עַל הַשֶּׁקֶט עַל הַבֶּכִי וְעַל זֶה הַשִּׁיר.
עַל כָּל אֵלֶּה, עַל כָּל אֵלֶּה...

For All of These

Guard the honey and the sting, Guard the bitter and the sweet.
Guard the baby and her teething ring, Guard it all, my God who is great.
Guard the hearth-fire which is burning, Guard the pure, cool, clean waters.
Guard the man, so prayerfully yearning to return home from distant borders.

All of these things all of everything, Guard over them, my God who is great.
Guard the honey and the sting. Guard the bitter and the sweet.
Please do not uproot that which is grown. Do not forget our heartfelt mission.
Bring me back, I want to come home, to the land of my hope and my vision.

Guard for me please, my dwelling, its garden and its fence,
Protect us from aerial shelling, Provide us with divine defense.
Guard our very little stipend, Our sunlight and our offspring
Our fruit which has not yet ripened, And our newly harvested planting.

All of these things, all of everything,…

Through the wind, the rustling of a tree, From a distance, the falling of a star
Through the darkness, my heart offers a plea, Petitioners of the Divine, we are.
Please, guard for me all these things,
Especially our loved ones for whom our souls long.
Guard the silence, and the tears, And guard this song.

All of these things, all of everything,…

Let it be

There is still a white sail in the distant
horizon facing a black heavy cloud
All we ask for is let it be.
And if this evening in the windows
the light of the holiday
candles shakes,
All we ask for is let it be.

Let it be, let it be, please let it be
All we ask for is let it be ...

In a small shaded neighborhood
there is a small red roofed house
All we ask for is let it be ...
This is the end of the road
please let them return to here
All we ask for is let it be.

Let it be, let it be,...

O Lord My God

O Lord my God I pray
that these things never end.
The sand and the sea
The rush of the waters.
The crash of the heavens
The prayer of the heart.

לוּ יְהִי

עוֹד יֵשׁ מִפְרָשׂ לָבָן בָּאֹפֶק
מוּל עָנָן שָׁחוֹר כָּבֵד,
כָּל שֶׁנְּבַקֵּשׁ לוּ יְהִי.
וְאִם בַּחֲלוֹנוֹת הָעֶרֶב
אוֹר נֵרוֹת הַחַג רוֹעֵד,
כָּל שֶׁנְּבַקֵּשׁ לוּ יְהִי.

לוּ יְהִי, לוּ יְהִי
אָנָּא לוּ יְהִי.
כָּל שֶׁנְּבַקֵּשׁ לוּ יְהִי.

בְּתוֹךְ שְׁכוּנָה קְטַנָּה מוּצֶלֶת
בַּיִת קָט עִם גַּג אָדֹם
כָּל שֶׁנְּבַקֵּשׁ לוּ יְהִי.
זֶה סוֹף הַקַּיִץ סוֹף הַדֶּרֶךְ
תֵּן לָהֶם לָשׁוּב הֲלוֹם
כָּל שֶׁנְּבַקֵּשׁ לוּ יְהִי.

לוּ יְהִי, לוּ יְהִי...

אֵלִי אֵלִי

אֵלִי אֵלִי שֶׁלֹּא יִגָּמֵר לְעוֹלָם
הַחוֹל וְהַיָּם רִשְׁרוּשׁ שֶׁל הַמַּיִם
בְּרַק הַשָּׁמַיִם תְּפִלַּת הָאָדָם.